Violence as Politics

Violence
as Politics
A Series of Original Essays

Edited by
Herbert Hirsch and David C. Perry
University of Texas, Austin

HARPER & ROW, PUBLISHERS
New York, Evanston, San Francisco, London

Sponsoring Editor: Alvin A. Abbott
Project Editor: Betsy Dilernia
Designer: T. R. Funderburk
Production Supervisor: Robert A. Pirrung

A different version of "The Chaos of the Living City," by Charles Tilly, was previously published in Paul Meadows and Ephraim Mizruchi, eds., *Urbanism, Urbanization and Change,* Reading, Mass.: Addison-Wesley, 1969.

Library of Congress Cataloging in Publication Data
Hirsch, Herbert, 1919-
    Violence as politics.

    Includes bibliographical references.
    1. Violence—Addresses, essays, lectures.
2.   Violence—United States—Addresses, essays, lectures.
I.   Perry, David C., joint author.   II.   Title.
III.   Title: Political violence.
JC328.6.H56   301.5'92   73-6227
ISBN 0-06-042834-1

To Jonathan, Candace, Diana, and Clayton

in the hope that when they are adults,
no book such as this one will need
to be written.

Contents

Preface

This volume contains a collection of essays reflecting interdisciplinary perspectives on political violence. The original impetus for most of the papers came from a Conference on Political Micro-Violence held at the University of Texas at Austin in March 1971. We are indebted to the University of Texas for its financial support of this conference, and, in particular, we wish to express our appreciation to Dean John Silber and Provost Stanley Ross for their sincere interest and continued support. We are also grateful to the Hogg Foundation, and particularly to Director Wayne Holtzman, for the support the Foundation provided. It is all but impossible to express our debt of gratitude to Carl Leiden for contributions he has made to this series of essays. Professor Leiden was instrumental in conceiving of the conference and enlisting sources of support. Beyond this he provided substantive advice and constant encouragement.

The contributing essays reflect sometimes conflicting, sometimes complementary, analyses of political violence. The process of putting together this collection involved a rigorous critical exchange among the participants in the original conference, to which a number of people made substantial contributions. Among them we wish to thank Francis Beer,

Arnold Buss, Nathan Cohen, David Edwards, H. George Frederickson, Murray Havens, Louis Masotti, Rick Piltz, Neil Richardson, and Karl Schmitt. Further, we are grateful to Bruce Grube for reading the entire manuscript and offering important suggestions. We would also like to thank Bill Hutchison and Sharon Scanio for their help in making arrangements and recording the proceedings.

None of the aforementioned groups or persons should be bound to share with us the adverse criticism that inevitably comes. Since we did collect, order, and attempt to influence, through editorial criticism, the overall nature of the book, we alone accept ultimate responsibility for the finished product.

Finally, we would like to note that the experience of putting this volume together brought about a definite strenghtening of the friendship and respect those of us involved have for one another. Moreover, it provided an opportunity to initiate a new set of professional and personal bonds among the members of the community of scholars gathered between the covers of this book.

Austin, Texas, 1973   Herbert Hirsch
                                                                  David C. Perry

Introduction

In the recorded history of the human species, there has not been a period when men have not been engaged in a war. Intraspecific violence is no stranger to humanity, nor to the United States. In our short history we have engaged in seven declared wars and have sent troops abroad over 165 times since 1798—an average of approximately one military intervention every year.[1] When human beings have not been engaged in international conflicts, they have occupied themselves with intranational conflict. Violence is an integral factor in the internal politics of nation-states. Richard Maxwell Brown points out that in the United States violence has coexisted with some of the "most constructive chapters of American history."[2] What most observers fail to point out is that violence has always been a tool used by the dominant powers within a nation to subdue the subordinate powers. Therefore what often appears to be a "constructive chapter" often turns out to have been achieved at

[1] Alphonso Pinkney, *The American Way of Violence* (New York: Random House, 1972), p. 25.

[2] Richard Maxwell Brown, "Historical Patterns of Violence in America," in Hugh Davis Graham and Ted Robert Gurr, eds., *Violence in America: Historical and Comparative Perspectives* (New York: Bantam, 1969), p. 75.

the expense of another cultural group. Thus the so-called occupation of the land[3] in the United States was accomplished by genocide foisted upon the American Indians. Despite the fact that violence is endemic to the internal and external relations of nations, most observers of violent behavior have argued that violence is an abnormal or aberrant form of human behavior. Edelman describes this violence-as-aberrance argument as the tendency of political scientists to "see collective acts that are violent . . . as atypical departures from a political process which is peaceful and rational."[4] This type of argumentation has been a main theme of social scientists studying violence; that is, most observers have uncritically accepted the assumption that the natural or normal state of humanity is one of peaceful rationality.

A second posture of social scientists that has traditionally been accepted concerns the assignation of legitimacy. Scholars examining political violence usually focus on violent acts that break state laws or are directed toward some representative of the state. Rarely are violent acts commited *by* existing governments considered to be violence. The rationalization runs in a common form.

Since the state has the de jure right,[5] or, in Eastonian terms, the authority, to allocate certain resources to some individuals and groups and to sanction and withold them from others, the government acts in the name of authority in order to preserve the existing social order. Its actions are, therefore, legitimate. Actions that break its laws or threaten its existence are illigitimate. Acts of civil disobedience are, therefore, considered aberrant not because they are irrational, but because they are counter to the existing authority — they are illigetimate. These two concerns are central themes of this book.

This collection of essays is directed to the student who is interested in questions concerning the rationality, normality, prevalence, and significance of violence. Through a variety of methodological and disciplinary perspectives, the contributors attempt to understand violence for what it is — an important, if not also typical, facet of human behavior. The essays discuss the phenomena of violence and politics at

[3] *Ibid.*

[4] Murray Edelman, *Politics as Symbolic Action: Mass Arousal and Quiescence* (Chicago: Markham, 1971), p. 1.

[5] Lewis A. Froman, Jr., *People and Politics: An Analysis of the American Political System* (Englewood Cliffs, N.J.: Prentice-Hall, 1962), pp. 3–6.

individual, collective, intra- and international levels, thus representing a broad variety of disciplinary perspectives. Scholars of violence have been mired in disciplinary provinciality. At their provincial best the disciplines that have studied political violence have emphasized one or the other components of violence. This book is an attempt to present a number of different perspectives within the covers of a single volume. Further, such a collection represents an initial step in the process Sheldon Levy calls the "redefinition of the working relationships among the members of the scientific community."

The essays in Part One demonstrate the interdisciplinary nature of the analyses that contemporary students bring to the study of political violence. In the first selection, Lupsha and MacKinnon turn the tables on the traditional political science approach and direct their analysis toward the patterns and styles of political violence initiated by political out-groups in the United States. They find that American society has evolved into a series of hierarchical relationships that have been perceived by these groups as being coercive. According to Lupsha and MacKinnon, these out-groups have responded with increasing levels of violence as their awareness of systemic coercion has increased.

While Lupsha and MacKinnon prefer to see violence as related to heightened political consciousness, in the second selection Berkowitz sees the increase of domestic violence in the United States partly as an example of contagion. A psychologist noted for his study of aggression, Berkowitz views political violence as a contagious pattern of imitative acts based on initiating violent events. He argues that proper stimuli can "evoke a range of implicit aggressive responses"—hence, Berkowitz notes, the importance of the violent stimuli presented by agents such as the media. According to his psychological argument, these stimuli may be catalytic in that they contain the proper aggressive content to spark a contagious pattern of violence.

The third essay, by Davies, draws upon the historical evolution of humanity to discuss the recurring patterns of superordinate and subordinate relationships. Davies describes violence as one of the consistently recurring patterns that characterize human relationships. He also attempts to work Maslow's need hierarchy into his analysis, arguing that man's common needs will "continuously affect political behavior including political violence."

On another level, Frohlich and Oppenheimer direct their attention away from violence as a physical event and present their analysis of violence as carried out by the legitimate institution of government through the function of taxation. They articulate a "somewhat formalized generalized theory of taxation" to clarify the logical relationships between the citizenry and its government, and make an argument for the potential of political violence as a normal practice engaged in by governments during their everyday interactions with citizens.

Part One thus provides a variety of conceptual and theoretical vantage points from which one may view political violence. Where Davies focuses on the broad hierarchy of social order and needs, Berkowitz focuses on the individual and the factors that might stimulate aggressive behavior. If there is any common thread running through this section, it is that there is a great deal of evidence to demonstrate that violent interactions are not exceptions to the rule—that, in other words, political life is not a placid pond but a storm-swept ocean.

The essays in Part Two follow closely the line of argument set up in Part One. This section deals with the institutional determinants of political violence, focusing primarily on the urban areas of the United States. The essay by Tilly is an exception. Tilly examines the urban environment in comparative perspective and finds that it is both chaotic and violent in its everyday interactions. While the city is not necessarily a pathologically violent place, it does, according to Tilly, exhibit a recurring form of collective disorder. In the second essay, Feagin and Hahn review urban riots in the United States and corroborate Tilly's thesis. They see urban riots as evidence of black America's impatience with the impediments the larger society has placed in front of its full entry into political arena. This topic leads into the third section of the volume, which deals with institutional reactions to political violence.

Part Three contains three diverse descriptions of institutional responses to political violence. The first essay, by Lipsky and Olson, examines the ways in which governmental commissions are used as a tactic to delegitimize riots and rioters. In the second selection, Feierabend and Feierabend review international patterns of violent responses to political violence and simply conclude that violence begets more violence. Finally, in the third essay Bill discusses the effects of revolutionary violence that may lead to real system transformation as opposed to the usual "systems maintaining" pattern of modification.

Part Four consists of the final selection of the book, in which Levy examines the nature of social science research on violence. His essay offers an analysis and critique of the current research on political violence, as well as a strategy for restructuring the study of violence in such a way as to bring about more comprehensive coverage and more precise conceptual and theoretical propositions.

Violence as Politics

Interdisciplinary and Theoretical Perspectives

The recent years of political assassination, urban and campus riots, and police violence have led to increased attention, by both governmental agencies and scholars, to the question of violence. As a result of this activity all social scientists agree upon one fact: There are as many ways of viewing violence as there are disciplines. Political scientists have a special interest in violence as both a political response and a political stimulus. Yet, if we perceive violence to be a social-cultural-behavioral problem with which we must deal forthrightly in the last quarter of this century, we must engage in interdisciplinary examinations of the problem. Part One of this book is designed to meet this task.

In this first section a variety of scholars from different theoretical perspectives present their views of political violence. In the first essay Lupsha and MacKinnon focus their attention on broad sociocultural concerns. Their essay examines incidents of domestic political violence in the sociocultural context of the United States in the last five years. Primarily concerned with what they perceive as the changing patterns and styles of violence, they analyze 1404 separate incidents and pose important questions about political authority and legitimacy in America. After examining a series of interrelated questions, they conclude that the bombing of the Capitol of the United States in March 1971 cannot be seen as a unique or aberrant event. Rather, according to their interpretation, "it fits into a consistent pattern of political consciousness expressed through political action which can be meaningfully interpreted as an expression of outrage and moral indignation by citizens, as their response to the aggravations of political institutions and events. In this broadest theoretical context, then, this paper sheds light on the shifting basis of the authority and legitimacy of American political institutions."

The second essay, by social psychologist Leonard Berkowitz, argues that certain forms of aggressive behavior are subject to contagious influences through a process similar to that of vicarious or observational learning. Berkowitz is concerned with how such crimes as airplane hijackings and urban riots as portrayed in the media present to certain individuals situational stimuli provoking impulsive aggression (that is, "expressive" rather than "instrumental" aggression).

In the third essay James C. Davies attacks the largest theoretical task in the volume. Interested in developing generalizations as to why people engage in political violence, particularly of a rebellious or revolutionary type, Davies develops what he refers to as the "dominance–submission nexus." Noting how "the most widely current explanations of political violence lack general applicability," he attempts to develop a more general theoretical typology based upon the ideas of dominance and submission. Generally, according to Davies's formulation, the dominance–submission nexus develops "when it serves various basic, innate needs of all those involved in the relationship." The dominance–submission nexus, therefore, serves "demands and expectations whose roots are in the nature of man as an organism." Modifying the scheme of basic, innate, organic needs originally developed by Abraham Maslow, he then fits it and the dominance–submission nexus into an analysis of a number of historical events of a violent nature. Davies concludes that what they all had in common was a "demand for power, for greater participation in the making of decisions on public policy that affect the protestants."

The fourth essay, by Norman Frohlich and Joe A. Oppenheimer, adds a new dimension to the analysis of political violence. Utilizing theoretical insights drawn largely from the study of rationality models in political economy research, they examine the relation between governmental violence and tax revenues. After developing their "decision calculus," they link their "explanatory schema" to larger questions of political legitimacy and the breakdown of the coercive capacity of governments. At the same time, the Frolich-Oppenheimer essay will raise fundamental questions concerning the very use of rationality modeling as an approach to an area of study that has heretofore been viewed as subject only to those behavioral humanistic approaches most traditionally aligned with the study of human behavior.

Part One concludes with a critique from a sociological perspective focused especially on the work of Davies and Berkowitz. In his critical analysis Louis Zurcher notes that "each of us, representing our respective disciplines and subdisciplines is at this time unwilling or unable to account for much of the variance among assorted independent variables

and the dependent variables of political violence." Zurcher focuses upon the "perpetuation of those dramatically violent events that involve
more than one individual at a time—such phenomena as the spread of
so-called race riots in the late sixties, the student rebellions, and in general those forms of violence that sociologists would put under the rubric
'collective behavior.'" Using Smelser's ideas of collective behavior as a
base, he then examines the theories of Berkowitz and Davies and concludes with the thought that perhaps "the necessity for such complex
models will be negated by the discovery that all of the causation for
political violence is encapsulated in the dorsomedial and ventromedial
nuclei of the hypothalamus."

If we can point to anything that these five papers have in common,
we must certainly admit to their provocative and, one can hope, catalytic nature. If we are to understand the base of violent behavior in
human beings we must certainly pursue the leads presented here.

1

A Sociocultural Perspective on
the Nature of Political Violence
Domestic Political Violence, 1965-1971:
A Radical Perspective

PETER A. LUPSHA
University of New Mexico
CATHERINE MACKINNON
Yale University

INTRODUCTION

Nearing the end of 1971, one wonders what we have learned over this
and recent years about the nature, form, and meaning of political violence in America. The year began with a bang, with the bombing of the
Capitol of the United States in March and the street disruptions and
mass arrests of more than 11,000 antiwar protesters in May. Though
the public was calmed by the apparent decline in campus violence and
by the apparent lack of mass violence in urban ghettos,[1] the executive
director of the violence commission could report by early fall:

We believe there has been a substantial rise in terrorism as seen in the
polarization of young blacks, in the prison uprisings and in the ambush
shooting of policemen, and terrorism is the most difficult form of violence to cope with.[2]

Indeed, the preliminary statistics indicate that violence in 1971 remained at a high level. In the first 8 months of this year the Justice
department reported 11 major civil disorders, 32 serious ones, and
133 minor ones, as compared with 19 major, 49 serious, and 93
minor for the same period in 1970.[3] Terrorist acts included 1425 bombings for the year ending July 1, 1971, and 116 police officers killed and
965 injured in violent clashes during the 13 months ending July 31,
1971.[4] All signs indicate that domestic political violence remains part
of the American scene. In addition, the 27 deaths at Attica State Prison

in New York after what guards report was the politicization of a "country oriented" prison population by transfer of radicals and militants from "downstate" prisons,[5] and the fact that the majority of the FBI's most wanted list still comprises political militants allegedly engaged in political violence,[6] attest to the fact that domestic political violence, and fear of it, still permeate our national life.

In this paper we wish to shed light on not only the phenomenon of domestic political violence but also the larger theoretical issues surrounding it. To this end we first ask a series of analytical questions about the state of domestic political violence in America.

1. Where does the current barometric reading of political violence stand?
2. Has this violence changed in intensity, shape, and form in recent years? If so, how?
3. Has the expected movement from "commodity riots" to more premediated planned actions taken place?
4. Have the targets shifted over time from diffuse attacks on visible authority representatives to more focused assaults on less obvious authoritative institutions?
5. Does there appear to be a relation between government policy (seen as aggravation) and violence (seen as response)?
6. What role have universities and college campuses really played in political violence?
7. Do students, who fit so neatly into Wolf's designation "peasants," really fit a "revolutionary" model?[7]

But as we are also interested in the larger theoretical issues that are part of, and take meaning from, the occurrence of domestic political violence, we shift to asking questions about order and legitimacy and about the changing nature of authority relationships. As steps towards accomplishing this, we indicate our position relative to other scholars of political violence; then we present our conceptualizations, usages, and paradigm before going on to present a longitudinal analysis of recent incidents of political violence. Finally, we present our thoughts and interpretations on the nature of political violence and its occurrence. Because this is secondary analysis of data collected for other purposes, it is important that the nature of the data base be clearly delineated. For that reason, a brief section on the data base will follow this introduction.

In this study we are part of a long tradition of scholarship that has sought to understand the place of violence in government and politics. In many ways we are theoretically closest to Georges Sorel[8] but have gained sustenance and insight from much recent work. One group of scholars (Rubenstein, Hobsbawn, Nieburg, Rude, Tilly) give emphasis to questions of power distribution and the socioeconomic and political bases of domestic violence.[9] Within this group, some (Rubenstein and Hobsbawn), like Sorel, place emphasis on economic and class conflict, while others (Tilly and Nieburg) tend to stress the role of political violence as a tool of mobilization and contention for political advantage. We concur in this. Questions regarding the distribution (and maldistribution) of power are critically important to understanding political violence. While this may be one root, we feel there is a need to go beyond this and probe the antecedent social conflict in the norms and belief systems of the polity (Edelman).[10] Any litany of recent scholarship on political violence must cite the work of Ted Gurr, who seeks to explain political violence in terms of individual and collective frustration, relative deprivation, and rising expectation.[11] We do not, however, find this approach as useful as the psychological approach of James C. Davies (see the third essay in this volume)[12] which stresses questions of basic human identity and needs for and patterns of subordination and domination as vital aspects of the process of political violence.

In our view, a person's conception of political reality is filtered through the learned value screen of his polity. Psychological mechanisms, blocking, thwarting, frustrating, are meaningless if the value set of that society justifies them as "good, right, and proper." Our work thus reflects our belief in the centrality of this value screen—beliefs in justice, "rightness," legitimacy—and the ways it filters and reflects events that lead to political actions, such as political violence.

For us then the critical research nexus is between political values and political action. Although, methodologically speaking, the data of this paper can only stimulate inferences and suggest insights into such questions, they can provide clues to ways of clarifying our hypotheses, narrowing our research focus, and tightening our methods so as to better grapple with the central relationship of political violence, political institutions, and political legitimacy.

THE DATA BASE AND ITS PROBLEMS

The data for this paper comprise 1404 incidents of "guerilla warfare and terrorism" covering the period February 12, 1965, to September 7, 1970, taken from *Scanlon's* magazine (No. 8, January 1971) and sample-verified in the *New York Times. Scanlon's* issue will be shortly published in book form by Simon & Schuster. *Scanlon's* lists the sources for these materials as follows:

U.S. Senate Permanent Subcommittee on Investigations
Report on Bombings in the United States
Seattle Post Intelligencer
San Francisco Chronicle
Milwaukee Journal
St. Louis Press Dispatch
Boston Globe
Cleveland Plain Dealer
Baltimore Sun
Atlanta Constitution
Denver Post
Los Angeles Times
Houston Post
Miami Herald
Washington Post
New York Times
Chicago Daily News
Detroit Free Press
Kansas City Star
The Lemberg Center for the Study of Violence, Brandeis University

Despite this apparently complete and impressive listing of clipping activity, we had doubts as to the veracity and usefulness of any *Scanlon* selection. Specifically, we feared a built-in slant toward the sensational defined from the "left-liberal" point of view (*Scanlon's* having been founded by disaffected staffers on *Ramparts* magazine). In addition, *Scanlon's* handling of the incident data left much to be desired. They simply cited each incident, listing it by date and location with a brief write-up, and coding it by target type (seven categories: government buildings, corporations, homes, high schools and elementary schools, colleges, police, and military) and weapons type (six categories: sniping, bomb or dynamite, time bomb, arson, molotov cocktail, and terrorism). The brief write-up of each incident, however, often included a great deal of additional information, such as whether the police officer was shot while stopping a robbery suspect or by a sniper after being called into an area on a false report.

This kind of evidence often led us to suspect that perhaps a number of *Scanlon's* incidents of "guerilla violence" were, perhaps, really not political violence. This suspicion suggested that recoding these incidents might provide clearer insights into the state of political violence over the last six years. Finally, we felt that this pool of longitudinal data, even recognizing its shortcomings, offered potentially the best and most extensive collection of such data that we had seen. At least, the dynamic characteristics of domestic political violence could be explored more completely. The *Scanlon's* issue itself contains only one longitudinal analysis (a chart of crudely coded targets by raw scores), which simply suggests that "guerilla" attacks have been increasing over time. By recoding each of the incidents, clarifying targets, weapons, and locations and separating the more political from the less political from the nonpolitical, the apparently planned from the more spontaneous interactive violence, we were able to develop a more complete and dynamic portrait of the nature of recent domestic violence since 1965. Figures 1 and 2, with accompanying analysis, more clearly illustrate this problem and our attempts to rectify it.

The data pose a number of problems that are familiar to anyone who works with aggregate data of this type. First, in any use of incident data, one is often comparing mice and elephants as equals. An incident such as the Watts riot, with its $45-million-plus damage and scores of deaths, is compared with a bombing of an ROTC building that fails. This reality can only be corrected by use of multiple controls. The Kerner Commission, for example, introduced magnitude dimensions as a control, and tried to limit their incidents to one specific type. As we have not sought to introduce multiple controls, the data contains the full box of animal-cracker differences. As our purpose in this paper is to spell out the general patterns of domestic terrorism and to relate implications of this changing shape of violence to vital theoretical questions about the nature of political order and legitimacy, rather than to make a detailed analysis of subgroups or actions, we feel this heterogeneity of data is acceptable to the present analysis. When one is interested in land forms, photography from 50,000 feet is useful; for an investigation of the ecology of birch trees it is not. In future studies we plan, with improved data, to introduce controls that will permit subgroup analysis.

A second problem with data based on newspaper clippings and governmental reports is that one never knows what has been passed over lightly, missed, or magnified. In short, one does not have full control of the reporting universe and over the elements reported in each case. This difficulty, common to much aggregate analysis,[13] is compounded in the present case, since we have chosen to rely on reporting of reporting. There is of course some consistency in this acceptance, but it does limit one's information. Such seems the price of secondary analysis. A third problem is that the time span of the data is not quite complete, for we are missing the last three months of the year 1970; *Scanlon's* report stops in September 1970. This is perhaps a minor difficulty, but it does skew the statistical profile for that year. It is our impression that political violence did indeed fall off dramatically in the fall of 1970. Certainly one of the most common campus comments was "What's happening? Why are things so quiet? The students, apparently so intent on action, are privatizing their lives." In order to check on this perception of "drop-off" or "activist drop-out" *the New York Times Index* was examined. It lists only nine major incidents for the period after September 9, 1970. While this verification is indeed limited, it does support the subjective evidence that fall 1970 was a cool spell compared with a heat wave of violence in the spring and early summer. (See Figure 6.)

DATA AND ANALYSIS

In addition to problems with the data, there are a number of conceptual problems that arise when trying to work with questions of political violence. While there have been many attempts to define and conceptualize political violence, each new research effort seems to encounter difficulties in fitting data to the existing models. Ours is no exception. In large part, our difficulty in fitting other models stems from the fact that we are using a very different data base from those of previous studies.

Most conceptual models of political violence were developed to describe or predict mass behaviors such as ghetto riots or civil insurrections; our data go far beyond this. We have everything from isolated incidents of bombing and sniping to apparently coordinated attacks on the Bank of America. Such data simply do not fit well into the existing paradigms for understanding or explaining domestic violence or violent social change.

Ted Gurr's sophisticated model of political violence clearly illustrates some of the difficulties of fitting existing models. Gurr's analysis is constructed around three basic forms of political violence:

Turmoil: Relatively spontaneous, unorganized political violence with substantial popular participation, including violent political strikes, riots, political clashes, and localized rebellions.

Conspiracy: Highly organized political violence with limited participation, including organized political assassinations, small scale terrorism, small scale guerrilla wars, coups d'etat, and mutinies.

Internal War: Highly organized political violence with widespread popular participation, designed to overthrow the

regime or dissolve the state and accompanied by extensive violence.[14]

Our data simply do not fall neatly into any of these categories. Few
of the incidents we describe—relative to the whole population of incidents—had substantial popular support. Few of these incidents could
be called instrumental in character.

Hannah Arendt argues that violence must be instrumental to be political.[15] We disagree, for many of our incidents are obviously political,
but noninstrumental. This disagreement may, however, be more apparent than real, based in the way one defines instrumental. We use it, as
the dictionary does, as "serving as a means to an end," and we place our
emphasis on both the immediacy and directness of that means to goal
attainment. Under our use of the word, the rash of ROTC building
bombings that occurred in May 1970 in apparent protest to the invasion
of Cambodia are not instrumental but expressive acts. Similarly, the
decoying and fatal ambushing of a police officer in the Oakland ghetto,
as a warning to "all Honkie pigs," is an expressive act indicating hostility to all white police authorities, and not an instrumental one for eliminating that particular officer, nor a step in a planned program to kill the
entire police force. We are reluctant, given our emphasis, to classify any
particular violent action as instrumental unless a fairly clear relationship
can be drawn from evidence about the direct connection of means to
ends. While this perspective demands greater caution and rigor in analysis, it seems more sensible to us than the inverse. To view the bombing
of the United States Capitol as an instrumental act aimed at overthrowing the government, or the bombing of a branch of the Bank of America
as an instrumental act towards overthrowing capitalism, seems inappropriate. But to deny them a political character, especially when their
perpetrators claim one, simply because they appear to be expressive
acts, seems even less appropriate.

Similarly, few of our incidents could be viewed as "highly organized"—
indeed, it is often part of their ideology that they are not—but this
does not mean that they necessarily lack planning. To plant a
bomb requires a degree of forethought and planning; it does not require any high level of organization or formal structure. Indeed, the
bulk of incidents we have examined appear to be *relatively* spontaneous
expressive outpourings of discontent, having limited participation, little
formal structure, and often a "symbolic" motivation. The issues that
call forth violent action are at times specific, but more often are as multidimensional and complex as the causes of urban riots. They relate
more to underlying political discontent than to specific surface issues.

In all, and to the point, our data do not fit neatly into Gurr's categories. Perhaps an example will illustrate this more clearly. Draft opposition and discontent over America's criminal war in Vietnam lie at the root of many campus bombings and the actions against Selective Service offices throughout the country in recent years. Similarly, the invasion of Cambodia in the spring of 1970 triggered off the wave of campus protest and ROTC bombings and culminated in the murders at Kent State. Irving Louis Horowitz notes:

Opposition to the draft was the primary motive in the anti-war protest movement in the United States during the 1960's; between 1965 and the fall of 1968 an estimated 7,000,000 people participated in some 170 anti-war demonstrations about 25 of which involved significant violence.[16]

As the data in this paper show, this escalation of protest coincided with a marked rise in bombings of military, particularly campus military, property. Indeed, it generally appears possible to juxtapose the escalation in domestic violence with major American increases in commitment and action in Vietnam. This upswing in domestic violence occurred, however, without what Gurr would call "vast domestic turmoil"; without concerted "conspiracy" by college students or others (except for the vaguest purposes of police harrassment); and without the development of internal war. In many ways it seems to us that these data are in a sense prior to that range of political violence that interests Gurr, though developments over time could lead to a dovetailing with his "domestic turmoil" form of violence.

A second aspect of Gurr's theoretical schema sheds further light on the problem of fitting models, as well as highlighting some aspects of the incidents we are working with.

Within each of Gurr's forms of political violence, he defines three critical components that can describe the magnitude of any incident of political violence. The first is the *scope* or extent of participation in the event. The second is the *intensity* or destructiveness of the action. And the third is the *duration,* or length of time the violence persists.[17] Such categories of magnitude are very useful, particularly for describing mass events like the recent ghetto riots. In fact, the Kerner Commission report contains quite similar "measurement" devices.[18] In our present analysis, unfortunately, such categories are of little use. For what do the extent of participation, destructiveness of action, or duration mean in a sniping incident or the destruction of utility towers? The incidents we are dealing with are qualitatively different from the mass uprisings of urban ghettos or the macrophenomena for which Gurr's model was

designed. We have no desire to take him to task for not addressing our
concerns, yet it is worth noting that even this outstanding work does not
cover the full range of events we normally term domestic violence.

Our data, in a sense, predate Gurr's categories. They come before what
Tilly terms "contention for power," and are prior to mobilization.[19]
The data we are examining here fit more into what Gurr calls "the de-
velopment and politicization of discontent" than into one of the stages.
In fact, if we were to propose a stage-wise paradigm of political activa-
tion, it would be as follows:

1. *Awakening of discontent:* the recognition of grievances and dissatisfactions.
2. *Politicization of discontent:* the recognition that the cause of discontent lies outside the self and in the structure, allocation, and
   distribution of economic and political power, and the authority
   structures that maintain it.
3. *Mobilization of discontent:* the publicizing of these recognitions to
   similar others, and the attempt at organizing those others into a coherent body for attempting change.
4. *Contention:* the active attempt to alter the situation politically
   (violently or nonviolently) through concerted mobilized action.

Within such a paradigm the incidents we are examining fall into stages
1 and 2, while the work of Gurr and Tilly seems to us to focus more
on stages 3 and 4. We hope, therefore, that despite the usual conceptual discontinuity, our efforts will add to and complement their
research.

In order to insure that the incidents we examined focused on the
"legitimacy-threatening" model of guerrilla warfare we wished to study,
we sought to separate actions that were definitely political from those
that were only probably political, and from those that were nonpolitical.
To this end we developed a set of consistent criteria for identifying and
coding the data.

1. *Political by Target.* For the incident to be political, the target had
   to be clearly a representative of the State or a symbol of state authority, and clearly focused upon as the object of attack.
2. *Political by Initiator Consciousness.* The degree of planning or connection with other incidents must indicate a consciousness of, or
   intent to further, goals that go beyond the immediate or instrumental destruction of the target. The incident should somehow indicate
   that it was intended to have political effect furthered by, but not
   completed by, the attack on the target. This means that the act

must be within the context of some larger political position or ideo-
logical stance that the target symbolizes.
3. *Political by Group Representation.* The action should be initiated
   by or in the name of a group with a particular interest or by a representative of a subgroup apparently directly concerned with the
   target and what it stands for.

An incident was only "probably political" if it met all three criteria.
To be considered "definitely political" an incident not only had to meet
these criteria, it had to be explicitly tied in planning and apparent motivation to obviously political issues, or the report had to state that political issues or motivations were attributed to the action.

In general we felt it better to err on the side of calling not political
some incidents that might be, than vice versa. The coding of this distinction was stringently conservative. We found that we disagreed with
approximately 10 percent of *Scanlon's* coding. By collapsing the "definitely political" and the "probably political" in Figure 1, the percent
of the *Scanlon* data that we felt was political, by year, is revealed.

Explanation of Figure 1
Since a high level of violence in society does not necessarily imply a high
level of political violence, we can assume that only a portion of all the
violence in a given year will be political.[20] *Scanlon's* selected what it
considered to be instances of "guerrilla warfare" from many sources on
presumably constant criteria across years. From the distinctly upward
trend (indicated in Figure 1) in the proportion of clearly political violence to ambiguous or less political violence, we can infer that political
violence as a *percentage* of total violence is increasing. This suggests
that political violence is increasing at a differential rate rather than as
a constant proportion of overall violence.

There are at least two plausible explanations for this differential
growth in political violence. First, we may be witnessing a displace-
ment of violent impulses—impulses that normally would be directed
elsewhere—onto politics; or, second, the customary explanations of
political violence may be mistaken in interpreting political violence as
merely a subcategory of violence per se. Perhaps by not focusing adequately upon what separates political from other violence, the psychological explanations, in particular, may account for less and less violence
as the motivations for such actions become increasingly more political
and less rooted in individual idiosyncrasy. Such thoughts depend,
however, on one's sense of the psychosocial portrait of the initiators
of political violence; until data are gathered they must remain matters
of conjecture.

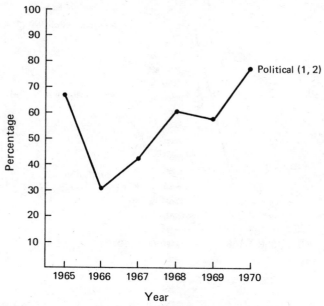

Figure 1   Percentage of Incidents Coded as Political by Year

Explanation of Figure 2

This chart further breaks down the trend shown in Figure 1, indicating the relative proportion of each of the four coding categories (representing varying degrees of "political") to each other and to the total number of incidents. The line indicating "not political" is a precise measure of our disagreement with *Scanlon's* on their selection of incidents.

The graph of "don't know" suggests several interpretations. First, its relative magnitude is a measure of the stringency of our criteria for coding an incident either "political" or "probably political." Second, it reflects the adequacy of the reporting of the incident. Third, it may indicate a change in the media's perception of the nature of the phenomenon. That is, if the reporter was sensitive to an emergent trend of increasing political violence, he may have been more likely to perceive (or create) political overtones to otherwise more straightforward acts of violence. All these factors probably contribute to this finding in varying degrees: the first at a constant rate, the second probably varying unpredictably, and the third probably tending to explain the dramatic decrease in indeterminate cases in 1970. The extent to which the

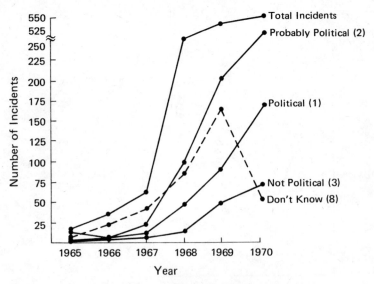

Figure 2   Number of Incidents as Coded by Year

actual and proportional rise in political violence is media-created or media-reinforced, then, cannot be decisively determined from these data.

Explanation of Figure 3

By revealing the changing regional patterns of political violence, this chart reflects a transformation in the central issues that have stimulated violent incidents over time. Certain issues are generally more salient in certain regions, but lead to violence at some times and not at others. It seems reasonable to suppose that, given a basic configuration of issue sensitivity in a region, changing governmental policies and other institutional factors could touch a nerve and aggravate citizens to violence. Levy implies this conclusion in his summary of his research findings:

Generally, the population is unlikely to endorse any but legal responses to remove different provocations, but given a sufficiently antagonistic political situation . . . substantial numbers agree that even armed action may be an appropriate response.[21]

A regional example of Levy's statement in our data is the American South, which accounted for 70 percent of the nation's violence in 1965. At this time the issues in the South were heated and primarily racial,

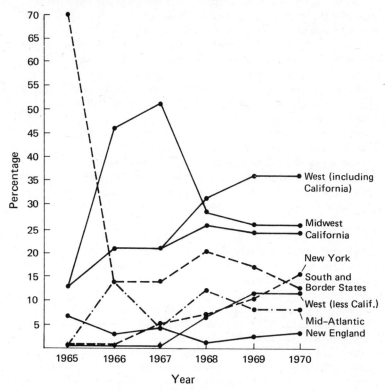

Figure 3 Percentage of Incidents by Region by Year (1, 2, 3, B/38)

centering around the growing pressures by civil rights organizations for enforcement of the government's integration policy.

For the Midwest the peak years of violence were 1966 and 1967, when the North began to realize that its cities also would have to integrate, and when black antagonisms and anger broke loose in the populous industrial areas. This pattern roughly parallels that of the Middle Atlantic states (New York being listed separately). One particularly interesting aspect of these data is that they imply that intensity is related to diffusion. By this we mean that each major riot in an urban center is recorded as only *one* incident; yet on this chart, corresponding to the times when the major riots occurred, we generally see an increase in the percentage of incidents occurring in the same areas as the riots.

Certain regions, such as New England, seem generally less volatile, whatever the issue, although perhaps this is because the "right" issue has not come along. The West (less California), long without political violence, has become markedly more violent. This chart supports the inference that 1968 was generally a critical year for the United States in terms of issue priorities, in that race as a stimulus to violence (for whatever reasons) began to take second place to the issue of Vietnam and the system of authority generally. The states of California and New York also exhibit this trend.

Finally, it is interesting to note that since 1969, with the exception of a great increase in political violence in New York (this may be a reflection of the explosions on campuses in 1970; see Figure 6 and Figure 7), the rank order of the regions has remained constant. Perhaps this indicates some stabilization in the issues salient to political violence, if one can speak of stability in these terms.

Explanation of Figure 4

This figure shows the percentage of incidents occurring each year in different types of locations. The analysis focuses more on the trend in the data than on the relative magnitudes, because of the natural bias in data collection toward urban events, both absolutely (because of the higher incidence of violence with higher population density) and relatively (because a rural incident has to make a bigger splash to be reported in the big city papers that form the data base).

This bias notwithstanding, these data present interesting and close parallels to the patterns and relative magnitudes by regions (Figure 3). Small-town violence, for example, parallels the trend in the South exactly, except for 1970. Large-city violence follows the Midwest pattern. Rural violence reflects the trend observed in the West (less California); and suburbs follow a New England-like pattern over time.

We are probably witnessing another reflection of the shift from racial violence to attacks on instituted authorities. Large-city and metropolitan violence has declined from highs in 1966 and 1967. The decline through 1969 in small-town violence, where much racial unrest occurred, also supports this suggestion. Small-city and medium-city violence have generally moved together; their increases could represent a diffusion of the antiauthority sentiment from the major cities to the more "typical" American city, from the urban elite to the middle-class masses. The dramatic increase in small-town political violence in 1970 may indicate an expanding political consciousness, but is more likely that it is because many colleges and universities are located in small towns. This should be investigated further.

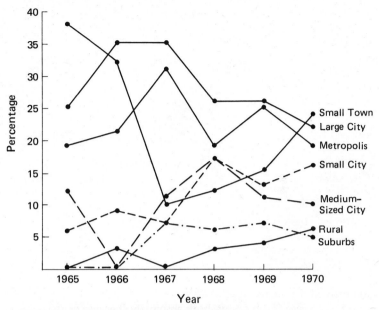

Figure 4 Percentage of Incidents by Place by Year

It is interesting that the suburbs have never been hit with political violence. After a modest increase during the pressured years of Northern integration (1967–1969), suburban violence seems to be on the decline. The intentional isolation of the suburbs from the clashes and tensions of American society apparently remains relatively unviolated.

Explanation of Figures 5 and 6
One of the most popular "folk theories" of political violence might be called the thermal or heat-wave hypothesis. Crudely put, it states in essence that when the temperature rises, the natives, particularly the urban natives, get restless. Figure 5, using *all* incidents, seems to suggest support for this view, with violence reaching its seasonal high in the warm summer season and dropping off when the cold sets in.

If one accepts this thermal view of politics, our paradigm is obviously wrong. These incidents do not suggest the first stages in the awakening of discontent or some emergent sense of politicization of grievance in the form of violent action. They simply reflect the discomfort and irritability caused by hot summer nights. But look again at the data.

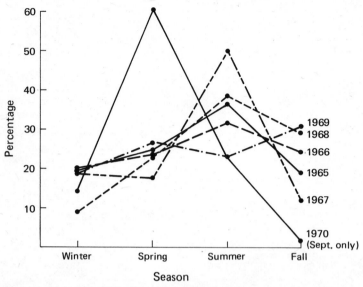

Figure 5 Percentage of Total Incidents Occurring Seasonally by Year

The year 1970 does not quite fit this sweaty explanation. Is it an aberration, an early summer, or something else? To find out, we reran the data using only the political incidents (Figure 6), and, indeed, a new pattern appears. Fall and spring now appear as the peak seasons for political violence, with winter and summer the new lows. The pattern of political violence seems now to fit the academic year better, while violence in general appears to correspond better with seasonal shifts in temperature. Given the nature of the political incidents we have been examining (campus arson, police sniping, military and corporate bombings) and issues that disturb college-age youths (university reorganization, the draft, the War, the bomb, racism, sexism, ecology, the military-industrial complex, police brutality and harrassment), it does not seem surprising that political violence tends to correspond with the academic year. J. Edgar Hoover had been telling the American people this for years; the interesting thing is how right and wrong he was.

Explanation of Figure 7 and Table 1

In 1971 President Nixon issued a call for 1000 new FBI agents, to be used, according to then-Chief J. Edgar Hoover, to "infiltrate college campuses." Since the incidents of May 1970, public officials and the

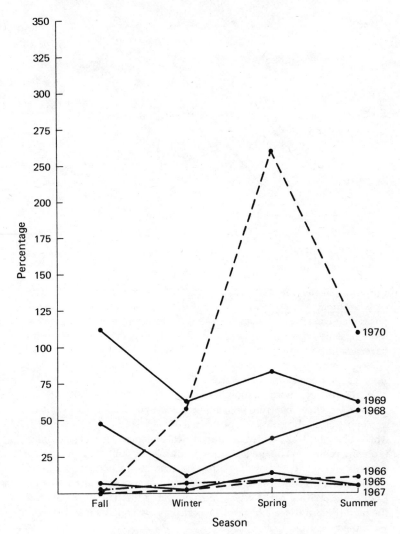

Figure 6   Number of Political Incidents Occurring Seasonally by Year

popular press, consistent with Hoover's analysis, have looked to college and university campuses as centers of violent activity against the State and its policies. While the events at Berkeley, Santa Barbara, Harvard, and Yale garnered much media space, analysis of Figure 7 indicates that

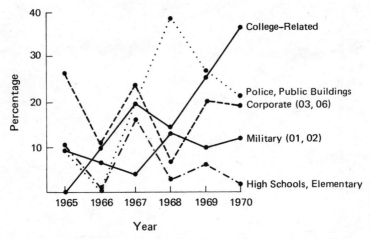

Figure 7 Var 17: Percentage of Political Violence by Target Type by Year
(Property Only)

this image of the universities as *the* hotbed of revolutionary radicalism
may be somewhat overdrawn.[22] That is, to a certain extent, the campuses may have become scapegoats for repression of what is actually a
more broadly based phenomenon of violently expressed antipathy to
government policies.

Table 1 supports this idea more conclusively. Although much political
violence has occurred in university towns and campuses (and when it
does, its character appears more consciously political than not), the
political violence occurring on campuses and in college towns is only a
small portion of the political violence occurring elsewhere. The year 1970,
when the high of 37 percent of the political violence was college-related,*
probably represents no great watershed of overall political violence, for
the bulk of it consisted of the nationwide campus response in the spring
(see Figure 6 on Seasons) to the Cambodian invasion and the killings at
Kent State. Without that violent outpouring in the first weeks of May,
the data (Figure 6, for example) suggest that the colleges may have been
less violent in 1970 than in 1969.

What one can say about campus-related violence is that (as of 1971)
it has been increasing and it appears to be consciously political. This
does not seem unreasonable, particularly if one takes the view that

---

*"College-related" is a sum of attacks on college campuses and clearly political
attacks in clearly college towns (e.g., a Selective Service attack in Ann Arbor).

Table 1 Crosstab: Political/Not Political, College-Related/Not College-Related

1965
%

	Political	Not Political
College-Related	0	0
Not College-Related	100 (N = 11)	100 (N = 31)

1966
%

	Political	Not Political
College-Related	9	0
Not College-Related	91 (N = 11)	100 (N = 23)

1967
%

	Political	Not Political
College-Related	20	12
Not College-Related	80 (N = 25)	88 (N = 32)

1968
%

	Political	Not Political
College-Related	14	7
Not College-Related	86 (N = 147)	93 (N = 88)

1969
%

	Political	Not Political
College-Related	25	6
Not College-Related	75 (N = 308)	94 (N = 209)

1970
%

	Political	Not Political
College-Related	37	8
Not College-Related	63 (N = 433)	92 (N = 112)

campus violence is simply part of a larger crisis of legitimacy that confronts American institutions. Universities are commonly held to be the repositories of the dominant social myths of a society, particularly those of "truth, beauty, justice, and wisdom." As such they act as signal mirrors transmitting and reflecting social values. But since there is usually a gap between theory and practice, idea and reality, the university often acts more like a fun-house mirror, reflecting and accentuating both the truth and distortion of the world around it. In the university anger at and questioning of myths and hypocrisy one has been sold does not seem strange.

Explanation of Figures 8, 9, and 10

These figures illustrate the changing face of political violence from 1965 to 1970. Prior to 1967 there were few terrorist actions against institutions of higher education or the corporate structure of the United States. Violence directed against public property was rare, and willfil attacks on symbolic public authority figures (policemen, firemen, and so forth) were uncommon enough to be surprising. Five years later, in 1971, things seem rather different. To read of policemen decoyed and shot from ambush, or a building burning because firemen were turned back by rocks and bottles thrown from rooftops, is now almost regular backpage newspaper fare. Perhaps the quick desensitization and callousness of our age is showing, but even the Bank of America no longer seems shocked by having another of its branches bombed.

Figure 8 shows the long-term antimilitary, anti-Vietnam feeling that has existed on college campuses, ROTC buildings being the favorite target since 1968. In the spring of 1970 events in Cambodia and Kent State catalyzed this longer-run antagonism in a massive outpouring of violence on college campuses, but it is interesting to note that over this period increases in attacks on other campus buildings also occur.

Figure 9 shows the shifting pattern of attacks on representatives of authority (police, military), their property, and other public buildings. Both 1969 and 1970 register an increase in attacks on the military as well as attacks on campus ROTC buildings. Although further analysis is needed to see what proportion of these other military attacks are campus-related, these data imply that the antagonism to the military, particularly the Selective Service system, which symbolizes coerced service in Vietnam, is not confined to the campuses. (The category "military" here is a combination of draft-related non-ROTC and non-draft-related military attacks.)

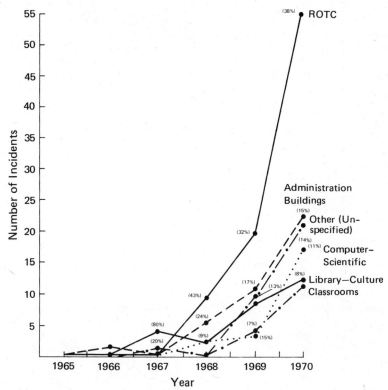

Figure 8 College Targets by Type* by Year

> *Attacks not included on graph are: attacks on specific individuals
> (1966 = 1, 1968 = 1, 1970 = 3); dormitories, fraternities, and sororities
> (1966 = 2, 1969 = 1, 1970 = 3); and faculty offices (1968 = 1, 1969 =
> 5, 1970 = 1). Data were particularly limited in these types.

Also increasing in the same pattern in the same years are attacks on public buildings, such as the CIA, courthouses, the FBI, and city halls. It seems
reasonable to suppose from these parallel patterns that antiauthoritarian-
ism, however aggravated by Vietnam, extends beyond simple antimili-
tarism. Figure 10, delineating the increases in attacks on corporations
(particularly banks), shows the same pattern, implying that a perception
of the connection between economic, military, and governmental power
may lie behind these attacks. Insight into the interrelatedness of these
parts of the social infrastructure also extends to the universities, where
computers and scientific facilities (Figure 8) have increasingly been seen
as the campus contribution to the military-industrial complex.

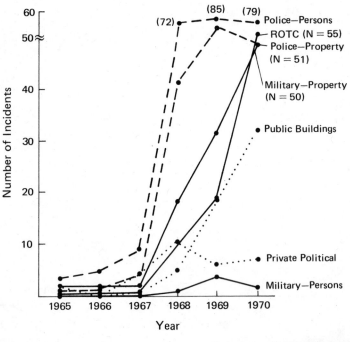

Figure 9 Attacks on Authority by Target Type by Year

Taken together, these figures suggest, we would argue, that there may have been a change in the political consciousness of the actors involved in these various acts of violence over the period studied. We realize that it is indeed tenuous to leap from very limited data to making statements regarding the awareness of the actors involved. Yet if we are to achieve fuller understanding of the phenomenon, it is at times necessary to make inferences that may be a bit risky. (We will happily admit error, if someone will provide the data.)

By changes in political consciousness we mean alterations in a person's awareness of what's happening and why. These changes in consciousness, we submit, can be sensed, picked up, observed, in the changing behavior (actions) of the individual. We further submit that while this change takes place "in people's heads" (that is, is an individual phenomenon)

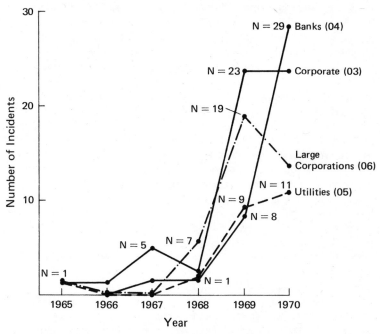

Figure 10 Corporate Targets by Target Type by Year

it can be taught, learned, and quickly spread to subgroups and collectivities who have the same or similar key recognitions, "vibrations," and identifications (in the language of social science, persons with similar life chances, styles, identifications, and social milieus). Common empirical examples are the growth of black consciousness, often called pride, and the increase in women's awareness of sexist attitudes or chauvinism in men.

In speaking of changes in political consciousness, we refer here to a new political recognition by persons and subcollectivities of where the power lies and who, or what, is responsible for the state of the world around us. (Note: this usually takes place in terms of "negatives"—that is, who is to blame—rather than as a seeking out of persons or institutions to praise.) One obvious change in political consciousness among middle-class white youth since the middle sixties is the decay of the notion that "the policeman is your friend." Another is the decline in the belief that "our leaders do not lie," or "American soliders do not kill women and children or their fellow young Americans."

President Eisenhower planted the seed of the idea that there is a vast "military-industrial complex" that is dangerous to the Republic and bears close scrutiny. He was virtually ignored, except by a handful of journalists and academics. Yet that seed grew, and by the time of the escalation of the Vietnam war, few antiwar Americans denied that connection. That is an example of changing political consciousness.

What we simply suggest is that, taken together, these incident data indicate in a crude way this changing political awareness—a realization that it is not just the policeman, or military, but the structures and institutions (governmental, economic, and even educational) that lie "behind it all." Given the data, it would be foolish to push this thesis too far. We would note, however, the way this conception of shifting political consciousness fits our earlier stage-wise paradigm. Stage two, politicization of discontent, signifies that point where individual awareness is changed to collective awareness, with the accompanying recognition of collective (institutional and structural) causation.

Another interesting trend in these data can be seen by comparing attacks on persons with attacks on property. The policeman, as a highly visible interface between constituted authority and the people, catches a great deal of antiauthoritarian sentiment. It is significant that attacks on police have increased rather than decreased as racial-related violence has declined. Certainly the "off the pigs" movement among the Panthers and the Weathermen registers success here. The figures for "police-persons" may be exaggerated, however, since many of the antipolice incidents were double-coded, including both persons and property when both were present and it was difficult to tell which was targeted. Further analysis will have to be done, and the slight drop in attacks on police in 1970 will have to be explored further. It may be that an awareness is growing that policemen may have a role beyond that as an instrument of oppression—that policemen may be exploited too.[23]

While these data do not permit us to prove our paradigm—that these incidents may constitute the first stages of an awakening and politicization of discontent—we have enough suggestive evidence to realize that something is happening underground. Violence is remaining steady over the years, political violence appears increasing, and the purely spontaneous actions appear to be dropping off while the planned, conscious political acts—though still what we have called expressive in nature—are increasing. Furthermore, as we have seen, the targets of the attacks have been changing from more obvious and visible authority figures to include institutions representing the economic establishment. In time, the incidents examined here may have no more meaning for the history of America than as a quiet and seemingly crazy echo of the

exploding bombs of the late nineteenth-century anarchists. Nevertheless, to us they remain important to understanding larger questions
that have significance across time.

In the section that follows we take a giant step from these data, going
beyond them to seek answers to questions they only suggest or imply.
We do this, first, to make a case for what has been a rather unexamined
perspective on political violence and, second and most importantly, to
raise questions about the nature of order and legitimacy and the place
of political violence in society.

INTERPRETATIONS AND IMPLICATIONS:
NOTES TOWARD A THEORY OF POLITICAL VIOLENCE

Much attention has been devoted in the literature to defining political
violence, locating it with respect to agents and objects, questioning its
functionality, and ascertaining its role in social change. Less attention
has been given to questions of whether political violence is justifiable—
for what ends, and for whom—or whether it is "rational" as a political
mode or style. These latter questions—justification, rationality, and
"properness"—interest us. They also raise a question about the desirability and effectiveness of tactical violence, which (as our incidents
indicate) seems settled, but inadequately examined, by a number of
real-world activists. In the following pages we present a brief and ten-
tative discourse comprising our thoughts on these questions. They are
generated by, and are generally consistent with, the data and with our
reading of American politics and current political thought.

As a point of departure, we will first explore the ways in which violence has become legitimized as a means of challenging authority and
attempting to change authoritative institutions in a relatively open representative democracy.[24] We will then examine the justifications of
the authoritative structures and institutions in response to that challenge. Finally, we will explore what these two different perspectives
imply for the explanation of current types and trends of political violence. It is hoped that this discussion will elicit comment and criticism
with a view to developing a more accurate and comprehensive picture
of the factors contributing to political violence.

To begin, let us seek to locate political violence with respect to two
basic and related social concepts: social order and political legitimacy.
Within any society the notion of order is closely connected, both
epistemologically and psychologically, to the structure of that society
and the normative notions underlying its perception as legitimate.

Political violence, on the other hand, is often viewed as an indicator of the breakdown in both order and legitimacy. As the data presented suggest—showing but the violent iceberg tip—both the orderliness and the legitimacy of political authority and institutions of America are being questioned. In turn, the orderliness and legitimacy of the act of challenging it are also being questioned. Those who wish to preserve the status quo perceive and explain away challenges to its legitimacy as threats to order. Order in this sense refers both to the structural order of society (as in the social order) and to orderliness in its everyday functioning (as in "law and order").

Those who hold the traditional conception of a crisis in legitimacy see the argument rather differently. They generally seek to stand outside the system and "objectively" gaze in. S. M. Lipset exemplifies this traditional view:

A crisis of legitimacy is a crisis of change. Therefore, its roots must be sought in the character of change in modern society. Crises of legitimacy occur during a transition to a new social structure if (1) the status of major conservative institutions is threatened . . . (2) all major groups do not have access to the political system . . . [and] if the political system is unable to sustain the expectations of major groups.[25]

Those within the system who also challenge it may perceive such legitimacy crises with different eyes. First, they may perceive that the system is not legitimate on its own terms. In what it sees as self-defense, the system violates the very values it is supposed to be defending (order among them), and in so doing it does not confine itself to its own channels for orderly redress of grievances. Two examples of socially legitimized violence that come to mind are those involving the military and the police. Both are conceived to have either a protective or retributive function, but they are supposed to protect for society at large just those values they most often violate in the pursuit of their protection—namely, person and property. This version of the critique, then, condemns the American pattern as lacking in *any* central logic, as headlessly running amok. Vietnam wars and the extermination of the Indians, for example, are seen as sins of omission rather than comission, as a series of semiconscious errors rather than as an intentional policy. This particular version of social order is seen as inherently disruptive of human life. Slater illustrates this point as follows:

Consider what happens when a defective traffic light fails to change from red to green. . . . At some point someone decides that the symbol of order is in fact in disorder and . . . goes through. . . . The initiator . . . is

challenging the specific rule about red lights in terms of a broader understanding which says that the purpose of traffic laws is to regulate traffic, not to disrupt it.[26]

The implication of this example is that the authoritative structures and
institutions of governance that require and sanction obedience can, in
certain circumstances, readily and perhaps rightfully lose their legitimacy. This situation occurs when the political system comes to be perceived as disrupting an order that is defined in terms that are not, in
themselves, dependent on the social definition of order. As society's
version of order ceases to make sense out of reality, as society fails to
live up to even its own legitimating myths, it ceases to deserve its claim
to allegiance. For those who can perceive order only in terms of social
structures, the more revolutionary would probably note that they will
be left standing at an eternal red light. In summary, one of the causes
of society's polarization, and one of the sources of mutual aggravation
and violent response, is that where society's defenders see order, the dissidents see chaos, and vice versa. Hence, just as repression is justified by
the society as a means to the legitimate end of preserving legitimate social
order, antisystem political violence can often be legitimized, by those
who desire basic change, as a means to the legitimate end of changing the
illegitimate social order. According to Bienen, Machiavelli accounts for a
rise in violence with a breakdown in legitimacy. "Machiavelli tells us that
in a corrupt age, greatness can be attained only by immoral means."[27] In
a corrupt society, who, it is asked, is to say that change is immoral, or
that any means to change need be anything more than appropriate?

A second, more thoroughgoing version of this critique stresses the inherent illegitimacy of the present configuration of authoritative structures and arrangements, for a host of reasons. From this point of view
everything makes a kind of invidious sense. Legitimized (but not legitimate) violence at home and abroad seems to form an all-pervasive and
encompassing network of order, which—when judged using commonly
agreed-upon standards of humanity and morality—appears to be creating a
vast web of human and psychological chaos. Hence, the society is criticized as inherently doing violence to human values. Tocqueville, writing
for his time, noted a similar conflict over the role of social structures:

Epochs sometimes occur in the life of a nation when the old customs of
a people are changed, public morality is destroyed, religious belief shaken,
and the spell of tradition broken. . . . [C]itizens have neither the instinc-
tive patriotism of monarchy nor the reflecting patriotism of a republic. . . .
[T]hey have stopped between the two in the midst of confusion and
distress.[28]

While one might argue about the present state of "confusion and distress," one feels that Tocqueville would quickly recognize the parallels in the current conflicts between the role of structures in the relationships of individuals to the state, and the role of hierarchy in social organization. It often seems that there may be something inherent to a hierarchical organization of power that tends to encourage violent responses, by constituted or superior authority, to refuse-to-be-coopted challenges from below. This applies not only to concrete structures (government or military) but also to relationships between the state and the individual. In this hierarchical relationship, which can be seen as part of a larger set of inequality relationships, the individual is often seen as occupying the inferior position and the representatives of the state as occupying the superior one. The state is conceived as exercising power *over* the individual, rather than *for* him.

Evidence of this view can be found by examining just what kinds of violence are considered legal by the system and what are not, for what is legal is a good index to what is considered legitimate from the standpoint of those in power. For purposes of the law, military and police violence are not defined as violence, because they are conceived as legitimate. Similarly, they are not seen as threats to order. This reveals an essential element in the definition of just what constitutes violence from the perspective of the system. To the system, only violence that comes from the bottom of the hierarchy is really "violence" and hence requires repression if control fails. Antiauthority violence is always illegal. But authorized violence, as Max Weber notes, is legal and hence legitimate, from the systemic perspective of the state, as "the rule of men over men based on the means of legitimate, that is, allegedly legitimate, violence."[29] Taken in the foregoing context, Weber also supplies us with a view of the state as inherently repressive. Restated, we could interpret his definition as that rule of men over men that succeeds in making itself authoritative (violence that succeeds) is what we shall call the constituted authority, or the *state*. In other words, Weber does not separate the legitimacy of a given state from the fact of its existence. Thus, all states that exist are legitimate—so long as they exist. This definition allows for no recourse other than successful violence to change the definition of what the state shall be, just as it allows by definition for no other concept of legitimacy than that power that makes itself supreme. In other words, the state's legitimacy is based on violence that is legitimate for the state, but, by implication, not as a challenge to the state, unless and until it succeeds. For if the state has monopoly on the means of coercion and also on legitimacy, where is the recourse to be found? On what grounds can one base a challenge to the state's legitimacy other than post facto—that is, after one has replaced it?

This supports the conclusion that, so long as society is hierarchically organized with the people at the bottom, it will be part of the definition of the state that it can legitimately use power to repress citizens, but violence against the state will be conceived as inherently illegitimate. This is particularly irksome to a nation nurtured on the myth that in a democracy the repository of power is with the people. As Gurr puts it:

If a highly legitimate regime imposes a policy that substantially violates popular expectations about what the regime should do, people are motivated to protest not only because of the direct deprivation it imposes, but *because it is inconsistent with their image of the regime.* (Emphasis added.)[30]

This image of the "regime" myth in America implies at least an equality relationship between the state and the people. Consequently, to the extent this is accepted, the people will view the government's legitimacy as somehow dependent on an equality (rather than an inequality) relationship with the governed. While this is a "recognized" ideal, the reality is that when citizens perceive inequalities of power, and accompanying distribution of benefits and sanctions, that consistently appear to give the benefit of the doubt to the government, they may begin to see the hierarchical relationship not as a compromise for efficiency, but as a disruptive mechanism blocking, delaying, thwarting, and rechanneling their desires. In such circumstances they will see the hierarchical structure itself as repressive, rendering such a government illegitimate. And if they accept the myth fully and argue for radical egalitarianism *within* the society as well as between the people and their government, they will arrive at a justification for participatory democracy that does not sit well with the present hierarchical structures. The logic of this argument, then, serves to delegitimize the present structures as well as their recourse to violence.

The argument can serve as a beginning explanation of much of the attack on authority seen in our data, as well as of the suggestion in the data that acts of repression only stimulate more violence. Implicit of course in the foregoing argument is an acceptance of the view that structural conduciveness promotes political violence. As Neil Smelser constructs it, the basic elements of structural conduciveness are (1) the availability of communication conditions that can promote crowd mobilization, (2) the failure of responsible authorities to deal forcefully and equitably with all the conflicting parties, and (3) the inadequacy of grievance procedures and mechanisms.[31] This latter point particularly concerns us here. Although one could argue that the failure of authorities to deal equitably with conflicts encouraged the perception that they were illegitimate, our impression is that this argument often does not go far enough and thus fails to explain the emerging kinds of political violence. The problem is not that a particular set of grievances have not been met, but that over time the whole idea of going to authorities with grievances begins to be questioned. Indeed, the idea of "forceful" authoritative dealing with conflicts may typify precisely the kind of hierarchical approach to social order that is under attack. Students, for example, do not seek out for attack representatives of constituted authority simply because they wish to replace them with *other* authorities. Their goal often goes far beyond urging "transforming aims which are incompatible with the continued power of the members of the polity."[32] This is where many appear to misunderstand the nature of many campus upheavals.

What is the view of the dissidents toward violence as a means of attaining such a redefinition of power? A partial answer has been provided by the previous analysis: Violence as a means is legitimized by the critique of the society it seeks to replace. But it seems somewhat paradoxical that violence has become legitimated as a means to this end. A second rationale for legitimating violence in this attitudinal context is that political violence may be the only remaining effective means to political change. Recognizing the general sense in which much behavior, particularly such thresholds as we are examining, may be influenced by socialization, there may be some validity to Chalmers Johnson's suggestion that "the fact that a revolution has not yet occurred illustrates the principle that socialized actors will resort to violence only when all other means have been blocked."[33] This logic of last resort for redress of grievances, which is also substantiated by Levy's research, underlies the recent statement from Jackson State: "We resent everyone ignoring us until we have a riot."[34] Justice Douglas generalizes and capsulizes the logic of this position:

People march and protest but they are not heard. . . . [W]here grievances pile high and most of the elected spokesmen represent the Establishment, violence may be the only *effective* response.[35]

In addition, there is another partial answer to the problem of how violence has become legitimized as a means to changing the present social situation. It lies in the feeling that the *basic sense of justice* has been violated by the established order. In this sense, violence is seen as appropriate retribution rather than as remedial, as *quid pro quo* for violence visited upon citizens. From this point of view, repression aggravates the dissidents' grievances and affirms their perception of society as inherently illegitimate and violent. In Arendt's terms, "under certain circumstances violence . . . is the only way to set the scales of justice right again."[36] David Horowitz applies this argument specifically to the Weathermen as a justification for their actions: "For if Vietnamese are dying and their land is being destroyed by American power, by what bizarre structure of justice in the universe does America expect to be exempted from the consequences of its deeds and have the war stop at its borders?"[37]

By extension, this sense of justice can be seen as intimately related to what is perceived as a just order. For what is clear from both defenders' and dissidents' criticisms of each other is that what causes a society to be perceived as both orderly and legitimate has to do with what is and what is not perceived as violent. And violence becomes legitimized in both cases through a process of delegitimizing the target. Moreover, as a step in between the status quo and social change, violence is often conceived as a short-term means of keeping the illegitimate order from proceeding in its inherently disruptive way.

When the regime is considered by challengers to be disruptive, when authority relations fail, then power relations take their place. In turn, when symbolic power relations (that is, the internalized inhibitions associated with feelings of legitimacy) fail, coercive power relations (the use of authority force and violence) take their place. The events at Attica State Prison in New York played out such a scenerio to its murderous end—all in the name of order. It is worth noting and remembering here that coercive power relations can be and have, historically, been established not by any necessarily conscious conspiracy at the top, but by decisions and nondecisions that allowed the impulses, attitudes, predispositions, and awareness of local administrative and police officials to pour forth. Students of political theory and decision making have given slight attention to this phenomenon and its ramifications. Yet, from the murder of Thomas Beckett, to the Chicago police riot of 1968, to My Lai, field cadres within the lower levels of the hierarchy have struck blows for authority not because such action was ordered but because their superiors (and perhaps the culture as a whole?) created a general atmosphere that condoned it.

Just as the repression of demonstrators and the burning of Vietnamese villages to "save them" are examples of regime attempts to impose order, so the student strikes and bombings of ROTC buildings are seen by dissidents as attempts to slow or stop (or at best transform) what they see as the disruptive order of society.[38] It is this view of the disruptive order of society, combined with the revolutionary's vision of the just order, that transforms violence (for him or her) from a weapon of chaos to an instrument of justice.

Where does this leave us in explaining political violence as a phenomenon? In an earlier paper [39] we criticized the psychological explanations of political violence, including the theories of rising expectations, relative deprivation, and frustration–aggression. The foregoing discussion indicates that these explanations are still considered to be inadequate.

One of the latest applications of frustration–aggression to explaining political aggressiveness in *thought* as well as action illustrates and reinforces our central objections to frustration–aggression theory: namely, its tendency to explain nothing in particular about political violence by explaining (away) everything in general.[40] Robert Lane's application of frustration–aggression shows to what lengths it has to be stretched to begin to explain political phenomena: He argues that the concept of frustration–aggression must include "anticipation and speculation." He continues:

A man who imagines that his future road to riches and power will be blocked by government taxes is frustrated, even when the government has done nothing to him as yet. In the same way a young radical who feels that his vision of a socialist society is made unlikely by the power of the capitalists is frustrated from a happy consummation of his pleasant dream. Like "power" the concept "frustration" must allow for potential and reserved and fantasied uses. In our political material, there is very little mention of actual experienced frustration: the isolationist cannot say that foreign nations have frustrated him, but he hates their "selfishness"; the man who has derogatory things to say about the Catholic Church has not had any real goal thwarted by the Church, but he thinks he might. The concept "anticipated frustration" is often more useful in accounting for aggressive political ideas than actual experienced frustration. Moreover, the symbol of the potential frustrator may quickly become a ready stimulus to aggressive thought. If the frustration–aggression theory is to have much application to political thought, it must be in this extended sense.[41]

One wonders what is now left out? The theory explains everything from small degrees of anger to large-scale attacks, both individual acts (and nonacts) and collective acts or failures to act. In other words, it explains very little. What is it about either violence or psychology that makes people think that violence is best explained by psychological concepts? The answer is simply that violence is conceived of as a form of *abnormal* behavior. Psychology is seldom called in to explain normalcy. At this point concepts contributing to society's definition of legitimacy and its definition of *normalcy* begin to converge. In psychology, there are few situations for the person on the bottom of a given hierarchy (parent-child, teacher-student, and so on) in which the inferior person is considered normal for responding in a violent or aggressive manner. The behavior is considered evidence of a maladjustment, symptomatic of a larger problem, which needs to be corrected. Violence is at most an unnatural response; at the least, it is evidence that the individual is not fully correctly socialized or he or she would respect the constraints as to person and property.

Such a perspective reduces morals to rationalization—hardly a valid justification for a violence. (Lane, for example, reduces morality to the "need to feel moral.")[42] On the other hand, spanking children is often conceived as a necessary form of discipline, analogous functionally to much police behavior. It seems to be part of the underlying theology of psychology that the top of the hierarchy, the authority, can be endowed by the psychologist with the knowledge of good and evil, whereas children and strangers, the disfranchised and the dispossessed, must be dragged kicking and screaming into normalcy. Sovereignty resides in the authority; it does not derive from the people but from the knowledge of the expert. As a result, it can always be used to justify the status quo arrangement of power. If we accept this psychological explanation, we have nothing to turn to as a source of legitimacy for asserting counterclaims to the system's power. Thus psychological explanations of violence can often be seen as one more outgrowth of the hierarchical arrangement of society, which allows violence by superiors but condemns violence by inferiors.

In this paper we have attempted to illuminate many facets of the problem of political violence. But we believe all reflect a central theme. In this last section, "Notes Toward a Theory of Political Violence," we have tried to shed light and understanding on the phenomenon of political violence, with sensitivity to the perspective of the dissenter in a regime. Here we have also attempted to show how one's concept of "order" may be relative to one's perspective, and that one's perspective in this representative democracy may not be that of one equal to the authorities. We have argued that power relationships not only create inequalities, but that the structure of organization and hierarchical relations promote dominance of and submission to supposed equals. Might, we have suggested, often makes right; the thin fabric of legitimacy cloaking force in the guise of authority. When this cloth of legitimacy tears, symbolic and then coercive power relations emerge. This form of relationship between government and governed can be particularly disruptive in a period of challenge, not only through conscious sins of commission or omission, but by simply creating an atmosphere of condoning official violence. Finally, we have sought to show how, in seeking to understand political violence, analysts often turn inward toward the individual and his abnormality or maladjustment, when it is the society, its political and economic configuration of control, that may be more in need of analysis.

NOTES

1. Morris Janowitz, "Patterns of Collective Racial Violence," in Hugh D. Graham and Ted R. Gurr, *Violence in America,* New York: Bantam, 1969, p. 433.
2. *New York Times,* September 26, 1971, p. 1.
3. *Ibid.*
4. *Ibid.*
5. Warren H. Hanson, "Attica: The Hostages' Story," *New York Times,* Section 8, October 31, 1971, p. 18.
6. Department of Justice, *Uniform Crime Reports,* Washington, D.C.: U. S. Government Printing Office, July 1971.
7. See Eric Wolf, *Peasant Wars of the Twentieth Century,* New York: Harper & Row, 1969.
8. Georges Sorel, *Reflections on Violence,* London: Collier MacMillan, 1950.
9. Richard E. Rubenstein, *Rebels in Eden,* Boston: Little, Brown, 1970; E. J. Hobsbawn, *Primitive Rebels,* New York: Norton, 1959; H. L. Nieburg, *Political Violence,* New York: St. Martin, 1969; Charles Tilly, "Revolutions and Collective Violence," unpublished manuscript, December 1970, pp. 30–42.
10. Murray Edleman, *Politics as Symbolic Action,* Chicago: Markham, 1971.
11. Ted Gurr, *Why Men Rebel,* Princeton, N.J.: Princeton University Press, 1970, p. 317.
12. James C. Davies, "Political Violence: Phenotypes and Genotypes," manuscript, March 1971.
13. Ivo K. Feierabend *et al.,* "Social Change and Political Violence; Cross-National Pattern," in Hugh D. Graham and Ted R. Gurr, *Violence in America: A Staff Report,* Washington, D.C.: U.S. Government Printing Office, 1969, Vol. 2.
14. Gurr, p. 11.
15. Hannah Arendt, *On Violence,* New York: Harcourt Brace Jovanovich, 1970, p. 46. We disagree with Arendt's interpretation that violence must be "instrumental" to be political, for our incidents are often obviously political and noninstrumental.
16. Irving L. Horowitz, "The Struggle is the Message: Protest and Violence," The National Commission on the Causes and Prevention of Violence, September 1969.
17. Gurr, p. 9.
18. Report of the National Advisory Commission on Civil Disorders, New York: Bantam, 1968, pp. 109–158.

19. Tilly, p. 31.
20. This has recently been tested and confirmed using European data quite similar to ours. See Betty A. Nesvold and Carolyn Stevenson, "World Patterns of Campus Conflict—the Mid 50's and the Contemporary Scene," paper: APSA Convention, Chicago, September 1971.
21. Sheldon Levy, in *Assassination and Political Violence* by James Kirkham, Sheldon Levy, and William Crotty, Washington, D.C.: U.S. Government Printing Office, 1969, Vol. 8, NCCPV Staff Study Series, p. 417, Appendix Supplement.
22. Clarification of Other Categories on Figure 7: "Police and public buildings" includes police cars and police stations (*not* individual policemen), city halls, CIA buildings, etc. (17, 16). "Corporate" includes a combination of small businesses, banks, utilities, and large corporations. "Military" includes all draft-related incidents less ROTC attacks, all attacks on military bases, trucks, ships, and ammunition plants. Most of the high school and elementary school incidents are coded as "don't know" in the political/nonpolitical breakdown, as their character was often highly ambiguous, producing a generally small N. Remaining target violence includes: (a) private political, including college presidents' homes, off-duty policemen at home, police informers, corporate executives' homes, etc. (N = 12); (b) public events (N = 1); (c) prisons (N = 1); (d) miscellaneous (N = 11).
23. Apparently this latter awareness extends to military personnel—perhaps because so many radicals narrowly escaped being one of them (one volunteers to be a policeman) or perhaps because soldiers are less visible, since most of them are abroad.
24. In Easton's terms we are most concerned with "authorities" and then, to the degree it represents basic authority structures, the "regime." At times, however, we feel that those aspects of Easton's "community" that form the basis for accepting or rejecting authority need somehow to be included. See David Easton, *A Systems Analysis of Political Life,* New York: Wiley, 1965.
25. S. M. Lipset, *Political Man,* New York: Random House, 1960, p. 78.
26. Philip E. Slater, *The Pursuit of Loneliness: American Culture at the Breaking Point,* Boston: Beacon, 1970, p. 31.
27. Henry Bienen, *Violence and Social Change,* Chicago: University of Chicago Press, 1968, p. 74.
28. Alexis de Tocqueville, *Democracy in America,* Vol. I, New York: Knopf, 1945, pp. 251–252.
29. Max Weber, *Politics as a Vocation,* in Hans Gerth and C. Wright Mills, ed., *From Max Weber,* New York: Oxford, 1958, pp. 78–79.
30. Gurr, p. 186.
31. N. J. Smelser, *Theory of Collective Behavior,* New York: Free Press, 1965, pp. 227–241.
32. Tilly, p. 40.
33. Chalmers Johnson, *Revolutionary Change,* Boston: Little, Brown, 1966, p. 90.
34. *New York Times,* March 21, 1971. Article by Stephen Lesher, "Jackson State a Year After," p. 25.
35. Justice William O. Douglas, *Points of Rebellion,* New York: Random House, Vintage, 1969–1970, pp. 88–89.
36. Arendt, p. 64.
37. David Horowitz, "Revolutionary Karma Versus Revolutionary Politics," *Ramparts, 9,* No. 8 (March 1971), 29.

38. Violence, as Nieburg has pointed out, can be the rational political response to many forms of governmental action, especially when it reciprocates government violence. See Nieburg, pp. 132–164.
39. Peter A. Lupsha, "Explanation of Political Violence: Some Psychological Theories Versus Indignation," *Politics & Society* (November 1971).
40. Robert E. Lane, *Political Thinking and Consciousness, The Private Life of the Political Mind,* Chicago: Markham, 1965, p. 155.
41. *Ibid.,* p. 156.
42. *Ibid.,* p. 190.

2

A Psychological Perspective
on the Nature of Political Violence
Studies of the Contagion
of Violence

LEONARD BERKOWITZ
University of Wisconsin

Over 80 years ago the French sociologist, Gabriel Tarde, described what he called "suggesto-imitative assaults." Epidemics of crime, he proposed, "follow the line of the telegraph." News of a spectacular crime in one community suggests criminal ideas to others and can even produce imitative crimes. Tarde pointed to the aftereffects of the Jack the Ripper murders as a notable example. The lurid news stories about these crimes evidently inspired a series of female mutilation cases in the English provinces (Tarde 1912, pp. 340–341). Police in this country have at times offered similar observations. According to Commander Francis Flanagan of the Chicago Police Department (*Look Magazine,* September 19, 1967), Richard Speck's murder of 8 nurses in Chicago in July 1966 and Charles Whitman's shooting of 45 people from the University of Texas Tower the next month instigated a rise in homicides in Chicago. At least 5 murders in Arizona were apparently influenced by the Texas Tower shootings. In November 1966, Robert Smith, an 18-year-old high school senior, walked into an Arizona beauty school and shot 4 women and a child. He told police he had gotten the idea for a mass killing from the news stories of the Speck and Whitman outbursts. He had been planning his murders from the time his parents gave him a target pistol 3 months earlier (*Ithaca Journal,* November 14, 1966).

Many other illustrations of apparently contagious violence can be cited. To single out just a few, in the winter of 1966–1967, a televised dramatization of a fictitious plot to blow up an airliner led to a sharp increase in hoax telephone calls warning about bombs aboard airliners (*Ithaca Journal,* December 20, 1966), and in the spring of 1968, a

German housepainter shot the student radical Rudi Dutschke, saying he had gotten the idea from the assassination of Martin Luther King (*Madison Capital Times,* April 13, 1968). The news stories may even lead to crimes that do not closely resemble the instigating event; in Gravesend, England, probation officers reported a sharp rise in offenses by local delinquents after a sex killing of two teenagers (*London Sunday Times,* April 24, 1966). Urban riots in this country also show a pattern suggestive of a contagious spread of violence. According to Lieberson and Silverman (1965), American race riots tend to be clustered together in time. No detectable riot occurred in 26 of the 51 years from 1913 through 1963, while there were 2 or more such riots in 15 of the years in this period, and 5 of the years actually had 7 or more riots—all of this before Watts exploded into our awareness. Can it be that any one racial flare-up somehow makes it easier for another similar outburst to take place soon after?

THE CONTAGION OF CRIMINAL VIOLENCE

Some time ago I wondered if these seeming "imitative" effects would be revealed in crime statistics. Through the cooperation of the Federal Bureau of Investigation, my associate Dr. Jacqueline Macaulay and I obtained the number of aggressive crimes in each month for the years 1960 through 1966 for 40 cities across the country (Berkowitz and Macaulay 1971). We were particularly interested in the possibility of increases in the frequency of these offenses after John Kennedy's assassination in late November 1963, and after the Speck-Whitman murders in the summer of 1966. The most reliable measure is the sum of the scores for the four violent crimes (murder, rape, aggravated assault, and robbery), and many criminologists have worked with an unweighted sum of these offenses as an index of total violent crimes. Analyses were also carried out for the separate crimes, but I will here focus my attention on the total score measure.

We found a significant, positively accelerated trend for these aggressive crimes across the 84 months and no reliable differences from one area of the country to another. More important, the analysis revealed a significant rise from the general linear trend after each of the sensational murders. There was a significant rise above the overall trend in December after the assassination and a still sharper jump in January. The total incidence of violent crimes then declined in February. President Kennedy's murder evidently had its strongest effect about a month or more after this tragic event. The FBI does not know of any widespread changes in police procedures that could have accounted for this jump. Going on to the summer of 1966, there was a reliable increase in violent crimes above the trend line in 4 of the 5 months following the slaying of the Chicago nurses. The other destructive outbursts occurring that summer probably strengthened the aggressive consequences of the Speck murders.

A graphic analysis of changes in the frequency of violent crimes also shows these effects. For these data we first calculated the mean number of aggressive crimes over all 40 cities in each of the 12 months. Using these monthly averages as a base, we then plotted the deviation from the monthly average for each month in the period from January 1960 through December 1966. The results are given in Figure 11. Here we see the sharp and startling rise in January 1964, after John Kennedy's assassination, the decline from January through July of that year, and then the gradual increase until the tragic summer of 1966. Another rise in violent crimes occurred at that time, but the Speck and Whitman violence evidently increased the incidence of aggressive crimes still further.

Albert Bandura has recently obtained even more striking evidence of behavioral contagion—this time in regard to airplane hijackings. Making use of governmental records, he simply tallied the number of such hijackings in this country and abroad every year from 1947 through 1970.

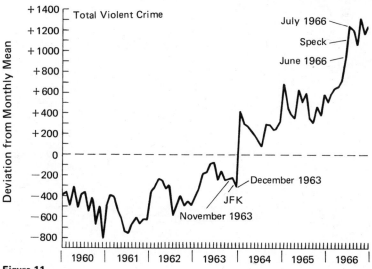

Figure 11

The results are shown in Figure 12. As you can see, a number of foreign airliners (primarily Hungarian and Czechoslovakian) were hijacked before 1951 without there being any American imitations. Then, beginning in 1958, Cubans seeking to flee their country resorted to this particular technique about 15 or so times, with a veritable rash of hijackings—from Havana to Miami in these years—occurring in 1960. Some Americans evidently got the idea, and 5 U.S. airliners were hijacked in 1961. But most impressive of all, other people around the world also learned this lesson. Particularly after 1967, news from one country seemed to influence the hijackings in other nations as well. The incidence of kidnapped foreign airliners dramatically parallels the number of hijacked American airliners in the 1967–1970 period. The contagion spread with the television camera and newspaper headline.

Many other examples of behavioral contagion could be provided if we were to get away from violence. It is enough for my purposes, however, merely to show that many kinds of aggressive events seem to be subject to contagious influences: reactions to filmed aggression, urban disorders, and violent offenses following sensational crimes. The problem now is to account for these violent outbursts. Why does the

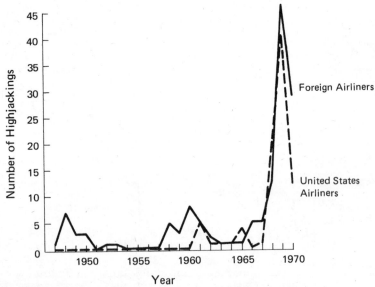

Figure 12

depiction of violence in the mass media so often incite people to act violently themselves?

SOME FACTORS INVOLVED IN THE CONTAGION OF VIOLENCE

Many of the leading theoretical analyses of the effects of observed aggression have emphasized three things: (1) the information provided by the model's conduct, (2) changes in the strength of the observer's inhibitions against aggression, and (3) the degree to which the witnessed event has produced a generalized emotional or motivational arousal. My own approach has been somewhat different. While I do, of course, recognize that the three types of reactions just summarized play an important part in determining the consequences of media violence, I have also been struck by the extent to which aggressive behavior occasionally seems to function like a conditioned response to situational stimuli. There are times, I suggest, where a classical conditioning model appears to be the best way of explaining the outcome. On these occasions the observer reacts impulsively to particular stimuli in his environment, not because his inhibitions have been weakened or because he anticipates the pleasures arising from his actions, but because situational stimuli have evoked the responses he is predisposed or set to make in that setting. Contagious violence often comes about in this way.

Simply put, it seems to me that reported or portrayed scenes of violence in the mass media often function as stimuli that can evoke a range of implicit aggressive responses. This happens because the stimuli and responses are associated semantically; they have aggressive meaning. The implicit reactions (probably ideas, feelings, and even motoric responses), I suggest, facilitate the occurrence of other actions having the same meaning—open aggression. These overt responses need not be made, but are more likely if the observer is set to act aggressively at the time, and if other facilitating conditions are also at work.

The argument I have been spelling out has an obvious implication: Stimuli having this aggressive meaning should be capable of eliciting aggressive responses from people who, for one reason or another, are ready to act aggressively. Weapons are prime examples of such stimuli, and an experiment I did in collaboration with LePage (1967) demonstrates that even their mere presence can instigate violent reactions for angry people. For many men (and probably women as well) in our society, these objects are closely associated with aggression. Assuming the weapons do not produce inhibitions that are stronger than the evoked aggressive reactions (as would be the case, for example, if the weapons were labeled as morally bad), the presence of the aggressive objects would generally lead to more intense attacks upon an available target than would occur in the presence of a neutral object.

To test this hypothesis, one group of male undergraduates were made to be angry with the experimenter's confederate who was posing as another subject; a second group were treated in a neutral manner by the accomplice. All of the men were then given an opportunity to administer electric shocks to the confederate. Some of the men saw weapons lying on the table near the shock apparatus; another group of subjects in both the angered and nonangered conditions gave the shocks without anything being on the table except the shock key. Finally, for a third group of subjects, two badminton racquets and shuttlecocks were close to the shock key. The purpose of this third condition was to determine whether the presence of *any* object near the shock apparatus would lead to relatively strong aggression, even if the object were not connected with aggressive behavior. The hypothesis guiding the study received good support. The strongly provoked men delivered more frequent electrical attacks upon their tormentor in the presence of a weapon than when nonaggressive objects (the badminton racquets and shuttlecocks) were present or when only the shock key was on the table.

Stimuli presented in the mass media that have this kind of aggressive meaning should also elicit aggressive reactions in audience members. It is for this reason that I believe Frederick Wertham (1954) is essentially correct in criticizing comic books that feature violent crimes. With Wertham, I suggest that these violent scenes can give rise to aggressive ideas and images in the reader even though the scenes are portrayed only on the printed page. An unpublished experiment by Parker, West, and myself demonstrates that comic-book violence can stimulate aggressive ideas even in "normal" people. Third-, fourth-, and fifth-grade school children were asked to select words completing a series of incomplete sentences both before and after they read a particular comic book. The youngsters given a war comic book to read (*Adventures of the Green Berets*) were much more likely to show an increase in their use of hostile words to finish these sentences than the control children, who were required to read a nonaggressive comic book (*Gidget*). For example, if the subjects had to complete a sentence such as "I want to_____the book," and could choose between "read" and "tear," the children who had read the war comics were more apt to select "tear."

These aggressive ideas and images evoked by violent scenes are probably usually too weak and short-lived to influence the behavior of most viewers. Under some conditions, however, these implicit reactions might lead to fairly open attacks upon an available target even by people who ordinarily have strong inhibitions against direct aggression. This is shown in an experiment in which college girls listened to a humorous tape recording (Berkowitz 1970). The subjects were required to rate another girl's suitability for a job as dormitory counselor after they heard a brief excerpt from a comedian's routine. Half of the subjects listened to a nonaggressive comedian (George Carlin), while the other girls heard the hostile comedian (Don Rickles) in a very aggressive routine. The subjects were much more hostile toward the job applicant after hearing the aggressive humor than after the neutral humor. Moreover, and contrary to some recent studies purporting to demonstrate the supposedly beneficial effects of aggressive humor, there was no evidence of a cathartic reduction of hostility in the aggressive humor condition; Don Rickles' comic routine led to heightened hostility whether or not the job applicant had previously provoked the subjects. In both cases, the hostile jokes had stimulated aggressive reactions in the listeners, which then caused them to evaluate the job applicant less favorably.

THE OBSERVER'S ANGER OR AROUSAL LEVEL

In our Wisconsin research we have generally obtained significant effects only when the subjects had been angered before seeing the movie. On the basis of other findings, however, it is clear that this anger is not absolutely necessary for media violence to have an effect; it facilitates the aggressive reaction, but is not necessary. Many different kinds of emotional arousal can have the same effect. As one demonstration of this, Geen and I (1967) have reported that task frustrations can also heighten subjects' responsiveness to the aggressive stimuli in their environment.

Other sources of heightened arousal could well have the same consequences—again, if clearly defined aggressive stimuli are present. Several interesting experiments are illustrative. Geen and O'Neal (1969) recently found that men who heard a loud but not painful "white noise" after seeing a prizefight film attacked their partners more strongly than did other subjects who had not watched the fight or who had not heard the sound. The excitation resulting from the noise had evidently strengthened the aggressive reactions stimulated by the aggressive movie. Similarly, when Tannenbaum and Zillman showed a brief sex film to one group of men who had been provoked by a partner, these sexually aroused subjects gave him stronger electric shock punishment than did men in the control group, who were similarly angered but not sexually aroused. The sexual arousal had evidently helped "energize" the aggressive responses elicited by the provocation and the opportunity to attack the partner. In a later variation on this study, these researchers obtained results consistent with the previously cited Berkowitz-LePage (1967) experiment. The strongest electric attacks on the tormentor were given by men who watched the sex film and at the same time heard a tape recording of the woman character's thoughts about killing her lover. In this case the viewers' sexual arousal apparently also strengthened the aggressive responses elicited by the aggressive tape recording. This kind of phenomenon, in which sexual arousal functions like other arousal sources to facilitate aggressive responses to aggressive cues, could contribute to the apparent connection between sexual and aggressive motivation posited by some writers.

JUDGING THE PROPRIETY OF THE OBSERVED AGGRESSION

We have already seen that the observer cannot be viewed as merely a passive recipient of the stimuli presented to him. He imparts meaning to these stimuli, sometimes classifying the witnessed event as "aggressive" and sometimes as "nonaggressive." He may also judge any observed violence he sees as "good" or "bad," "moral" or "immoral," "justified" or "unjustified." Five separate experiments employing college students have demonstrated that the interpretation of the propriety of the witnessed aggression can influence the observer's own aggressive behavior immediately after the movie.

In four of these studies (Berkowitz and Rawlings 1963; Berkowitz, Corwin, and Heironimus 1963; Berkowitz 1965; Berkowitz and Geen 1967) the "champion" prizefight scene was introduced to deliberately provoke students in one of two ways: By varying a supposed summary of the plot, the fight loser (the main character in the movie) was portrayed in either a favorable or relatively unfavorable manner so that the beating he received was generally regarded as either unjustified or justified aggression. Immediately afterward, when the men had an opportunity to attack their tormentor, they displayed weaker aggression toward him after seeing the film victim get the less justified beating than following the more justified injury to the movie character. It is as if the justified aggression on the screen legitimated the subjects' own attacks on the person who had provoked them.

IDENTIFICATION WITH FILM CHARACTERS

In addition to defining the meaning of the actions he sees and judging their moral rightness, the observer may play a fairly active role in the situation by imagining himself to be one of the film characters. This process, often termed "identification," has frequently been discussed by film writers but has received surprisingly little systematic research attention.

When a person identifies with someone on the screen, he does more than watch this individual closely. In imagining himself to be this character, he is also thinking of doing what he believes this other is doing. He is implicitly copying the actions he observes. As a result, we might say, he is also particularly ready to carry out the same kind of behaviors openly and should be highly responsive to those situational cues that could evoke such responses. Turner and Berkowitz (1972) applied this reasoning to film violence.

After each subject was informed that the study was an investigation of physiological reactions to complex stimulus situations and was hooked up to supposed autonomic recording apparatus, the experimenter's accomplice deliberately angered the subject by giving him a large number of shocks as his "judgment" of the subject's work. For the second stimulus situation, the subject and the confederate then watched the "champion" boxing scene. Instructions written on an index card that had been given to the subject (without being seen by the experimenter) created the set the subject was to employ in watching the violent film. One-third of the men were asked to think of themselves as the character named Dunne, Kirk Douglas' opponent in the movie fight. Another third were to think of themselves as a judge watching the fight whose job was to observe Dunne specifically and judge his performance. Finally, the control group were given no specific "imagine self" instructions.

The results indicate that identification with the fight winner had heightened the aggression-evoking effect of the witnessed violence. The men who were asked to imagine themselves as Dunne (the winner) administered a greater mean number of shocks for each idea evaluated, and inflicted reliably longer punishment in doing so, than either the subjects who had only watched Dunne or the control subjects not given any particular instructions. This increased aggressiveness evidently also produced a greater general hostility toward the experimenter and the experiment. Here too, then, as in the other experiments in the Wisconsin program, observed violence did not have a cathartic effect. Rather than lessening hostile desires, identification with an observed aggressor led to stronger displays of aggression.

CONCLUSION

The present paper does not pretend to be an analysis of all human aggression or even necessarily of the most dramatic forms of violence. Nor does it offer a comprehensive interpretation of all of the influences the mass media can have. I have dealt only with relatively quick, impulsive reactions to events portrayed in the media. Much of the speculation advanced here, however, probably applies to other forms of impulsive aggression as well. Although they are often called "expressive" behaviors, these outbursts are governed by environmental cues as well as by internal excitation. Situational stimuli have elicited aggressive responses from people who were predisposed to display such behavior.

Viewing impulsive aggression as something like a conditioned response to a particular stimulus does not imply that cognitive processes have no part in this behavior or that the human being is merely a passive responder to the world around him. He quickly categorizes the stimuli impinging on him and then reacts, even when the reaction seems fast and spontaneous, in terms of the meaning the dominant stimuli have for him. Even very rapid explosions of violence can be governed by the aggressive meaning the individual has imparted to aspects of the situation confronting him as well as by his level of emotional arousal. Other kinds of ideas also influence the individual's reactions to witnessed violence. It may be that the sight of aggression, or of an object associated with aggression, elicits aggressive thoughts (together with an imaginal representation of the stimulus) in virtually everyone. However, this perceptual-cognitive reaction will not necessarily lead to open attacks upon available targets. Other cues in the environment may tell the person that aggression will bring unpleasant consequences (so that he inhibits this response) or that the behavior will be rewarded (so that the action comes forth). More than this, as I tried to show earlier, the viewer may think of the observed violence as "good" or "bad," "justified" or "unjustified," and these ideas will also influence what he does.

The role of thinking must not be exaggerated, however. Impulsive behavior is not carried out with deliberation and forethought. It bursts forth, relatively free of control by intellect and cognitive processes. When this happens man is more like the lower animals than he is otherwise and is subject to many of the same influences that operate on them. One of our most important tasks as psychologists is to determine the conditions that govern these different levels of human functioning. What makes a person respond impulsively, automatically, and with a minimum of thought, and when are his cognitive processes more dominant in regulating his actions?

REFERENCES

Geen, R. G., and L. Berkowitz, "Some Conditions Facilitating the Occurrence of Aggression After the Observation of Violence," *Journal of Personality, 35* (1967), 666–676.

Geen, R. G., and E. C. O'Neal, "Activation of Cue-Elicited Aggression by General Arousal," *Journal of Personality and Social Psychology, 11* (1969), 289–292.

Lieberson, S., and A. Silverman, "The Precipitants and Underlying Conditions of Race Riots," *American Sociological Review, 30* (1965), 887–898.

Tarde, G., *Penal Philosophy,* Boston: Little, Brown, 1912.

Turner, C., and L. Berkowitz, "Identification with Film Aggressor (Covert Role Taking) and Reactions to Film Violence, *"Journal of Personality and Social Psychology* (1972), in press.

Wertham, F. C., *Seduction of the Innocent,* New York: Holt, Rinehart & Winston, 1954.

3

A Systemic and Extrasystemic Perspective
on the Nature of Political Violence
Political Violence:
The Dominance-Submission Nexus

JAMES C. DAVIES
University of Oregon

The most widely current explanations for political violence lack general
applicability. They fit some riots, rebellions, and revolutions, but not
all. The Puritan and the French Revolutions, for example, may be reduced to the conflict between the rising bourgeois and the declining
feudal socioeconomic classes. The conflicts between India and Great
Britain and between Algeria and France may be analyzed as confrontations between the colonized and the colonizers, in the twilight of
imperialism. Or imperialism itself may be reduced to class-conflict
analysis. The strife in North Ireland between Irish Catholics and Scotch-
Irish Protestants may be deemed ethnic or religious—or it, too, may be
seen in Marxist terms as fundamentally socioeconomic class conflict.

There is, however, an explanation that does have more nearly universal applicability. It is, of course, not a complete, a sufficient, explanation
for all political violence, but it specifies a necessary common element,
including the genotypical element common to the analyses of all the
conflicts mentioned. This is the dominance–submission nexus, the relationship between those who have and those who lack political power. As
an explanation, the relationship seems to be almost tautological, but
when its origins and functions are examined, its apparent tautology
disappears. In discussing the thesis, I will first state it and then specify
its foundation in human needs that are universal to all men everywhere

This is a revised version of a paper read at the Conference on Political Micro-
Violence, at the University of Texas at Austin, 25–26 March 1971. Copyright
© 1973 by James C. Davies.

and how they function in all developing societies. Then I will compare this psychologically based dominance–submission explanation with other basic analyses of political violence.

THE DOMINANCE–SUBMISSION NEXUS

As a phenotype, dominance–submission includes all visible forms of interaction between superordinate and subordinate groups. The superordinate group may be an economically ruling group—a managerial or other ruling group whose basis for political control is the production and distribution of material goods. The superordinate group alternatively may be a group of settlers, of colonials who control an undeveloped society that has large but unexploited natural and human resources for the production of both material and nonmaterial goods. The superordinate group may be one that controls people whose distinguishing characteristic is not necessarily either low economic status or geographic location in an undeveloped territory but skin color or other ethnic difference.

In actuality, these three types of relationship between those who rule and those who are ruled usually overlap. A ruling group typically has superior economic power to go with its political power and in many instances exerts this economic and political power over people who are geographically or ethnically distinguishable, or both. Most analyses have emphasized the economic relationship and applied it promiscuously to colonial and ethnic power relationships. Other analyses, whether or not they include economic factors, rest primarily on a colonial or an ethnic basis.

The dominance–submission nexus is theoretically universal, because it contains all status and power relationships, including the economic, colonial, and ethnic variations. What is involved in status are such things as prestige and deference, which may be manifested in a variety of ways that include superior wealth, culture, and different (and therefore superior) skin color.* What is involved in power is the ability to control the production and distribution of material and nonmaterial goods. That

---

*From the beginnings of exploration in the fifteenth century to the (capitalist or socialist) colonialism of the twentieth, white skin color has been considered superior by overweening whites. There is little evidence to support the idea that the reverse may not also develop. That is, at another time, overweening people of brown (or black) skin may well consider brown (or black) skin color to be superior to all other skin colors. Hence the more general adjective "different" is applied to skin color here.

is, power may be exercised not only in ways that have to do with who gets how much land and housing and commodities but also in ways that have to do with who gets how much deference, education, and authority to make basic policy decisions for the entire society.

The dominance–submission relationship is phenotypical in its socioeconomic, colonial, racial, and other manifest forms. A genotypical examination of the phenomenon is useful as a step in the process of establishing more generally applicable classifications. If we use dominance and submission as the nouns and socioeconomic, colonial, and racial as adjectives applicable to various circumstances, we then avoid having to say things that are almost self-evidently inaccurate. We need not say that the domination by whites of blacks is really socioeconomic when socioeconomic describes only part of the picture and skin color is also important. We need not say that the exploitation of Indonesians when they were called Dutch East Indians was based on skin color *or* economics *or* geographic separation from the "mother country"—when all these factors were involved. We need not say that the attempts of Japan to conquer Indonesia in the 1940s or of Indonesia to absorb Netherlands New Guinea (also called, politically, West Irian and, ethnically, Papuan) in the 1950s were economic, colonial, or racial—or use some other adjective. By using the phrase dominance–submission, we are indeed describing the relationship in its universally basic form.

But names and classifications are only a first step. Whatever improvement there is in analysis that avoids synecdoche—that in this case avoids using adjectives as though they were nouns, subsets as though they were sets—we have not gone very far in explaining *why* the relationship develops, continues, and finally ends. To reduce the dominance–submission nexus from its socioeconomic or other adjectival form does not tell us why, in certain social relationships during certain periods, some people dominate and others submit. Dominance–submission may begin and end in a sheer struggle for power, but during its intervening, continuing period the nexus may rest on authority, on the acceptance by those who are subordinated of the fact of their submission and of the dominance of those who have superior wealth, prestige, and political power.

My argument is that the dominance–submission nexus comes into existence because it serves the needs of both those who dominate and those who submit. It is stable as long as it serves the needs of both parties to the relationship. Thereafter, those who are dominant tend to demand its continuance, because it serves their continuing needs for wealth, prestige, and power. And correlatively thereafter, those who are subordinate tend to wish and demand an end to the relationship, because it no longer serves their now increased needs—for wealth, prestige, and power. During its continuation, the nexus is functional to the needs of both. When it is no longer functional to the needs of the subordinate group—and I would argue also no longer functional to the needs of the superordinate group—it then becomes an unstable relationship. It finally comes to an end when the subordinated group loses its tendency to submit and the dominant group its tendency to demand submission. When the process occurs relatively voluntarily, it takes place rather peaceably. When the dominant group resists vigorously the change in the power relationship, it usually takes place with violence. If the resistance to change is prolonged and intense enough, the violence becomes widespread and the process is a revolution.

In a commonsensical and evident way, the utility, the functionality, of the dominant–submissive relationship in certain circumstances is rather widely acknowledged. Its utility is most often stated by the dominant parties. Poor people who can get jobs in a factory, at whatever is the going wage rate, may indeed be better off if the alternative is semistarvation or mere subsistence in the country village. This may well be the case when the society involved is generally but not universally advanced, like Sweden or the United States. It may also be the case when the employer is an oil company based in a technologically and economically advanced country and the employee is an Arab in Saudi Arabia or when the employer is an American copper corporation and the employee is a onetime Chilean peasant. It may be the case when the employer is a New England-based textile manufacturer and the (black) employee lives and works in a mill town in South Carolina.

On noneconomic grounds also, the relationship may be mutually beneficial. A peasant moving to a city may experience more than the pleasure of earning substantial wages after living in a mainly barter rural economy. He may experience better medical care, the chance to get formal education, and other welfare benefits. He may also experience the freedom and excitement of urban life, free of the restraints of his tradition-dominated home community. Such observable benefits can develop within a dominance–submission relationship of any of the adjectival sorts mentioned—socioeconomic, colonial, or ethnic.*

---

*And they may develop, for a time, in other, nonpolitical, dominance–submission relationships, as when the exciting male takes unto him an innocent maiden, who, for a time, is really happier as his handmaiden than she was as her parents' subordinate daughter. This could be called the Cinderella syndrome, if the phrase did not make these relationships seem to be only legendary and not really common dominance–submission relationships in the twentieth century, both among traditional and among supposedly emancipated partners to the liaison.

The benefits to the dominant party are mostly correlative. If the peasant-turned-factory-worker lives better than he otherwise would without the relationship being established, so also do the boss and the ruler—people who are, as I said earlier, as a category usually indistinguishable.*

That is, people in the dominant group enjoy more wealth, prestige, and power than they did before their dominant position was established with respect to others in the society. If the peasant enjoys prestige when he returns to his native village with his transistor radio and reports how he can read and write and drive a truck, the boss or ruler can exhibit his paintings purchased at a London auction and send his son to America for his higher education. If the peasant enjoys a new-found power to manipulate his largely nonpolitical environment (by driving a truck and buying a forged labor card in order to get a new job in a new town), the boss or ruler can exercise his power economically and politically. He can break a threatened strike of his field hands or factory workers, with the help of police or military forces responsive to his command.

But in due course and inevitably, the relationship changes. The subordinated individuals and groups acquire, under tutelage of the dominant ones, social skills of urban living, the technical skills of the division of labor, some of the vision and power that education gives, and more of the same kind of expectations that the dominant ones have. Having acquired these competencies and expectations, they—the subordinated ones—change. They wish to end the dominant–submissive relationship, replacing it with one in which there is at least greater equality of material reward, more equal prestige and more mutual deference, and more equal political power.

The dominant groups have gained greatly during the stable period of the relationship and naturally wish it to continue. They naturally want to continue to get a high material reward. Also, and naturally, they want to continue enjoying greater prestige and deference, and power disproportionate to their numbers and to their usefulness to the subordinated ones. That is, they want their absolute and their relative portions of material and nonmaterial goods to continue. It is usually the case that only when these groups see as the alternative losing everything they have gained in material and nonmaterial goods do they recognize

*They are usually indistinguishable as members of the "ruling class," whether it be in societies in which the dominance–submission is largely socioeconomic, as in the United States or the Soviet Union; colonial, as in parts of Africa during their colonial period or in the satellites of the Soviet Union; or ethnic, as in the South of the United States or in Rhodesia and South Africa.

the need for accepting the demands of the subordinate ones. As I said earlier, when they do accept these demands, the change in the dominance-submission relationship is peaceful. When they do not accept the demands, the change is usually postponed while the subordinate ones gather their strength, but it occurs then, nevertheless, and typically with enormous violence.

What I have just said about the diminishing utility of the dominance-submission nexus to both those who dominate and those who submit is indeed on the manifest level. It does little more than focus attention on what is, at least on second glance, rather obvious: When people have a choice, they don't like to get shoved around. However, subordinated people become so very passionate in their demands not just because, let us say, they are no longer satisfied with transistor radios and now want television sets. They become so passionate not just because they want to end imprisonment for debt or exile to Australia for crimes against property. They become so passionate not just because they want the vote. In sum, they are not passionate from a simple desire for gadgetry and for symbolic political recognition. They want substantial wealth and prestige; they also want substantial power.

And it is possible to go deeper in our analysis. By doing so, we can explain the intense passion that becomes evident on both sides when the nexus has lost its utility—I would argue its bilateral utility—and the subordinate ones demand change. The goods described are only visible manifestations of what fundamentally the subordinated ones want. What fundamentally they want is what the superordinate ones want: the chance—by their own voluntary individual and collective action—to satisfy their basic needs. This is a process as continuing and endless as life itself, for rich and poor alike. These needs are not just the physical ones for food, clothing, shelter, and physical safety. And during a particular epoch in a particular society, the most prominent basic needs of one group will differ from the prominent needs of another group. Subordinate groups differ from dominant groups, not in their needs, but in the time historically when each kind of need emerges.

To reiterate briefly, those who are dominant at a particular time in a particular culture have secured more complete satisfaction of more of their basic needs and wish the satisfaction pattern to continue. Those who remain subordinate have secured less satisfaction of fewer of their basic needs and wish the satisfaction pattern to change. The difference between the two categories is not one of differing basic needs but of differing degrees and kinds of need satisfaction.

Thus, my general explanation for the dominance-submission nexus is that it develops when it serves various basic, innate needs of all those involved in the relationship. That is, at a particular point in history in a particular culture, some needs are being generally satisfied in one group in the culture and other needs then become prominent in that group. At that same time, in another group in the same culture, a different set of needs have been satisfied and other needs have then become prominent. This is shown in Table 2 on the following page.

In Table 2, Group A may be considered the ruling group and Group B the ruled group.

At any particular time in any actual culture, there are inevitably other kinds of groups than rulers and ruled, and there are inevitably individual crossovers from one group to another, including from Group B to Group A and from Group A to Group B.

For example, at Time One an individual whose group of origin is Catholic and working class may therefore start his adult life in Group B; but he may be entering Group A as a rising administrator in the governmental bureaucracy of a developing and Protestant-dominated culture. He will have role conflicts. Similarly, at the same Time One in a different culture, an individual in Group B may be a "native" in a colony dominated by the "settlers" or "colonials" who compose Group A; this individual may also be a rising public official. He, too, will have role conflicts.

Correlatively, at Time Two, a person born into Group A may, for failure to gain satisfaction of his own private demands that fall into Need-Set Four, identify himself with Group B and he may articulate the grievances of that group. He may thereby become, at least for a time, an accepted member of Group B. He, too, will have role conflicts. Meanwhile (as indicated in the table) most of those in Group B, the ruled group, will have demands for satisfaction of needs that fall into Need-Set Two or Need-Set Three.

The role-conflict problem for real-life participants is indeed severe for marginal men, those who move into or out of, particularly, the ruling group (but also into and out of other groups). This difficulty helps explain why such people are inordinately tense and may take to drink, to women, men, drugs, fantasy, or ideology. If students of society find it difficult to locate, to categorize, such individuals, they should appreciate how easy is their task as observers when compared with the task of real-life participants. Yet the group location of people, whether done by participants or observers, is necessary to the understanding of fundamental processes of change—as these processes affect both participants and observers.

The dominance–submission nexus thus serves demands and expectations whose roots are in the nature of man as an organism. By organism

Table 2 Satisfied, Prominent, and Latent Needs in a Particular Culture

At Time One

Group	Need-Set One Physical Needs	Need-Set Two Social Needs	Need-Set Three Dignity Needs	Need-Set Four Self-Actuali- zation Needs
A	satisfied	nearing satisfaction	prominent	latent
B	prominent	latent	latent	latent

At this time, conflict between Groups A and B is likely to develop over the denial by Group A to Group B of its demand to satisfy needs that fall into the category of Need-Set One.

At Time Two

Group	Need-Set One	Need-Set Two	Need-Set Three	Need-Set Four
A	satisfied	satisifed	nearing satisfaction	satisfaction
B	satisfied	nearing satisfaction	prominent	latent

At this time, conflict between Groups A and B is likely to develop over the *acceptance* by Group A of Group B's demand to satisfy needs that fall into the category of Need-Set One and the *denial* by Group A of Group B's demand to satisfy needs that fall into the category of Need-Set Two.

At Time Three

Group	Need-Set One	Need-Set Two	Need-Set Three	Need-Set Four
A	satisfied	satisfied	satisfied	nearing satisfaction
B	satisfied	satisfied	nearing satisfaction	prominent

At this time, conflict between Groups A and B is likely to develop over the *acceptance* by Group A of Group B's demand to satisfy needs that fall into the category of Need-Sets One and Two and the *denial* of Group B's demand to satisfy needs that fall into the category of Need-Set Three.

I mean the complex somatic and psychic bundle of bone, muscle, and nerve tissue that is genetically programmed at the time of conception and gestated in the womb for nine months. This complex bundle, this organism, thereafter gains indispensable substance and facilitation from its natural and cultural environment, but it never is totally programmed by its environment. It spends the balance of its existence in continuous search for satisfaction of those needs whose roots are in the genetically programmed organism. These needs do not emerge all at once and they do not remain static throughout life. Their dynamic quality profoundly and always effects the content and at times even the style of political action.

Four things have to be borne in mind in considering basic needs as here conceptualized. The first is that the needs deemed basic are those that are innate. The second is that they emerge in sequence: most of them are latent at birth. During the process of the organism's maturation, each successive need as it emerges depends on the continuing satisfaction of prior needs. The process is cumulative, epigenetic. The third is that the visible manifestations of these needs are highly structured and stylized by the natural and cultural environment, the circumstances within which the organism is able to develop. And the fourth is that, during a particular historical epoch, the most prominent innate needs of a subordinate group may be manifest in the demand for a *larger* share of material goods and a *larger* measure of mutual respect, whereas during that same epoch the most prominent innate needs of a dominant group may be for a continuation of the *same* proportion of material goods and nonmaterial esteem, and for a *greater* opportunity to live the exciting life of men of influence, culture, and artistic creativity.

BASIC NEEDS

My scheme of basic, innate, organic needs is derived mainly from the work of Abraham Maslow (1943), a clinical psychologist who never really turned his attention to politics, political development, or political violence. But he did produce a need hierarchy that is, I believe, an essential part of any explanation of political behavior under any circumstances, whether stable or unstable, constitutional or anticonstitutional.

The Maslow hierarchy as I modify it (Davies 1963 and 1970) lists these basic substantive needs, and in the following order of emergence from latency to manifestation:

1. The physical needs, for food, clothing, shelter, health, and physical safety (freedom from bodily harm).

2. The social-affectional needs, for interpersonal love and a sense of mutual belonging and identification.
3. The self-esteem or dignity needs, for recognition in one's own eyes and in the eyes of others as an individual of worth, meriting regard and having value for his or her own sake.
4. The self-actualization needs, for the opportunity to develop one's own unique potential for spontaneous and often creative activity of whatever kind is appropriate to the particular personality of the individual.

In addition to these basic substantive needs is a set of implemental or instrumental needs (Davies 1970). These are the needs for understanding and for security and power. They are always linked to the substantive needs as means are linked to ends, but even though they are implements, instruments, or means, they nevertheless are also innate.

The manifestations of the need for understanding range from the first scanning of the visible and audible and tactile environment by a newborn babe to the mature speculation of a philosopher, the research of a natural or social scientist, and the ruminations of an octogenarian trying vainly to reduce a baffling world to the one ultimate cause of all causes.

The manifestations of the need for security range from the infant's crying, to be *sure* that it will be fed and comforted, to the mature person's purchase of life insurance, and to the old person's preoccupation with old age and medical insurance. Some grossly political manifestations include, in addition to the obvious ones like the demand for unemployment and health insurance, the support for local and national police and for various forms of armament justified in terms of national defense.

The manifestations of the need for power range from the infant's crying to bring mother, in order to exert control over her, to the old person's expressed wish that the FBI would take care of all those radicals who bomb public buildings (because the old person sees no way that he can himself directly control radicalism). Some other manifestations of the need for power include the revolutionary who blows up the bank to increase his sense of being able to influence the course of events and the oppressed working man or colonial native or black man who sometimes violently demands recognition of his right as a working man (or native or black) to become part of the process of political decision making. The need for power is of course high among economic and political leaders—corporation executives and politicians.

The basic needs—both substantive and implemental—naturally and continuously affect political behavior, including political violence. It is necessary to appreciate this to explain any political behavior. It is necessary to understand the emergent quality of the substantive needs, and their emergence in a general sequence, in order to explain how dominance–submission changes from being healthy to being pathological.

The physical needs are the first to emerge. They appear at birth and continue throughout life. Only later and after the satisfaction of the physical needs can be taken for granted (but very soon after) do the needs for affection emerge—and they also continue throughout life. And only after the affectional, social needs have been fairly well satisfied do the needs for self-esteem and dignity emerge, manifest usually in the demand for equality. And only after these have come to be fairly regularly satisfied do the self-actualization needs emerge. Moreover, it must be remembered that at no time, once they have emerged generally in this order, do the physical, social-affectional, dignity, and self-actualization needs ever disappear, during an individual's entire life. However latent an artist's demand for food and rest may be during a period of intense creativity, sooner or later the nerve signals from his brain and his muscles will make him stop working in order to eat and sleep. However latent may become the need for affection of a person with a loving and beloved mother or wife or friends, if in the course of actualizing himself by solitary creativity in the studio or in the library he is for a long time alone, he will seek companionship. A person's self-esteem and public recognition as an individual of equal worth may be well established, and he may be well into the process of actualizing himself, but if he is deprived of esteem by a sudden insult that seems to drop out of the blue, when someone yells at him "Hey, nigger," his need for dignity will be activated.

There appears to be no empirical basis for establishing an order to the emergence of the instrumental needs. Whether indeed the needs for knowledge, security, and power are instrumental to the substantive needs or, as some would argue, are enjoyed for their own sake, it is hard to see any sequence in their appearance. If one is or remains ignorant or becomes baffled about the satisfaction of any of the basic substantive needs, he will be frustrated and will continue his pursuit of understanding how things work in his world and the universe. If he remains or becomes insecure about the provision of any of his basic substantive needs, he will also be frustrated and may compulsively seek security by overeating, by a sequence of love affairs, by a continual demand from those about him that they appreciate him, or by a fussy insistence that people around him maintain complete quiet while he works at his painting. And if a person is or remains unable to have some control over his environment—if he is powerless—he will be deeply frustrated.

It is in all of these—in pursuit of the satisfaction of substantive needs as well as of the implemental needs for knowledge, security, and power—that we may and must look for our own understanding of why people turn to political, to revolutionary, violence. But we must recognize a common ingredient in all such violent activity: the profound frustration among people whose position in society has been subordinate with respect to the satisfaction of their need for power, their need to *control* the satisfaction of all their needs.

This is to say that in any political protest movement its participants demand political influence, political power. They want a part in the process of making the basic decisions that affect them—in whatever social or economic condition they may be and in whatever state of need satisfaction they may be. That is, even if their political concern relates to physical needs and takes the form of a cry for bread or (in the case of young people) freedom from the physical dangers of military service, they will have in common the desire to participate in political decisions. To move to the other end of the need hierarchy, even if people are well fed, beloved, and dignified, their political concern may likewise be active. It will be based on the demand that the government let them alone to do their thing. They will want to be part of the policy process as it affects them.

BASIC NEEDS AND THE DOMINANCE-SUBMISSION NEXUS

Now let us see more specifically how needs relate to the dominance-submission nexus. If a person must depend on the kindness, the graciousness, and the sense of justice of others, he will remain frustrated in the desire to control himself and the world as it affects him—even if the "ruling class" provides for his substantive needs. It would be gross oversimplification to say that the demand for equal political participation, for both democracy and autonomy, are innate. It is fully as gross oversimplification to say or assume that all of the roots for these demands are in the environment and none of them in the organism. Beneath the desire for democracy and for freedom lies the desire of the individual for power, for the ability to control his own destiny. It is not the only and not the first desire to become manifest. But it does manifest itself early, when the child first utters an explosive "No" when told to do something. And it manifests itself in a political form when an indigenous population roars a massive "No" to continued colonial domination.

These comments help explain in rather fundamental ways why it is that people burst into political violence. They do not of course explain all the particularities of a specific revolution or all the fundamentals of revolutionary processes. But they do help explain why a seemingly compliant general public will become a rebellious one. Let us take a very brief look at some actual incidents.

BASIC NEEDS IN THE CONTEXT OF HISTORICAL EVENTS

When the President's announcement of an invasion of Cambodia on 30 April 1970 was followed by the explosion at Kent State University on 4 May and other explosions on campuses across the country, the students who took part in these protests were profoundly frustrated by the threat to their physical survival. This was rooted in the low-level and chronic fear of military service. It became dominant when four students protesting the Cambodian invasion were killed. The shock was indeed profound when this physical need, this need to live, was so suddenly activated. The sense of community of interests among young people (rooted in the social need), along with the activated physical needs, caused protests in sympathy with Kent State students to spread like wildfire. The depreciation of their dignity, when the President indefinitely referred to the bums on campuses, the perpetual malcontents, was likewise acutely felt. And of course the Southeast Asian war and efforts to repress protest meant that young people were frustrated in their desire to do their thing, to develop careers and interests of their own choosing. Correlatively, their frustration was derived from their failure to understand it all, their insecurity as to particularly the physical needs, and their great sense of powerlessness to do anything about it.

Two dominant themes were operating in the 1955-1956 Montgomery bus boycott: the desire for equal dignity in public places and—I think newly and crucially—the determination of black people in Montgomery to have a participant voice in decisions that affected them. This is to say that in addition to the demand for self-esteem and dignity there was the newly manifest demand for power, which among virtually all of the participants had had to remain dormant throughout all their lives. Mrs. Rosa Parks was not just insisting on her equal worth when she refused to give her seat on the bus to a white man. She was uttering that explosive "No" that subordinates have been uttering since time out of mind—when they saw some chance of the utterance having impact, and some chance of gaining some power, some control over their own destinies, some end to subordination.

The link between dominance–submission and the need hierarchy helps explain even such a gigantic revolution as the sixteenth-century Protestant

Reformation. Germany in the sixteenth century was in the very midst of the process of rapid economic growth in Central Europe. Along with the development of trade came the emergence of powerful banking and trading houses, the Medici family in Italy, and the House of the Fuggers and the Hanseatic League in Germany. Furthermore, metal mining was increasing rapidly, to feed the shops of artisans making weapons and tools and clocks out of iron and brass. Germany's economy was perhaps the most rapidly advancing of any in Europe at this time. There was not much division of labor in the sense of dividing tasks in a modern factory, but there were at least the bold beginnings of a differentiation of function such that the same families were no longer both farmers and weavers. Towns developed as centers of special and skilled crafts, and the countryside supported the towns with food. Germany was enriching itself, and it was enriching Rome.

The Church in Rome, the focal point for the exciting cultural developments that became known as the Renaissance, began increasingly to depend on Germany, in what became sensed in Germany as pure but sanctified exploitation. Churchmen were wont to describe the hardworking and productive German people as stupid cows that must be milked for the greater glory of God—and the Italian Renaissance.

Analyses of the Protestant Reformation have emphasized theological arguments and the indignation at the corruption of the Roman Church. Or they have emphasized struggle between German (and Swedish and French) princes and kings in their swirling, shifting dynastic and territorial alliances and conflicts with each other, with Charles V of the Holy Roman Empire, and with the Roman Church. Or, generally under the Marxist frame of reference, the Reformation is analyzed in terms of economic class conflict. With the exception of the class-conflict analysis, such explanations of the Reformation appear superficial and too phenotypical. The incredible intensity of a human struggle that led to such an enormous commitment of lives, fortunes, and profaned honor was no superficial event. Elites might go to war only to fight corruption or to save or destroy a dynasty or simply to enlarge territory, but general publics do not fight so fiercely for the interests of elites. They have their own reasons, their own interests.

As a necessary part of any explanation of the Protestant Reformation must be included the intense nationalist reaction to continued semicolonial exploitation of Germany and Sweden by the Roman Church. This exploitation, I argue, was not resisted wholly or perhaps even primarily on economic grounds. It was resisted as an affront to the emerging sense of dignity among individual Germans and to the growing frustration of that sense of dignity by a host of large and small acts by churchmen, who thereby depreciated and degraded Germans. They acted toward Rome the way Algerians in the 1950s acted toward France.

There were other frustrations of a profound sort; frustrations of species-wide, basic, innate needs such as these had emerged in Germany during that epoch of its development. One of the catchphrases and, in a sense, battle cries of the Reformation was the "priesthood of all believers." As German principalities grew in wealth, prestige, and power, they ran into the competing demands of both the Roman Church and the forces of Emperor Charles V. The "priesthood of all believers" was the spiritual expression of a deep urge for freedom to control earthly fates as well as those involving God. As there was to be no intervenor between each man and his God, and therefore no church hierarchy, so there was to be no higher earthly civil authority. Each man was to be master of his spiritual and material destiny. As princes and lords and as cities saw this, it meant autonomy and a fulfillment of the desire to control one's own destiny. As peasants saw this, it meant the same thing—and when in 1525 the logical peasants confronted the inconsistencies of a rebelling class of princes, the peasants lost. The principle of self-determination, of autonomy, was indeed a universal one, but peasants were not to be included in the new universe.

The wars of the Reformation lasted for a century. The struggle was an intense one. It devastated towns and cities and it decimated the population, perhaps far more "totally" than all the wars and revolutions of the twentieth century put together. But the Reformation was the first crucial postmedieval political step in the continuing movement toward equality and self-rule, toward what is now called democracy.

The intensity of the Reformation wars cannot be explained without including as causes the innate tendencies of men to demand dignity and the power to control their own destinies. Having experienced deprecation and degradation at the hands of the Church, in scores of ways, Germans in the sixteenth century insisted on being regarded as equals by their God, their fellow men, and themselves. And they demanded power, the ability to control their own destinies, both individually as human beings, facing their God alone, and collectively, facing their God and their problems together and making their own decisions that affected their individual and collective well-being. All this is to say, as I think Luther was saying in his Address to the German Nobility in 1520, that perhaps the most neglected and surely the deepest forces producing the Protestant Reformation were the natural demands of subordinated people for equal dignity and for power.

A RECAPITULATION

In discussing phenotypes and genotypes of political violence, this is what I have tried to say: that such violence occurs when dominance-submission no longer serves the needs of either those who have submitted or those who have dominated, and that the crisis arises from an intense and widespread frustration of the most basic needs of men at the point in time when these develop and emerge. There are many varieties of the disease, as illustrated by the various events I have mentioned, from the violence in America in 1970 after the Cambodian invasion back to the violence in Germany in the sixteenth century that followed the opening of the Protestant Reformation.

It bears reemphasis and explication that domination-subordination is not under all circumstances pathological, a disease that requires immediate treatment. This is true under various circumstances both in and out of political life. There is nothing inherently unhealthy about parents guiding a child in ways that at times include their making certain decisions for the child. There is nothing inherently unhealthy about a political elite in certain circumstances dominating a general public.

Indeed, it would be a pathological situation if a child willfully decided to walk across a busy street and were allowed by its mother or father to do its thing and get killed in the process. I would argue that it is similarly pathological if a child that is angry at not being allowed to do something is then allowed to vent its anger in ways that can injure other people, even its parents. The unequal influence exerted by parents and children is not per se pathological, and thus the dominant-submissive relationship that is established when a child is born and that persists through childhood is appropriate to both the dominant and the submissive parties to the interaction process.

The relationship of dominance-submission is, however, clearly pathological when it persists beyond its utility in serving the needs of the parents for nurturance of a beloved child and the various needs of the child for sustenance in the form of food, affection, recognition, and encouragement of its own development. That is, when in the interaction process the child quite naturally begins to resist the power exerted by parents over it—that is, to deny parental authority—and when the child shows ability to function on its own, a continuing dominant-submissive relationship becomes pathological.

A mother too ready to wipe a child's nose, to pick it up when it falls, to coddle it when it fails at early attempts to interact with any new situation, is herself exercising her power over the child in ways that are

destructive of its maturation and of its ability to realize its own autonomy, its own ability to control, to govern itself. Minimally it will produce neurosis, not just in the child but also in the parents. And when
this neurosis develops, it reflects the buildup of tensions within both the
child and the parents reflecting the frustration of their various needs.

The tensions that rise from lingering domination, when they become
too great—following increasingly rote behavior on both sides and a
hardening and polarization of positions—can produce rebellion, even
violent rebellion, on the part of the child. This may take the form of
direct retaliation against the parents, but it is more likely to be dis-
placed in violence against other objects in the environment (including
friends and strangers outside the home) and against self.

In political life, there are numerous kinds and occasions of healthy,
functional dominant–submissive relationships. These have occurred
and continue to occur in circumstances where an asymmetrical distribution of power is of use not only to those who have more of it but
also to those who have less. The ever-repeated case is that of young
people below voting age. In any society many decisions are made by
its government and its adult citizenry that affect children but do not
permit them to vote or otherwise politically participate. Many—let us
hope, most—of these are taken in the interests of children, in such matters as public education, immunization against disease, and child-
support laws.

Even in colonial situations, many of the decisions made by the colonizers during the early period may be beneficial to the colonized. This
surely was the case in Spanish America when, along with all their own
violence and brutality, the conquistadors and their successors quite
successfully suppressed the practice of sacrificial killing. It was also the
case when at last, for example in the British empire, the slave trade was
abolished, in the face of the willingness of both white slave traders from
the English homeland and black slave traders in the colonized territory
to continue buying and selling human beings. It was surely also the
case when a uniform system of court justice was introduced and took
hold in such places as India and Africa, despite the occasional or frequent violations of the principles of this justice by the colonists. And it
has been and continues emphatically to be the case when a colonizing
nation introduces new technologies in mineral exploitation and industrial development that speed up the process by which poor, colonized
peoples can learn, rather quickly, invaluable skills that the pioneers in
modern technology took many centuries to learn.

There has always been exploitation by colonials of the peoples they
colonized. This has been said often enough and truly enough to quiet

sonorous protestations about the white man's burden. That there have been also enormous benefits to the colonized is almost never acknowledged. It need not be acknowledged, as long as its reality is recognized. This reality becomes unavoidable when one observes people whose fathers were illiterate villagers operating complex industrial machinery, flying jet aircraft, and conducting war against the colonizers with close social collaboration and highly skillful use of very advanced machines of destruction. It is absurd to argue that dominant–submissive relationships in political life are in all times and circumstances unhealthy.

And it is absurd to argue that these relationships, profitable, during a period of development, not only to exploiter but also to exploited, are of an enduringly stable sort. The problem arises, as it does between children and parents, when a dominant political class fails to recognize the political maturation of those it has historically dominated and persists in monopolizing power rather than welcoming them to the group of decision makers. Those who are demanding a share in that process—including those who sometimes have successfully run a protest movement that has become a shadow government, a revolutionary counter-government—are clearly showing their ability to make political decisions.

To understand the pathology of domination requires, therefore, an explanation of the fundamental causes for the initiation, the persistence, and the resistance that occur as a dominant–submissive relationship changes toward one of potentially equal sharing of power. My argument has been that it is the most basic forces within men, their innate fundamental needs, activated in a general sequence from the physical to social-affectional to dignity (including equality) and to self-actualization, that gradually generate the pressure to remove the dominant–submissive relationship. Along with these basic substantive demands are the instrumental needs to understand, to be secure, and to have control over the satisfaction of these substantive needs.

As these needs develop over time, as the politically undeveloped individual increases in his desire to control in his own ways the satisfaction of his own needs, he becomes frustrated when the government—as it usually does—continues to act toward him as though he had not developed in the ways that end up in and indeed sum to political development. Usually, no one is so aware of his own needs as the individual who senses them. Usually, no group is less aware of these changes than a ruling group, whether it be those whose influence has been socioeconomic, or colonial, or ethnic, and who have luxuriated in political power.

In mentioning the specific cases of political violence, I have suggested that the pattern of needs activated in a particular case will vary greatly and that in no revolution or rebellion can they be reduced to one single

need. Food riots relate to the physical needs. The demand for integration on buses and in schools relates to the self-esteem or dignity needs.
The protests of students against a quasi-colonial war in Southeast Asia
relate to physical needs and to the need to develop one's unique self by
continuing one's education and career training. In each of these instances and in the others mentioned, there is the common theme of a
demand for power, for greater participation in the making of decisions
on public policy that affect the protestants.

What I have tried to say is that analysis limited to such overt phenomena as the visible relationships and the visible conflicts between classes
and races remains unsatisfactory, surface analysis. Even an explanation
that rests content with setting up the model of conflict resulting from
the persistence of dominant–submissive relationships is inadequate.
While it does indeed establish a broad categorization that can successfully subsume class and race analysis, it is not itself an explanation.
Understanding of the development and the successive activation of those
needs in man that are fundamental and innate does, I believe, make a
large leap forward in the analysis of political violence.

ACKNOWLEDGMENTS

I wish to thank the organizers of the Conference on Political Micro-Violence,
notably Herbert Hirsch, Carl Leiden, David C. Perry, and Karl M. Schmidt, and
also the University of Texas, for crucially catalyzing the generation of this paper.

REFERENCES

Jerry L. Avorn *et al., Up Against the Ivy Wall,* New York: Athenaeum, 1968.
    Explains some of the frustrations of rebellious American college students.
W. J. Cash, *The Mind of the South (1941),* New York: Vintage, n.d.
Bradford Chambers, ed., *Chronicles of Black Protest,* New York: Mentor, 1968,
    "The Montgomery Bus Boycott: 1955, and 'I have a Dream': 1963," pp. 177–
    187.
J. C. Davies, *Human Nature in Politics,* New York: Wiley, 1963, Chapter 1.
J. C. Davies, "Violence and Aggression: Innate or Not?" *Western Political Quar-
    terly, 23* (No. 3) (September 1970), 611–623, at 617.
Frederick Engels, *The Peasant War in Germany* (1850), New York: International
    Publishers, 1966.
Frantz Fanon, *The Wretched of the Earth* (1963), New York: Grove Press, 1968.
    Perhaps the best work explaining the indignation at lacking dignity and the
    frustration of powerlessness among colonized people.
Martin Luther, "Address to the Christian Nobility of the German National Re-
    specting the Reformation of the Christian Estate" (1520). It is reprinted in C.
    W. Eliot, ed., *The Harvard Classics,* New York: Collier, 1910, Volume 36,

pp. 263–335. This letter at numerous points shows the indignation at the depreciation of German dignity, the economic exploitation, and the political control practiced by Rome.

O. Mannoni, *Prospero and Caliban* (1956), New York: Praeger, 1964. An excellent analysis of the change from dependency toward equality among colonized people.

Abraham Maslow, "A Theory of Human Motivation," *Psychological Review,* 50 (1943), 370–396.

E. G. Schwiebert, *Luther and His Times,* St. Louis: Concordia, 1950, especially Chapters 4 and 15.

4

A Political Economy Perspective on
the Nature of Political Violence

Governmental Violence
and Tax Revenue

4

4

NORMAN FROHLICH
JOE A. OPPENHEIMER
University of Texas, Austin

For many students of politics, government and coercion have long been
related. Thus, for example, Weber defined modern politics in terms of
the state: " 'Politics' for us means striving to share power or striving to
influence the distribution of power either among states or among groups
within a state."[1] And for Weber, the salient characteristic of a state
was a coercive one: "A state is a human community that (successfully)
claims the *monopoly of the legitimate use of physical force* within a
given territory."[2] With such an important social scientist defining such
a critical social organization in this manner, one would have expected
that many studies would have been undertaken to examine the use of
this monopolistic physical force within a given territory or social unit.
However, contrary to such expectations, there have been few studies of
the use and threatened use of violence by a government.

   Those studies that have been made regarding the actual or threatened
use of force by governments have usually dealt with politics between,
rather than within, states. Furthermore, if one examined the studies of
the actual or threatened use of coercion within a state or social unit, one
would find that most of them do not deal with governmental coercion.
Rather, such studies have been primarily concerned with the use of violence by nongovernmental groups.[3] The only two major "families" of
exceptions to this have been, first, the study of allegedly dictatorial
governments in which the violence of the government is examined by
"democratically biased" analysts,[4] and, second, the relatively marginal
literature by social scientists interested in police and the role of police

in society.[5] Such omissions as have occurred in this situation are all the more surprising given that one of the most common uses of violence, and the threats of violence, by a government has been virtually ignored.[6] The area in question is the use of coercion, by a government, to raise monetary and other resources.[7]

Not only has this area been ignored, though it is rather central to some of the most accepted definitions and processes of politics, but it has been ignored even though there are a number of very sound theoretical reasons for believing this would be an interesting area for social science research. Let us mention but two of these reasons: First, coercion in raising resources is a methodologically interesting subject because the product that is being exchanged is often measurable (tax revenues). Indeed, in modern tax relations, the substance being exchanged is money, and money is not only quantifiable but is also a generalized medium of exchange. These characteristics have often been cited as precisely those that have made it easier to theorize about and empirically test hypotheses concerning economic phenomena than hypotheses about political ones.[8] Second, if a few general hypotheses could be formulated or, even better, if a general theory of taxation could be developed, it could have applicability in a number of related areas. For example, such hypotheses could be generalized to cover any coercive extraction of resources from a group of individuals—such as a draft or corvee. Furthermore, with suitable modifications, it may be possible to use such a theory to analyze (the strategic problems of) law enforcement and resistance in general.

By now, it should be clear that what is to come are the basic elements of a somewhat formalized general theory of taxation.[9] The formality of the presentation is a means of clarifying and making unambiguous the logical relationships between the variables.[10] But a few qualifications are in order at this time.

First, the theory that follows is clearly an "elementary" theory of taxation. It does not deal with some of the more complicated tax relations that can develop, since that would constitute a book in itself.[11]

Second, although it is assumed that the "taxer" has (in Weber's terms) a monopoly of the use of force, we do not explicitly deal with the problem of legitimacy in this paper. There are a number of reasons for this omission, and perhaps they should be made explicit at this time. Regardless of perspective, it would appear obvious that legitimacy cannot be maintained when the government does nothing but tax the members of the society. The current formulations, by omitting the more complicated situation of taxation in conjunction with the supply of positively valued goods (see footnote 11), seems to preclude the con-

sideration of legitimacy. Indeed, given the isolation of the taxation relationship in what follows, the "tax deal" is a "losing proposition" from
the perspective of the average member of the society. The implications
of this, for the governmental leaders as well as the citizenry, are clearly
revolutionary, but are not a fundamental concern of the analysis to be
carried out in this paper. That is, the pressure on the tax collector to
"protect" his operation and revenues would require the supplementing
of his program.[12]   In this vein, we would contend that the question of
legitimacy can be subsumed under the problem of supplying positively
valued goods to the individuals of the social structure, with the resultant
subjective desirabiltiy (on the part of the citizens) of maintaining the
government.[13]

Finally, the reader should note that the theory presented here could
easily be integrated into a more inclusive theory of political behavior,
based on expected value and utility maximization assumptions. The
connections between those behavioral assumptions and the hypotheses
put forward here have been worked out elsewhere.[14]   To integrate the
theories here would lead us into a work of considerable length. Thus,
in what is to come we will analyze a particular type of social relationship, one that has the following characteristic: One of the individuals
in the relationships under examination attempts to obtain resources
from others by threatening to decrease the welfare of any individual
who refuses to surrender a specified amount of resources. In common
parlance, such a relationship is referred to by many names. These appear to vary as a function of two factors: the type of resource demanded and the social role occupied by the individual who is demanding
the resources. Some of the names it has received are blackmail, protection rackets, conscription, and taxation. In everyday language, taxation seems to connote, or seems to be characterized by the idea, that
(1) the resource being demanded is money, and (2) the social position
of the individual doing the demanding is a government official.[15]   Let
us examine how one can analyze such relationships.

TAXATION

As an introduction to the taxation relationship, let us first consider a
very simple case: the taxation of a single individual by another. Here
there are only two individuals:[16]   a taxer (symbolically represented as
A) and a potential taxpayer (represented as a_j). From our previously
given definitions it follows that the taxer possesses an apparatus for
imposing sanctions on the potential taxpayer. In particular, imagine
that A can impose a punishment, t, on a_j.[17]   The taxer can propose to

a_j the following proposition: "If you don't give me a certain payoff, I will impose my punishment, t, on you." How can a_j be expected to react to this sort of situation?

First note that if the taxer is to obtain any resources from a_j as a result of his threat, a_j must place a negative valuation on the sanction (he must prefer avoiding it to receiving it).[18] If a_j does indeed value the sanction negatively, then to avoid the sanction, he would be willing to lose, through paying A, an amount almost as great in magnitude as the potential discomfort of the sanction. Thus, if we designate a_j's valuation of the pain of receipt of t as $U_j(t)$, he would be willing to surrender things he valued up to (but not beyond) $-U_j(t)$, which is a_j's value of avoiding that punishment.[19] Then a_j's decision as to whether to pay or suffer the punishment is relatively straightforward. If A threatens a_j with a sanction t (which he can certainly impose) and asks a_j for some resources that a_j values less than $-U_j(t)$ (a_j's positive value of avoiding the sanction) for freedom from the sanction, the *best a_j can do is to pay tribute requested and free himself from the sanction.* If on the other hand the taxer demands more of a_j than his value of escaping punishment [that is, if he asks more than $-U_j(t)$], *the best a_j can do is to refuse to pay and suffer the punishment.*

Thus the decision of the potential taxpayer is relatively uncomplicated. His decision as to whether to pay or not depends only on his relative valuations of the punishment and the tax demanded. The analysis is unexceptional, and the situation is, admittedly, unrealistic. When several individuals are subject to a tax concurrently, the situation becomes more complex and the analysis more interesting.

Suppose now that A attempts to obtain tax revenue from more than one individual. The basic structure of the interaction would be similar. If the taxer employs the same basic sanction, t, and if he is attempting to obtain tax revenues from a number of individuals, then he must threaten each with the application of t. But given that there is more than one taxpayer, the situation may be radically altered. For the taxer to *threaten all* taxpayers simultaneously, he must face the possibility of attempting to *sanction* them *all* if they all refuse to pay the tax he demands. Assume that he has the capacity to punish m individuals simultaneously: He can deliver a sanction, t, to each of m individuals if they fail to pay their tax.

If the group he is taxing consists of fewer than m individuals, the form of the interaction is much as it was when he was threatening only one individual whom he could punish with certainty. Those individuals who value freedom from the sanction more than the loss of their tax choose to pay their tax, while those who do not, suffer the punishment.

But (and here is a *crucial* but) if the taxer attempts to tax more than *m* individuals simultaneously, the interaction is fundamentally altered. If the individuals in question number more than *m*, they know that the taxer cannot sanction them all at once. Thus, when faced with the taxer's demand for payment of taxes, each must consider the possibility that if he refuses to pay his tax he may escape punishment. If more than *m* individuals choose not to pay the tax, the taxer will be unable to punish them all and some will go free.

The taxer in this situation cannot guarantee that he will be able to deliver the sanction, *t*, that he threatens. His ability to punish all nontaxpayers (or evaders as they will be called occasionally) rests on the aggregate behavior of the members of the group he is threatening. If only a few evade, he can punish them. If many evade, he may be able to punish only a fraction of the evaders. In evaluating the alternatives of payment and nonpayment, therefore, the individuals must take into account the possibility that they can evade en masse and hence "crowd" *A*'s sanction mechanism. The likelihood of their escaping punishment will be a function of the taxer's capacity to punish *and the behavior of their fellows.*

The various factors that enter into the individual's decision calculus regarding payment or nonpayment when there are more potential evaders than sanctions can be represented in a formal fashion. This is done graphically in Figure 13, which represents the expected value of a sanction in such a situation as well as the elements that contribute to that expected value.

Figure 13(a) represents a_j's loss of utility from the receipt of a sanction as a function of the number of others who evade. In this case the graph is a straight line. His loss of utility from the actual receipt of a punishment is independent of how many others evade. Five years in jail are five years in jail.

Figure 13 (b) represents the conditional probability of actually receiving a sanction as a function of the number of other evaders. In this case the conditional probability is dependent on the number of other evaders. As long as the number of evaders is less than *m*, each evader gets a sanction with probability of 1.0. If, however, there are more evaders than sanction units, each evader receives a sanction with some probability less than 1.0. In particular, if there are *k* evaders, and *k* is larger than *m*, then each evader would receive the sanction *t*, with a probability of *m/k*. Those who actually receive the sanction, however, suffer a utility loss that is not affected by the number of individuals who evade, as indicated in Figure 13(a).

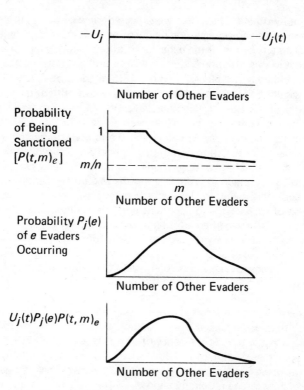

Figure 13 The Expected Value of a Sanction to an Individual When the Potential Number of Evaders is Greater than the Number of Units of Sanction
    (a) The Individual's a_j's, Valuation of the Receipt of a Sanction, t, as a Function of the Number of Other Evaders
    (b) a_j's Probability of Being Sanctioned as an Evader When the Taxer (A) Can Sanction m Individuals
    (c) a_j's Expectations Regarding the Number of Evaders
    (d) a_j's Valuation of the Sanction for Each Level of Evasion*

*The area under this curve is a_j's valuation of the sanction. This can be expressed as the following summation:

$$\sum_{e=0}^{n-1} U_j(t)\, P_j(e)\, P(t,m)_e \qquad (7{:}2a)$$

Thus, when an individual, a_j, is subject to a tax, his expected valuation of the sanction is based not only on the size of the punishment but also on the probability of receiving the sanction for each possible level of evasion by others. His subjective expected value of the punishment, and hence his choice regarding payment or evasion, is now subject to change as a function of the behavior of others. How is he to reach his decision in this situation?

The probability depicted in Figure 13(b) is the probability of receiving a sanction for each level of evasion by others. But a_j must reach his decision without the certain knowledge of how many others will evade. Each individual must decide whether to evade or pay on the basis of how many others he *thinks* will evade. Thus, every individual's decision is based on an estimation of how others will act, while those others are deciding on a similar basis. This situation, obviously characterized by strategic interaction, is inherent in the taxation situation where it is possible, collectively, to "crowd" the taxer's capacity to coerce. The analysis of such a situation contains potential indeterminancies stemming from strategic interactions and the accompanying incomplete information. Since every decision is made with reference to those of others, no one can be sure of the aggregate outcome.

Thus, a_j cannot pick a particular level of evasion and the associated probability from Figure 13(b), multiply it by his evaluation of the receipt of the sanction, and obtain his expected valuation of the sanction threatened by the taxer. He cannot take that specific figure, compare it with the tax demanded of him, and choose the alternative he prefers. His inability to predict the behavior of others leaves him in a risky situation. Since he cannot know with certainty what others will do, he cannot know the exact expected value of the taxer's threatened punishment. Hence, how can he rationally choose whether to pay or to evade his taxes? To do so, he must make some efforts to take the probable behavior of others into account. His behavior is like that of individuals involved in potential free-rider problems. In calculating the expected value of A's sanction, the individual must assign probabilities to the possible occurrence of different levels of evasion by others.

At this point further assumptions (or empirically derived parameters) must be introduced regarding the individual's expectations. We assume the individual's probability estimates regarding the various levels of evasion by others is unimodal. That is, we assume the individual estimates the most probable level of evasion by others, assigns a probability to the occurrence of that level, and assigns ever-lower probabilities to both ever-lower and ever-higher levels of evasion. In other words, we assume a unimodal distribution of probability estimates regarding levels of evasion by others. A graph of such a function appears in Figure 13(c). We designate a_j's estimation that there will be e other evaders as $P_j(e)$.

Having assigned a probability estimate regarding the levels of evasion he can expect, the individual is in a position to decide whether or not to pay a tax demanded by the leader. His decision rests on a combination of the considerations depicted in Figures 13(a), (b), and (c), and a comparison of them with the tax demanded. The individual can calculate the expected value of the sanction he would receive were he not to pay his taxes. The elements in his valuation are given in those graphs. For any level of evasion by others, e, his expected valuation of the sanction consists of his valuation of the receipt of the sanction for that level of evasion: $U_j(t)$ [Figure 13(a)] times his probability of receiving the sanction if that level of evasion occurs, $P(t,m)_e$, [Figure 13(b)], that is, $U_j(t)P(t,m)_e$. He must take these estimates into account. Thus, his expected value of sanctions from the taxer for a level of evasion by others, e, would be $U_j(t)P(t,m)_e P_j(e)$. And in calculating his total expected value of sanctions from the taxer if he fails to pay, he must take into account all such possible levels of evasion by others. Thus, his total expected value consists of a sum of terms, each representing the expected punishment attributable to a given level of evasion by others. His total expected valuation of punishment would be:

$$U_j(t) \sum_{e=0}^{n-1} P(t,m)_e P_j(e). \tag{1}$$

This sum algebraically represents the area under the curve in Figure 13(d): the total expected value of the receipt of punishment. Then the decision of the individual a_j regarding payment or evasion can be represented in these terms. If the area under the curve represents an expected utility loss that is greater than the loss suffered by paying the tax (call it T_j), then a_j will pay. If not, he will not pay. He will take the lesser of the two evils; that is, he will take the smaller loss.

The analysis above presents the factors entering into an individual's decision regarding payment and nonpayment of his taxes in graphical form. The same considerations can be represented algebraically in matrix form. The matrix formulation is derivable directly from our formulation of the individual's decision regarding whether to support the procurement of a collective good.[20] The logical connection between the decision to pay taxes and the decision to contribute to a collective good in general stems from the fact that a decision not to pay one's tax affects the government's ability to punish all of the other individuals who do not pay their taxes. Nonpayment crowds the government's coercive apparatus, and this crowding is supplied to all tax evaders collectively. Thus, at one level, the individual's decision not to pay his taxes is a contribution to a good supplied to all evaders: the crowding of the government's coercive apparatus.

This decision can be represented in matrix form. The individual's two strategies (to pay or not to pay) are represented by rows two and three in Matrix I (Table 3). His payoffs, the entries in these rows, are a function of how many other individuals evade. Hence, within each strategy different payoffs will be associated with different levels of evasion by others. To represent this, different columns are titled so as to represent each possible level of evasion by others (see row 1 of the matrix). In particular, if an individual is a member of a group of size n who are subject to a tax, there must be $n - 1$ columns in the matrix. Evasion by others can, in that case, range from 0 to $n - 1$. Let us examine how to use the matrix to analyze his choice situation.

The second row represents the individual's payoff if he pays his taxes. Paying his tax means giving up valuables amounting to T_j, or an expectation of $-T_j$ regardless of the behavior of others. This is represented in the matrix by having a $-T_j$ in each of the logically possible outcomes, or columns. To show the identity of the matrix formulation with our verbal one, note that the expected value of the payment of taxes is the sum of the expected value payoffs in row 2. That is, if the individual pays his taxes, he can expect to receive any of the possible outcomes. His expected value of each is its value multiplied by the probability of that particular outcome's occurring. These are contained in row 4, where each entry represents the individual's estimate of the probability that each of the indicated aggregate levels of evasion by others actually will occur. In other words, the expected value of paying one's taxes is the weighted sum of the payoffs in row 2, or, as we will refer to it, V_0:

$$V_0 = \sum_{e=0}^{n-1} -T_j P_j(e) \text{ or } -T_j \sum_{e=0}^{n-1} P_j(e) \tag{2}$$

But note that

$$\sum_{e=0}^{n-1} P_j(e)$$

represents the sum of the probabilities of each of the columns actually occurring. Since one of them must occur, this sum must equal 1.0. This

Table 3 Matrix I—Payoffs from Paying Taxes Versus Evading for a Member (a_j) as a Function of a_j's Expectations Regarding the Behavior of Others When the Sanction is Fixed at t and the Taxer Can Deliver m Units of Sanctions

Total number of other evaders	0	1	$\cdots$	$m-1$	m	$\cdots$	$n-1$
a_j pays his taxes $P_j(t_j) = 0$	$-T_j$	$-T_j$		$-T_j$	$-T_j$		$-T_j$
a_j evades his taxes $P_j(t_j) = 1$	$U_j(t)$ $P(t,m)_0$	$U_j(t)$ $P(t,m)_1$		$U_j(t)$ $P(t,m)_{m-1}$	$U_j(t)$ $P(t,m)_m$		$U_j(t)$ $P(t,m)_{n-1}$
a_j's estimate of the probabilities associated with the possible number of other evaders (e)	P_j	$P_j(1)$		$P_j(m-1)$	$P_j(m)$		$P_j(n-1)$

allows us to simplify the above expression for $V_0 = -T_j$. Thus, the verbal and the matrix formulations are consistent in this case.

Let us now examine the expected value, to the individual, of not paying his tax. His lot, in this case, is indicated on row 3. Again, the expected value of the strategy is the sum of the expected value payoffs in the row, or the entries in each of the columns times the estimated probability (in row 4) that the particular column will occur. In other words, the expected value of not paying one's taxes is the weighted sum of the payoffs in row 3, or, as we shall refer to it, V_1:

$$V_1 = \sum_{e=0}^{n-1} V_j(t) P(t,m)_e P_j(e) \quad \text{or} \tag{3}$$

$$V_1 = V_j(t) \sum_{e=0}^{n-1} P(t,m)_e P_j(e). \tag{4}$$

Then, when a_j values paying his taxes more than accepting the probabilistic sanction—that is, when $V_0 > V_1$—he will pay; if $V_0 < V_1$ he will not pay.

So far we have concentrated on the decision of the individual subject to a tax. But what of the decisions of the government (the taxer)? What considerations are they predicated on? We have indicated that in pure taxing relationships, the government is interested in getting increased revenues, given certain cost constraints. With this in mind we can examine the sorts of manipulations that are open to the government.

The government is clearly interested in keeping down the number of evaders. One possible way of doing this is by reducing the tax rate for any given set of punishments available. Of course, lowering the tax rate will lower the maximum expected revenue per capita, but under some circumstances the net result may be an increase in revenue (even neglecting such complications as the economic multiplier). Another tactic available to the government is an increase in its capacity to punish, that is, an increase in m. The larger the group the government can punish, the more likely are potential evaders to be punished, and the more likely are they to pay their tax. Of course, the government is constrained in its ability to increase its coercive capacity by cost considerations and must weigh increased revenue against increased cost. Finally, the government also has the option of increasing the severity of the punishment meted out (that is, of increasing t).

In all these manipulations the government has a definite interest in manipulating the subjectively expected levels of evasion: $P_j(e)$. If these levels of evasion are high, then, *ceteris paribus,* the people will have a low incentive to pay. If the levels are low, they will have a higher incentive to pay.

But the manipulation of the expected levels of evasion acts as a two-edged sword. Just as the government has an interest in generating low levels of $P_j(e)$, those who would oppose the government have an interest in generating high levels of $P_j(e)$. Indeed, when the government is involved only in taxation, there is considerable scope for an opposition leader to generate support for a program involving coordinated evasion and rebellion.

To preclude this form of evasion, the government has a possible strategy not discussed heretofore. The government can provide to the victims of taxation positively valued programs that are tied to the receipt of taxes. In this way the government can make support of opposition based solely on the overthrow of the taxation system less appealing. And, indeed, opposition becomes a much more complicated problem when positively valued goods are provided along with a program of taxation.

We started out analysis with a discussion of the purely coercive extraction of resources, admitting that this was a somewhat restricted case. But the direct thrust of our analysis leads us to the conclusion that when governments tax, they have incentives to supply other positively valued programs as well. The interaction of these two types of programs points to interesting paths of analysis, which cannot be pursued in this limited discussion.[21]

CONCLUSION

At this point, a number of things can usefully be brought together. Examining the nature of the preceding analysis, we note that it contained a formulation that was quite general, and could be applied to any number of situations with certain common characteristics. In each of these situations, the decisions of the individuals involved were said to be determined by a few variables. These variables have been identified as determining not only the individuals' decisions regarding the tax payment decision, but also as determining the outcome of the aggregate social interaction regarding taxation. Often the variables were those one might identify by "common sense"; what is new here is the codification and formulation of the links between these variables, and their incorporation into an explanatory schema.

The particular variables, $e, t, m, P_j(e)$, and T_j, all can be manipulated by the government, or by an opposition movement to the government. It was shown that manipulation by an opposition group can threaten the revenue-raising ability of the government. Therefore, this theoretical formulation can be used to examine both the governmental processes and the opposition processes in politics.

Theoretically, if a state is defined in terms of its monopoly of the use of force, then the rise of an opposition that breaks this monopoly implies the decay of the state. At the microlevel, this decay would be reflected in shifting levels of expected evasion: $P_j(e)$ and e in our notation. Empirically, this sort of political decay should be observable in real countries in a variety of ways.

For example, we can imagine situations where people have ascertained that certain illegal behavior is so widespread that the probability of being punished is greatly reduced. Such a situation exists currently in New York City where masses of people park their cars in no-parking zones and estimate that the number of others who will also do so is so high that punishment is unlikely. They expect to get away with it because there will be too many evaders to be handled by the government's limited coercive capacity.[22] The city government's sanctions fail to be effective in that instance. The same analysis applies to urban riot behavior. In riots an anticipation of large numbers of rioters is necessary before individuals choose to riot. If individuals feel that there is sufficient coordinated discontent to motivate large numbers of their fellows to riot, the expected personal costs of participation are reduced. Only at such times is such behavior attractive to the individual.

Such examples of the breakdown of governmental coercion may be found even in the absence of any opposition movement aiming to break the government's monopoly of force. Yet these examples underscore the potential for planned disruptive activity on the part of opposition movements. The theory explicitly identifies the variables that any opposition can manipulate for success. In particular, planned manipulation of the expectations of the people so as to lead to increasing expected payoffs for evaders will increase the viability of such movements.[23]

Yet the theoretical relationship examined in these pages is a relatively unrealistic abstraction of the taxation relationship as we find it in society. As discussed, taxation is *always* a losing proposition for the person being taxed. If such a situation were duplicated in the real world, it would be unstable. One could expect to find great support for any opposition leader who promised to disrupt such a tax program. To forestall such opposition and, hence, to stabilize his position, the taxer would sweeten the deal he was offering by supplying positively valued goods out of his tax revenue. He would attempt to make the total return (the value of the goods minus the tax) positive to at least *some* individuals who would then have a stake in his regime. Such policies would decrease the support available for opposition aimed at disrupting his programs.

In this context, the whole question of governmental legitimacy can be brought into focus. Legitimacy hinges on the balance and distribution of positively valued programs and coercive extractions in the society. The greater the surplus of positively valued goods over taxes, for any individual, the greater the subjective desirability (for him) of maintaining the government. The more the government does for any individual relative to the demands placed on him, the more legitimate the government for him. And if governmental violence were to rise without the provision of additional valued programs, legitimacy would decline.

Elsewhere[24] we have argued that consequences of this line of reasoning would manifest themselves when one government gives aid to another government to "beef up its capacity to tax." Thus, for example, if the United States were to increase the South Vietnamese government's ability to extract taxes from the peasantry, certain consequences could be predicted. In the absence of more governmental services to the peasants, the short-range effect of such a program would be a more solvent South Vietnamese government but, in our terms, a less legitimate one. Such increased coercive capacity would also increase the peoples' valuation of opposition movements to the government. Potential leaders of such movements could expect greater rewards to be available from the masses of the people.

If we now add to the theory some assumptions regarding the motivations and behavior of taxers, we can predict more precisely the kinds of goods that will be supplied along with taxation. For example, taxers who seek material rewards will consider complementarities between the taxation operation and potential goods in their selection of goods to be supplied. Such taxers would have incentives to use their coercive apparatus to provide domestic tranquility and to supply protection from outside threats. These are, in fact, traditional functions of governments. Why all governments would provide such services can be explained using the logic of the taxation operation.

Thus, although the current model is oversimplified and unrealistic, it should not be considered to be without empirical value. Additional factors such as positively valued programs, behavioral patterns of taxers, and the existence of opposition movements can be easily introduced.

These considerations, which need to be brought into the model to gain greater realism and greater specificity, would have encumbered a simple presentation of the basic tax relationship and, hence, have been omitted here. Nevertheless, the material presented here can be integrated into a much more general model of the political process, one that explicitly assumes particular motivations of the taxers and the taxpayers. Such a model, for example, could rest on assumptions of profit maximization for the taxer, as has been utilized in our earlier models of politics.[25] If such an integration is performed, the relationship between tax programs and opposition or resistance groups can be used to explain the diversification of the activities of the taxer. In particular, the expansion of positively valued political programs and the development of "constitutional rules" may be linked to the interactions between a profit maximizing taxer and the growth of opposition groups.[26]

NOTES

1. Max Weber, "Politics as a Vocation," in *From Max Weber: Essays in Sociology,* ed. by H. H. Gerth and C. Wright Mills, New York: Oxford University Press, 1958, p. 78.
2. *Loc. cit.* Further discussion of this definition and the notion of territoriality may be found in Max Weber, *The Theory of Social and Economic Organization,* ed. by Talcott Parsons, New York: Free Press, 1964, p. 156.
3. A fine example of this sort of bias can be seen in Hugh Davis Graham and Ted Robert Gurr, eds., *The History of Violence in America* (a report submitted to the National Commission on the Causes and Prevention of Violence, 1969), New York: Bantam, 1969.
4. Many books deal with governmental violence of authoritarian regimes. They range from the relatively analytic, Alexander Dallin and George W. Breslauer, *Political Terror in Communist Systems,* Stanford: Stanford University Press, 1970, to the more historical case studies exemplified by Robert D. Crassweller, *Trujillo,* New York: Macmillan, 1966.
5. Being the current fashion, a number of books have recently been published on this subject. Perhaps the reader should note Eliot Asinof, *People vs. Butcher,* New York: Viking, 1970; Paul Chevigny, *Police Power,* New York: Random House, 1969; and James Q. Wilson, *Varieties of Police Behavior,* Cambridge, Mass.: Harvard University Press, 1968.
6. A few very recent contributions to the literature are exceptions and, indeed, are related to the approach taken in this essay. The reader is referred to Gorden Tullock, "An Economic Approach to Crime," *Social Science Quarterly, 50* (June 1969), 59–71; J. M. Buchanan and M. Fowlers, "An Analytic Setting for a Taxpayer's Revolution," *Western Economic Journal, 7* (December 1969), 349–359; and Raymond Jackson, "A 'Taxpayer's Revolution' and Economic Reality," *Public Choice, 10* (Spring 1971), 93–95.
7. And this in spite of the fact that every man in the street knows that "nothing in life is certain except death and taxes."
8. See, for example, Karl Deutsch, *Nerves of Government,* New York: Free Press, 1966, pp. 120–122, and James S. Coleman, "Political Money," *American Political Science Review, 64* (December 1970), 1074–1088.

9. The original version of this model, and a much more lengthy discussion of it, can be found in Norman Frohlich and Joe A. Oppenheimer, *An Entrepreneurial Theory of Politics,* unpublished doctoral dissertation, Princeton University, 1971, especially Chapters 7, 8, and 10.

10. The use of mathematics in formal theory construction has been competently dealt with by a number of scholars. See, for example, Hubert M. Blalock, Jr., *Theory Construction,* Englewood Cliffs, N.J.: Prentice-Hall, 1969, Chapter 2.

11. In particular, we are not considering how the supply of other goods might affect a taxation operation. Thus, for example, what if the tax receipts were used, at least in part, for the securing of positively valued goods? These sorts of considerations would bring us far afield from the current thrust of the paper. The interested reader is referred to formulations contained in Frohlich and Oppenheimer, Chapters 8 and 10.

12. This in no way is meant to imply that the tax relationship empirically or analytically "precedes" the supplying of other positively valued programs. For an analysis of the opposite sort of process see Norman Frohlich, Joe A. Oppenheimer, and Oran R. Young, *Political Leadership and Collective Goods,* Princeton, N.J.: Princeton University Press, 1971, pp. 40–43, 50–57, and 60–65.

13. This question, of course, cannot be closed until alternative theories are tested to see which holds up better. It may well be that the formulations we propose, without an explicit additional "legitimacy factor," would not stand up to tests. We merely ask for indulgence until the tests are made.

14. In particular, see Frohlich, Oppenheimer, and Young.

15. Of course, it is also possible that one would wish to withhold the name "taxation" from relationships where the "tax collector" does *not* supply positively valued goods. The authors feel that this would be an arbitrary distinction, given the basic analytic similarity of the two situations. To see this, the interested reader is referred to Frohlich and Oppenheimer, Chapters 7 and 8, where the theory is developed to cover taxation with the supply of positively valued goods.

16. Although in this case we talk of two individuals, one of the "individuals" may be an aggregated actor. Thus the taxer may be a government or other organization.

17. There exists a range of punishments that could be imposed on a_j. That is, t may have many values. Here we will assume that t is fixed. In later sections we will discuss some of the implications of allowing t to vary.

18. In the empirical world of imperfect information and strategic interaction, it is not always easy to determine what any particular individual views as a negatively valued punishment. Thus, in one well-known Uncle Remus story Br'er Fox captures Br'er Rabbit; wishing to inflict maximum pain on Br'er Rabbit, he tries to do so and Br'er Rabbit escapes unharmed.

19. Since the punishment t is negatively valued, $-U_j(t)$ represents a positive number and the positive value of the resources that a_j would be willing to forego to escape.

20. "I Get By With a Little Help From My Friends," *World Politics, 23* (October 1970), 104–120.

21. A fuller discussion of many of the issues raised and hinted at here can be found in our *An Entrepreneurial Theory of Politics.*

22. Gordon Tullock has a related analysis of illegal parking in "An Economic Approach to Crime," *Social Science Quarterly, 50,* No. 1 (June 1969), 59–71.

23. For a discussion as to how this coordination occurs and what forms it takes, see Frohlich and Oppenheimer, Chapters 3 and 4.

24. In "Entrepreneurial Politics and Foreign Policy," in *Theory and Policy in International Relations, World Politics,* 24, Supplement (Spring 1972), 151–178. R. Tanter and R. Ullman, eds., we discuss some foreign policy implications of a taxation relationship when the taxers are profit-motivated political entrepreneurs.

25. How this might be done, given the assumption that taxers maximize profits, is suggested by the formulations in Frohlich, Oppenheimer, and Young. The current formulation of the tax relationship differs from the one found in that volume. However, the inclusion of the taxation relationship in the calculations of the political leader can be accomplished in an analogous fashion.

26. These links are developed in Frohlich, Oppenheimer, and Young, Chapters 8 and 10.

5

A Critique from the Perspective
of Sociology

The Arguments of Berkowitz and Davies:
Two of the Stages in the Development of
Political Violence

LOUIS A. ZURCHER, JR.
University of Texas, Austin

The essays by Berkowitz, a psychologist, and Davies, a political scientist, reflect their perspectives on factors salient to the emergence of political violence. These two perspectives, along with those presented in the essays by Lupsha and MacKinnon and by Frolich and Oppenheimer, may be taken as evidence for the interdisciplinary nature of the study of political violence. They may also be taken to indicate that each of us, representing our respective disciplines and subdisciplines, is at the present time unwilling or unable to account for much of the variance among assorted independent variables and the dependent variable of political violence. I now happily contribute to the confounding factors.

Berkowitz's essay is provocative, if for no other reason than that it dares to resurrect "imitation" as a simple and sovereign explanation for a form of social behavior. He cites evidence to support the contention that Tarde may have *accurately* assigned "imitation" a central and significant role in the evolution of contagious violence. Berkowitz's review of selected studies and crime statistics is interpreted to indicate that such dramatic phenomena as mass murders, assassinations, airplane bombings and hijackings, and race riots seem linked with subsequent increases in similar or other crimes of violence. I am not prepared to dispute directly his association of such dramatic events with the ensuing increases, even though the acceptance of such a relationship depends upon holding many other social variables constant—social variables that might account for as much or more of the variance than a specific dramatic event (for example: the state of the economy, the rate of employment, the existence of a current war, the aggressiveness of the police). What I do wish to suggest is that the kinds of dramatic events that Berkowitz offers as imitation-motivating stimuli come to have significance for behavior *only* if they are part of a series of value-added stages that summate to yield the behavior.

In offering the following interpretation, I wish to eliminate from consideration the case of the individual psychotic or, perhaps, psychopath. The violent example of one Whitman may appeal directly and with little social complication to the Whitman-like. But even in the individual case one needs to know (if one wants more fully to understand and perchance even to predict) more about the personality structure of the imitator, more about the etiology of that person's pathology, before resting with the conclusion that one man's rifle shots elicited similar behavior from him. Why did he imitate? What was the payoff? Was it really, as Berkowitz suggests might often be the case, simple classical conditioning? Or must more be discovered about the *reward* for the violent behavior?

In this discussion I wish to focus on the perpetuation of those dramatically violent events that involve more than one individual at a time—such phenomena as the spread of so-called race riots in the late sixties, the student rebellions, and in general those forms of violence that sociologists would put under the rubric "collective behavior." Essentially, collective behavior is taken to define those relatively uninstitutionalized behaviors engaged in by a number of interacting people who act according to a generalized belief that has been forged from perception or experience of strain and stress (Smelser 1962). Such social forms as riots, publics, crowds, fads, and social movements are types of collective behavior.

Smelser (1962) argues that a type of collective behavior, including any that may be hostile or violent, emerges only after each of a series of value-added stages has been implemented. The stages, each of which is a necessary but not sufficient prerequisite to the next, are as follows:

1. Structural conduciveness: The form of collective behavior must be physically and socially possible.
2. Structural strain: Within the context of the conduciveness there must be some social or social-psychological disequilibrium, inconsistency, or conflict.
3. Growth and spread of a generalized belief: The strain must be articulated, and its source identified and labeled.
4. Precipitating factor: An event or situation must focus the generalized belief more clearly, or give evidence that the source of the strain is correctly identified and labeled.

5. Mobilization of the participants for action: Events and/or the leader(s) must develop and implement a course of action based on the generalized belief—that is, a course seen to be able to alleviate the strain.

6. Operation of social control: Counterdeterminants to the first five stages must be activated, which shape the form, direction, and intensity of the collective behavior.

If one is willing to accept these stages as useful analytically, then Berkowitz's dramatic violent event might be seen, upon inspection, to have been the *mobilization for action* resulting from a whole series of other salient social and psychological phenomena. More importantly, *the dramatic event might serve as the precipitating factor for other similar or related kinds of behavior, including violence.* "Imitation" is thus translated into "precipitating factor" and given, perhaps, a more relevant and significant conceptual role in the analysis of political violence. A publicized ghetto riot spawns similar riots in other ghettos, not simply because of imitation, but because the violent behavior is seen by other individuals, in similar structurally conducive settings and experiencing similar strains and beliefs, to be an effective mobilization toward resolving the strain. Some forms of violence, for example assassination of the president, can be interpreted (according to the value-added stages) to contribute to widespread and severe structural and psychological strain, engendering potential for many kinds of social pathology.

Berkowitz does not ignore the possibility—or, even more, the probability—of antecedent and intervening variables saliently operating around and between imitation and violence. He specifically mentions the relevance of cognitive set in the emergence of some incidents of violent behavior. Furthermore, he demonstrates by his own and by other experiments that stimuli having aggressive meaning are "capable of eliciting aggressive responses from subjects who, *for one reason or the other, are ready to act aggressively.*" What I am suggesting here is simply an extension of his own argument, as I read it. In the larger social setting, a dramatic violent event can trigger similar or related violent events, *not because of imitation,* but because the event serves as a *precipitating factor* to mobilize people for action—people who already had implemented or experienced the earlier stages of conduciveness, strain, and belief, and *were ready to act aggressively.*

One more quick comment about the Berkowitz essay. It seems to me that when one discusses the imitation by viewers of aggressive models on television or film, one might profitably consider those media not only as generators of aggressive models, but as reflecting a societal value for violence and aggression. Does the program or movie actually only reaffirm the societal legitimacy of behaviors typified by, let us say, John Wayne? Among audience members, who was moved toward pacifism by the Easy Riders? Who was moved toward violence by the shotgunners? Why?

Like Berkowitz, Davies looks for an explanatory commonality underlying episodes of violence. He reviews several cases of what he takes to be political violence, although some of the examples are less specifically hostile outbursts than they are value-oriented or norm-oriented social movements. Davies argues that class conflict, colonial–colonized conflict, and ethnic conflict are idiosyncratic analytical constructs. What is genotypical to all the cases he cites is a pattern of frustrated innate human needs. This frustration is particularly acute when people are forced into subservience by a dominating government.

Allport (1954) suggested that all social scientists implicitly or explicitly define the essential nature of man (including assumptions about his "basic" needs) at the onset of every piece of research they conduct. Davies has early gotten his explicit definitions "up front," and I find that refreshing (since it fits with my biases). At this point, I choose not to argue whether the postulated needs are indeed innate or acquired. I suppose, were I to argue, I would still be influenced by Dollard and Miller (1950) and urge the derivation of secondary or social needs from primary or physiological needs, though I would listen to arguments for the functional autonomy of secondary needs. For the purposes of this discussion, I prefer simply to accept that various social needs exist (such as those noted by Davies: social-affectional, self-esteem or dignity, self-actualization, understanding, security, power). But I would like to add that, innate or learned, those needs are subject to wide and complex variation in meaning, importance, and permanence not only culturally, but situationally. Thus such needs, and the values, attitudes, and perceptions with which they are intertwined, are subject to unevenness in expression, acceptance, and opportunity for satisfaction. What is self-actualization to one person, for example, may be perceived as a threat by another.

Consequently, I suggest that the idiosyncratic factors noted by Davies (class conflict, colonial–colonized conflict, ethnic conflict) *and* the variations and frustrations of need-constellations can be placed analytically in the *structural strain* category of the value-added stages. Each one of those factors could have important implications for the emergence of political violence *if* the violence is physically possible, *if* there is a generalized belief about the source of the strain, *if* a precipitating factor confirms the belief, *if* there is enough slippage in the social control to allow the burst of violence. The strains that are attendant on restrictive domination will not yield political violence, or any other action form of collective behavior, unless the other value-added stages are satisfied.

Even if we accept Davies' postulation of political violence as the result of dominance-frustrated basic needs, and take that dynamic to account for all of the structural strain, analytically the value-added stages help him to explain the diversity of forms of political violence which stem from the same strain.

In conclusion, I would like to submit that Davies has suggested some interesting factors that contribute to those that can be subsumed primarily under structural strain in the value-added stages toward political violence. Berkowitz has contributed some interesting factors that can be subsumed primarily under precipitating factors. But to get at the complexity of the correlates and causes of political violence, it seems that the broader model, which includes all of the stages, must analytically be considered. Perhaps, however, the necessity for such complex models will be negated by the discovery that all of the causation for political violence is encapsulated in the dorsomedial and ventromedial nuclei of the hypothalamus.

REFERENCES

Allport, G. W., *Becoming,* New Haven, Conn.: Yale University Press, 1954.
Dollard, J., and N. E. Miller, *Social Learning and Imitation,* New Haven, Conn.: Yale University Press, 1950.
Smelser, N. J., *Theory of Collective Behavior,* New York: Free Press, 1962.

PART TWO

Institutional Determinants of Political Violence

We are no longer a rural nation; values and theories relevant to bygone eras are no longer applicable to an urban, highly technological, hetero- geneous society. Old theories must be renovated or totally discarded and new perspectives must come into use in order to give us insight into the problems associated with the rapid changes of contemporary society. One usual observation is that the move from rural to urban society re- sults in increased dehumanization and in increased levels of violence and brutality. Part II examines the current status of this perspective, in par- ticular, and opens it up to serious challenge. In doing so the authors here take an institutional perspective on political violence, using the city as their empirical referent.

In the first essay Charles Tilly examines the "Chaos of the Living City." Tilly asks whether the city itself is the source of disorder? Using material from the French archives, Tilly analyzes about 2000 distur- bances (defined as "any event occurring within the country in which at least one group of 50 or more persons took part, and in which some person or property was seized or damaged over resistance") in the gen- eral sample, 500-odd in the intensive one; a dozen disturbances were singled out for special analysis. Tilly concludes that, in the chaos of the living city we do not see "the lawless disorder" nor do we see "bucolic bliss"—we see "men held to their routines by commitments and controls, often dismayed by their routines, sometimes articulating and acting on their dismay, mostly singly, mostly in nonviolent ways, but occasion- ally being trained in another way of understanding and combatting the evils of their present situation and joining with other men to strike out against the situation itself. There is a kind of order to the city's collec- tive disorders, if not the one the forces of order would like to see prevailing."

Cities, then, according to Tilly, are not pathological. They are "living cities, and in the last analysis not nearly so chaotic as widespread sociological ideas imply."

While Tilly's conclusions are interesting, it is important to ask whether or not they are culturally and historically limited to the French experience. In the second essay of this section Joe Feagin and Harlan Hahn focus on the politics of violence in American urban areas. According to their formulation, "an adequate understanding of collective violence in urban areas is dependent on an understanding of the process and consequences of urbanization." Like Tilly, they note problems in theoretical and empirical conceptualizations of violence. After questioning the idea that violence grows out of the "sickness in the center of our cities," they "review conventional assumptions about the nature of urbanization and adaptation of black Americans as well as to examine existing theories of collective violence that appear to be grounded in these theories and related assumptions." They present "an alternative view of urbanization that emphasizes the structural rather than the pathological nature of cities" and then attempt to "develop a different framework for the examination of urban riots." They conclude that ghetto riots should be viewed "as politically disruptive acts in a continuing, politically motivated struggle between competing interests on the urban scene," which arise not "from the failure of ghetto residents to adjust satisfactorily or normally to the tensions and strains imposed on them in an urban context," but are mainly "occasioned by the failure of the existing urban political system to respond adequately to ghetto residents' desires and aspirations, to allow them a proportionate role in the urban structure of power." Black Americans, therefore, according to Feagin and Hahn, seem "to be pressing a demand for significant powers of self-governance and for the right to control their own lives."

The essays in this section suggest a new view of violence in urban settings. Tilly and Hahn and Feagin agree that urban violence is not a pathological inability to adjust to urban environments, but grows out of certain logical assumptions underlying the nature of cities. These somewhat unorthodox interpretations of urban violence assume even greater importance as we attempt to view the future of politics in the American urban setting. The hardening of value assumptions, coupled with the continued activity of emerging groups such as the Young Lords in northern cities and La Raz Unida Party in Texas, means that we will be confronted with potential political activity of an intense nature for several years. The system's response to challenges emanating from these and other sources becomes a key to understanding whether or not violence will persist. The essays in Part Three will address themselves to the institutional reactions to political violence.

6

The Chaos
of the
Living City

CHARLES TILLY
Institute for Advanced Study
and
University of Michigan

As life is disorderly, so is the city. But is the city itself the source of disorder? Since the rise of the industrial metropolis, generations of Western men have proclaimed it so. The nineteenth-century sociologists who argued that the mobility, complexity, and scale of the modern city were bound to strip men of social ties, disorient them, and thus push them toward individual and collective derangement were simply articulating a well-established tradition. The tradition has not yet died.

We find the precise tone in Baudelaire:

Swarming city, city of dreams
Where ghosts grab strollers in broad daylight . . .

How admirable it is, he tells us elsewhere, to join the few who are free of the spectral grasp:

And so you go your way, stoic, uncomplaining
Through the chaos of the living city . . .

"Through the chaos of the living city!" A great motto for the study of urban disorder.

"Under the aegis of the city," declares Lewis Mumford (1961: 43), "violence . . . became normalized, and spread far beyond the centers

This paper is a top-to-bottom revision of "A travers le chaos des vivantes cités," presented to the Sixth World Congress of Sociology (Evian-les-Bains, France), 1966. The original version was published in Paul Meadows and Ephraim H. Mizruchi, eds., *Urbanism, Urbanization and Change: Comparative Perspectives,* Reading, Mass.: Addison-Wesley, 1969, pp. 379–394.

where the great collective manhunts and sacrificial orgies were first instituted." Again we encounter the image of the city as destroyer, of urban
life as the solvent of social bonds, of violence as the price paid for living
on the large scale. While peasant revolts leave faded souvenirs here and
there, the word "revolution" recalls city streets. As deprived millions
limp hopefully into the cities of Africa or Latin America, political observers hold their breaths. When will the cities explode? Urbanization,
it seems to go without saying, means social disorder.

It does, in a way. Huge wars and devastating revolutions only came
into man's life with the flowering of cities. But whether urbanization
and collective violence have a necessary or a contingent connection—or,
indeed, any genuine causal connection at all—is far from clear.

Some small observations on the nature of that connection form the
substance of this essay. I want to comment on the ways urbanization
might incite or transform collective violence, raise some questions about
the relationship between violent and nonviolent forms of political participation, sketch some means for investigating the political consequences
of urbanization, and review some relevant findings from a study of the
evolution of political disturbances in France since 1830.

Why and how does urbanization affect collective violence? Sociologists have some well-frozen ideas on the subject. After stressing the disruptive personal effects of migration and the "frictions" produced by
the rubbing together of urban and preurban value systems in expanding
cities, Philip Hauser (1963: 212) tells us:

Another group of serious problems created or augmented by rapid rates
of urbanization are those of internal disorder, political unrest, and governmental instability fed by mass misery and frustration in the urban
setting. The facts that the differences between the "have" and "have
not" nations, and between the "have" and "have not" peoples within
nations, have become "felt differences," and that we are experiencing
a "revolution in expectations," have given huge urban population ag-
glomerations an especially incendiary and explosive character.

In Hauser's view, the breaking of traditional bonds and the conflict of
values feed disorder, while the swelling city's combination of misery
and heightened hopes nearly guarantees it. Change produces tension,
tensions breaks out in collective explosions, and a form of action more
frenzied than that of stable, developed countries erupts into life.

Hauser's analysis, I believe, sums up the predominant sociological
position. Seen from the outside, the set of ideas looks solid and chink-
less. From inside, it seems much less likely to withstand pressure. For
one thing, it contains a notion of the equivalence of different types of

disorder. Personal malaise, moral deviation, crime, and political upheaval are supposed to flow into one another.

Almost mystically, Louis Chevalier announces that essential unity.
Outside the major outbursts, he says,

> the political and social violence which have been studied so often and so
> minutely is replaced by other forms of violence—more continuous, more
> complex, harsher, involving greater numbers, taking from the rise and
> the bulk of the masses their progress, their unity and their force. Here
> is another form of connection among crises: Private dramas, daily ones,
> add their weight to the public ones, developing outside them, but ac-
> cumulating and culminating in them (Chevalier 1958: 552–553).

Chevalier does not hestiate to call nineteenth-century Paris a sick city,
or to consider misery, crime, suicide, street violence, and popular rebellion so many expressions of the same pervasive pathology. That is one
side of the standard sociological formulation.

Turn this set of ideas over. On the other side is stamped a complementary set: that there is a sharp disjunction between healthy and
pathological social states, between the normal and abnormal, between
order and disorder, which justifies treating different specimens of disapproved collective behavior as manifestations of the same general phenomenon—"deviance." The responses that other people give to the
disapproved behavior win another general label—"social control."

Collective violence almost automatically receives both the complementary treatments. It is easy to treat it as the final expression of a
fundamental pathology, which also shows up as a crime, delinquency,
family instability, or mental illness. It is even easier to treat it as radically discontinuous from orderly political life. Long before Taine and
Le Bon had dismissed the mass actions of the French Revolution as the
work of demonic guttersnipes, Plato had shuddered over the outbreaks
of man's "lawless wild-beast nature, which peers out in sleep," and
James Madison had warned of "an unhappy species of the population. . .
who, during the calm of regular government, are sunk below the level of
men; but who, in the tempestuous scenes of civil violence, may emerge
into the human character, and give a superiority of strength to any party
with which they may associate themselves."

More recently, Hannah Arendt (1963: 9–10) has argued that "violence
is a marginal phenomenon in the political realm," that "political theory
has little to say about the phenomenon of violence and must leave its discussion to the technicians," that "insofar as violence plays a predominant
role in wars and revolutions, both occur outside the political realm." And
the political realm, to Miss Arendt's mind, contains normal social life.

Here two ideas intertwine. One is that violence appeals to the beast in man and to the beasts among men. The other is that men in becoming violent step over an abyss which then separates them from coherent rationality.

Despite their devotion to death-dealing automobiles, aggressive detectives, and murderous wars, it is true that men ring round most forms of interpersonal violence with extraordinary tabus and anxieties. Yet collective violence is one of the commonest forms of political participation. Why *begin* an inquiry into the effects of urbanization with the presumption that violent politics appear only as a disruption, a deviation, or a last resort? Rather than treating collective violence as an unwholesome deviation from normality, we might do better to ask under what conditions (if any) violence disappears from ordinary political life.

That is, however, a mischievous question. The treatment of collective behavior in terms of change:tension:tension-release and the assumption of drastic discontinuity between routine politics and collective violence cling to each other. Most students of large-scale social change cling to both. Challenging either the fit between the two notions or their independent validity therefore smacks of rabble-rousing. Yet there are some alternatives we simply cannot ignore.

First, collective violence often succeeds. Revolutionaries do come to power, machine-breakers do slow the introduction of labor-saving devices, rioters do get public officials removed. The local grain riot, so widespread in western Europe from the seventeenth through the nineteenth centuries, often produced a temporary reduction of prices, forced stored grain into the market, and stimulated local officials to new efforts at assuring the grain supply (L. Tilly 1971). I do not mean that, by some universal calculus, violence is more efficient than nonviolence. I simply mean that it works often enough in the short run, by the standards of the participants, not to be automatically dismissed as a flight from rational calculation.

Second, whether or not it succeeds in the short run and by the standards of the participants, collective protest is often a very effective means of entering or remaining in political life, of gaining or retaining an identity as a force to be reckoned with. Eugene Debs boasted that "no strike has ever been lost," and American advocates of Black Power consider their appeal the only means of mobilizing blacks as an effective political force. Although there are always Revisionists to argue that the dispossessed will gain power more cheaply by circumventing revolution— even though the Revisionists are often right—collective violence does frequently establish the claim to be heard, and feared. In that sense, too, it can be a rational extension of peaceful political action.

Third, acts of collective violence often follow a well-defined internal order. The order goes beyond the Freudian logic of dreams or that symbolic correspondence Neil Smelser finds between the beliefs embodied in collective movements and the strains that produce them. In many cases it is sufficiently conscious, explicit, and repetitive to deserve the name "normative." Many Western countries on the eve of intensive industrialization, for example, have seen a recurrent sort of redressing action against what the people of a locality consider to be violations of justice: mythical avenging figures like Rebecca or Ned Ludd; threats posted in their names; outlandish costumes (women and Indians being favorite masquerades); routine, focused, roughly appropriate punishments inflicted on the presumed violators of popular rights (see Hobsbawm and Rudé 1968, Hobsbawm 1969, C. Tilly 1969). Disorder displays a normative order.

Fourth, the participants in collective violence are frequently rather ordinary people. Recent studies of popular disturbances in France, England, and elsewhere have shifted the burden of proof to those who wish to claim that mass actions recruit from the lunatic fringe (for example, Belvèze 1959, Bezucha 1968, Cobb 1961–1963, 1964, and 1970, Cornelius 1970, Davies 1969, Fogelson and Hill 1968, Furet, Mazauric, and Bergeron 1963, Godechot 1970, Gossez 1967, Hofstadter 1970, Kirkham, Levy, and Crotty 1970, Masotti and Bowen 1968, Mazauric 1970, Nelson 1970, Peacock 1965, Rudé 1970, Rule and Tilly 1971, Sewell 1971, Skolnick 1969, Saboul 1958, C. Tilly 1964, L. Tilly 1971, R. Tilly 1971, Tønnesson 1959, Vidalou 1959, Vovelle 1965, Williams 1968). Not that these studies portray the recruitment as a kind of random sampling: real grievances, local economic conditions, established paths of communication, the character of local politics, all help determine who take part. But the rioters and local machine-breakers commonly turn out to be fairly ordinary people acting on important but commonplace grievances. The "dangerous classes" stay out of sight.

Finally, the large-scale structural changes of societies, which transform everyday politics through their effects on the organization, communication, and common consciousness of different segments of the population, also transform the character and loci of collective violence. As the scale at which men organize their peaceful political actions expands, so does the scale at which they organize their violence. As workers in mechanized industries become a coherent political force, they also become a source of disorder. The correlations are obviously complex and imperfect; that is precisely why they are interesting. But they are correlations rather than antitheses.

So there are five reasons for hesitating to assume that collective violence is a sort of witless release of tension divorced from workaday politics: (1) its frequent success as a tactic, (2) its effectiveness in establishing or maintaining a group's political identity, (3) its normative order, (4) its frequent recruitment of ordinary people, and (5) its tendency to evolve in cadence with peaceful political action. The five points are debatable and worthy of debate—not to mention empirical investigation. To the extent that they are valid, they lead to somewhat different expectations from the usual ones concerning the development of political disturbances in the course of urbanization.

Urbanization *could* affect collective violence in three main ways: first, by disrupting existing social ties and controls; second, by exposing more individuals and groups to urban institutions and living conditions; and, third, by changing relations between city and country. In fact, an abundant (if largely theoretical and anecdotal) literature asserts the disturbing effects of each of these changes. The disruption of ties and controls is commonly supposed to incite disorder either by removing restraints to impulses that would under normal circumstances be muffled or by inducing anxiety in individuals detached from stable, orderly surroundings. (Mass migration to cities is the standard example.) Exposure to urban institutions and living conditions is usually considered to promote collective violence in two respects: (1) by imposing intolerable privations in the form of material misery and unfamiliar disciplines, or (2) by communicating new goals via heightened communication within large groups sharing common fates and interests, and via the diffusion of higher standards of comfort and welfare from the existing urban population to the newcomers. Thus rapid urban growth is said to exacerbate the "revolution of rising expectations." The changing relations between city and country are often thought to engender disturbance in the country itself as cities expand their claims for goods, men, taxes, and subordination, while rural communities resist those claims. Thus regions of distinct tribal character presumably become ripe for rebellion.

If the disruption of existing ties and controls, the exposure of individuals and groups to urban institutions and living conditions, and the changing relations between city and country all uniformly encourage collective violence, then matters are delightfully simple: the pace and location of upheaval should be closely correlated with the pace and location of urban growth. That hypothesis easily lends itself to testing. The surprising thing is that it has not yet been truly tested.

Even in the absence of good data on either side of the relationship, however, we may legally doubt whether it is so splendidly straightforward.

In no western European country have the peak years of urban growth since 1800 also been the peak years of political upheaval. Such quantitative international studies as we have of the twentieth century give relatively little weight to the sheer pace of change in the explanation of the frequency of protest and violence; instead, they tend to substantiate the importance of political structure and of short-term deprivation. So a global connection of upheaval to urban growth seems unlikely.

Happily, the various components of urbanization also lend themselves to separate analysis. We can, to some extent, isolate the political correlates of rapid migration from rural areas to large cities, of miserable urban living conditions, or of the expansion of central control into the rural backland. Rather than the amassing of case studies of violence or the statistical manipulation of general indices drawn from samples of whole countries, two strategies getting at differentials within countries seem particularly suitable. The first is to compare segments of the country—communities, regions, classes, as well as periods—in terms of the frequency and intensity of collective violence, of the forms violence takes, of the participants in it. Whereas international comparisons ordinarily make it tough to disentangle the correlates of urban poverty from those of rapid migration to cities, and case studies usually hide the significance of negative instances, systematic comparisons within countries promise the opportunity to examine the differences between turbulent and placid periods or settings in meaningful detail, with reasonable controls.

The second strategy is to separate—and, where possible, to index—the appearance of different *forms* of collective violence. This means eschewing summary indices of "turbulence" or "instability." It also means paying as much attention to variations in the form of collective outbursts as to shifts from calm to fury and back again. Here the illuminating work of George Rudé and of Eric Hobsbawm, who have depicted the characteristic preindustrial disturbances and stressed their replacement by other kinds of disturbances with the advent of industrialization, offer questions and hypotheses galore.

The power to close in on such hypotheses gives these two strategies their attraction. The ideas about urbanization and collective violence I earlier characterized as the standard sociological treatment immediately suggest predictions: Those periods and regions in which the most intense urban growth goes on should be the richest in disturbances; misery, mobility, and cultural diversity will have separate and roughly additive effects; while collective violence and other forms of "deviance" will be positively correlated in gross and will recruit in the same parts of the population, at a given level of urban concentration or a given pace of urbanization they will be negatively correlated, since they are alternative expressions of the same tensions; collective violence will recede as new groups become formally organized, integrated into the nation's political life.

There is surely something to all these hypotheses. They deserve checking. But the second thoughts on the nature of collective violence we encountered earlier suggest some different predictions: a weak connection of political disturbances with crime, misery, or personal disorder; a corresponding rarity of the criminal, miserable, or deranged in their ranks; a strong connection with more peaceful forms of political contention; a significant continuity and internal order to collective violence where it does occur; a long lag between urban growth and collective outbursts due to the time required for socialization, organization, and formation of a common consciousness on the part of the newcomers; a tendency for disturbances to cluster where there is a conflict between the principal holders of power in a locality and more or less organized groups moving into or out of a *modus vivendi* with those holders of power; a marked variation of the form of the disturbance with the social organization of its setting. On the whole these hunches are harder to verify than those deducible from the standard sociological treatment. Still they can be tested, and should be.

For some years now, a group of sociologists and historians at several different universities in Europe and North America have been working on the relevant comparisons for Germany, France, Italy, and a few other European countries since around 1830. The work on France is at present further along than the studies of the other countries, so we are not yet in a good position to make systematic comparisons *among* the countries. But we do have over a century of French experience well documented and enough information about the other countries to give some sense as to which features of France's experience are peculiar, and which commonplace. This paper deals exclusively with the French evidence.

France of the last century and a half is a good starting point. Its territory is fairly constant, the general lines of its political history well known, its violent incidents abundant. The period 1830 to 1960—the main one under examination here—contains several important surges of industrial expansion and urban growth. And the records are remarkably rich—often richer, contrary to our sociological prejudices, for the earlier years than for the later ones.

The raw materials come from French archives, newspapers, political yearbooks, government reports and statistical publications, occasional memoirs, and specialized historical works. For information on collective violence, our basic procedures are (1) to enumerate as many as possible of the violent conflicts above a certain scale occuring in France each year and code them all in a summary, standard way; (2) to select a systematic sample of them for intensive analysis, gathering as much additional information about them as possible from the archival sources and historical works, coding them in a very detailed fashion according to a regular scheme; and (3) to organize studies of especially informative periods or conflicts.

The basic unit in the analysis of collective violence is the "disturbance"— any event occurring within the country in which at least one group of 50 or more persons took part, and in which some person or property was seized or damaged over resistance. The disturbances in the general sample are all such events trained readers encountered in scanning two national newspapers from 1830 to 1860 and 1930 to 1960, plus three randomly-selected months per year from 1861 to 1929. There are about 2000 disturbances in the general sample, 500-odd in the intensive one, and a dozen disturbances that are singled out for special analysis.

A good deal of general information about the social settings of disturbances, of course, enters the analysis in the form of observations on the disturbances themselves. But that way of accumulating information slights the settings with few disturbances or none. We have tried to get around that difficulty by assembling comparable information on major social changes—for example, urban population, net migration, labor force shifts—year by year for France as a whole, for its 80 to 90 departments, and for the larger cities.

We have also begun to deal with other forms of collective conflict by putting together roughly comparable information on most of the strikes (some 100,000 of them) reported in France from 1830 to 1960. The two sets of conflicts overlap usefully, since a small proportion of the strikes turned into violent encounters. Despite this extensive standardization of the sources, however, the sorts of questions this research raises often drive us back to other materials in order to account for contrasts in violent propensities between different years, areas, and segments of the French population. In short, the data collected offer the possibility of moderately firm tests of existing hunches concerning differentials in collective violence, plus some good leads for further investigation; they cannot conceivably provide a total explanation of France's turbulent political history.

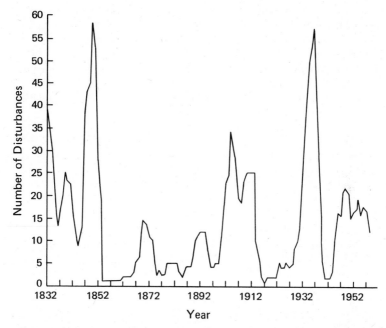

Figure 14 Number of Disturbances Per Year in France, 1832–1958 (Five-Year
        Moving Average Centering on Year Shown)

Figure 14 presents our count of the number of disturbances per year
in France from 1830 to 1960, smoothed to five-year moving averages.*
Despite the considerable smoothing, the curve reveals the tremendous
bunching of violent events in time. That bunching in itself rules out

*The estimates for 1861 to 1929 are based on a 25 percent sample of the months
in that interval, and have not been verified as carefully as those for 1830–1860 and
1930–1960; they are therefore subject to considerably greater error. Both general
knowledge of the government's treatment of the press and close study of our own
data lead me to conclude that censorship probably reduced the number of disturbances reported in the newspapers on which we relied during the postwar periods
of 1870–1874, 1918–1921 and 1944–1954. On the other hand, such detailed
comparisons as we have been able to make with other full sources (e.g., with all
disturbances mentioned in the inventories of the major national series of police
reports in Archives Nationales BB 18 and BB 30) indicate that the sharp drops in
disturbances during the two world wars and after Louis Napoleon's assumption of
power in 1851 are real. For control of the press, see Bellanger, Godechot, Guiral,
and Terrou 1969; Collins 1959; Hatin 1859–1861; Kayser 1958 and 1963; Manévy
1955; Mottin 1949; Weill 1934.

many of the interpretations of collective violence as a response to structural change, which lead us to expect more gradual crescendoes and decrescendoes of violence. Collective violence is unlike crime, suicide, fertility, marriage, or migration, all of which the pace of industrialization or urban growth does affect directly, and all of which display large but very gradual long-run swings. It resembles strike activity more closely, since strikes come in sudden surges superimposed on massive long-run trends. That is more or less what we should expect of a form of action clearly dependent on slow processes like unionization, industrialization of the labor forces, and changes in the organization of firms, but also responsive to short-run economic and political crises affecting the position of organized labor (see Shorter and Tilly 1971). But the fluctuations of collective violence correspond most directly with the ebb and flow of political conflict at the national level. The periods of the Revolution of 1848 and of the Popular Front—both of them times of massive popular mobilization—dominate the curve.

The swings of collective violence, on the other hand, do not correspond to the pace of urban growth, which was most rapid in the 1850s, the 1920s, and the 1950s. If anything, the correlation runs the other way: rapid urban growth, less collective violence. I expect, in fact, that more detailed studies will reveal a general tendency for collective violence to *decline* when and where urbanization is most rapid, because rapid urbanization means both that many people are leaving the countryside, where they are embedded in communities organized for collective action, and that many people are arriving in cities where it takes a long time for them to acquire the means of collective action, or to be drawn into the ones that already exist. My premise, obviously, is that violence flows directly from organized collective action instead of being an alternative to it.

Let us close in on the first 30 years of the period, from 1830 to 1860. The three decades lead us through several major upheavals and changes of regime in France: from the Restoration to the July Monarchy via the Revolution of 1830, through the Monarchy with its insurrections in Lyon and Paris, from the July Monarchy into the Second Republic via the Revolution of 1848 and its turbulent aftermath, to the Second Empire through Louis Napoleon's *coup d'état.*

The 30 years also bracket an unprecedented push of economic expansion and urban growth. The expansion was slow in the 1830s, punctuated by depression in the 1840s, and extraordinarily vigorous in the 1850s. During that third decade the railroads proliferated and modern industry got under way. Correspondingly, the growth of big cities accelerated from moderate in the 1830s and 1840s to fast in the 1850s.

While at the beginning of the period the leaders were mainly the old regional capitals—Toulouse, Strasbourg, Marseille, Lyon, Paris, with St. Etienne and Roubaix–Tourcoing starting to represent the newer industrial centers—by the 1850s the entire region of Paris and all the industrializing Northeast were full of spurting cities.

On this smaller stage, we still do not see collective violence dancing to the rhythm of urban growth. The turbulent years of this period, even leaving the major revolutions aside, were 1830, 1832, 1848, and 1851. Roughly two-thirds of all the disturbances we have enumerated in the entire three decades from 1830 to 1860 occurred in the seven years from 1830 through 1832 and 1848 through 1851. The later 1850s, those peak years for urban growth, were practically empty of violent disturbances; so were most of the 1860s. Again the correlation over time is inverse: rapid growth, little disturbance.

This does not mean, however, that the cities were calm and the countryside turbulent. The pattern was much more complicated than that. It is true that short-lived disturbances flourished in the smaller towns and rural areas of France in the 1830s and 1840s. Three types of events recur again and again: food riots, violent resistance to taxation, and collective invasions of forests, fields, and other rural property. (A fourth frequent form of collective violence of the mid-nineteenth century—the smashing of machines by unemployed or fearful workers—did not reach its stride in France until the Revolution of 1848.) Here we have the recurrent, and somehow coherent, "preindustrial" forms of disturbance described by Edward Thompson or Eric Hobsbawm. The food riot, with its regular combination of grumbling against price rises, massing in markets, seizure of grains being shipped or held in storage, and forced public sale at a price locally determined to be just, sums up their character.

Even in the 1830s, however, the larger conflicts and the ones that most seriously affected the distribution of power in France clustered in and around the great cities. Paris usually led the way; Lille, Lyon, Rouen, Marseille, and Nantes rarely stayed out of the action. During any substantial block of time, therefore, we see three broad classes of disturbance: major conflicts centered on the great cities; ramifications of those major conflicts in smaller cities and in the hinterlands of the great cities; smaller-scale events, only indirectly linked to nationwide conflicts, spread through the rest of the country.

The Revolution of 1830 and its aftermath display this pattern clearly. The central events were no doubt Paris' Three Glorious Days of July 1830; with large demonstrations and extensive street-fighting across barricades, a coalition of workers and bourgeois brought down the

Bourbon monarchy of Charles X and installed the house of Orleans, with Louis Philippe as king. Yet much happened outside of Paris. Almost immediately, struggles for power broke into violence in Dijon, Nantes, Amiens, Bordeaux, Lille, and Toulouse and went on without public confrontation in most other big cities. As the new government attempted to reestablish its control over the provinces, resistance to taxation and to other actions from the center produced clashes throughout large regions of France. The struggles continued into 1831 and 1832, most notably in the great Lyon insurrection of November 1831, the counterrevolutionary guerrillas of the Vendée and other parts of the West in 1832, and the incessant conflict among segments of the revolutionary coalition in Paris itself.

A map of participation in disturbances during the years 1830, 1831, and 1832 (Figure 15) reveals the considerable spread of involvement in

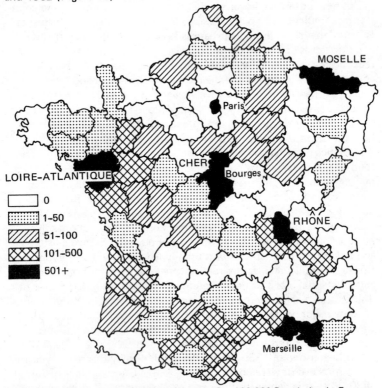

Figure 15 Participants in Collective Violence Per 100,000 Population in France, 1830–1832 (Corrected to Annual Rate)

violent conflict. The map, which shows estimated participants in each department per 100,000 population, singles out Paris as a small spot of intense participation in the midst of a region where conflict was under control. It also shows the high involvement in collective violence of the Rhône (which is essentially that of Lyon), the influence of several major conflicts over taxes in Bourges and elsewhere in the Cher, a long series of food riots in Moselle, the repeated conflicts in the West, and the widespread resistance to central power in a whole band of departments running across southern France from Bordeaux to Marseille.

Let us sum up the pattern statistically. Suppose we calculate rates of participation per 100,000 population for the revolutionary months of July and August 1830, for the period of consolidation during the remainder of 1830, and for the period 1830–1832 as a whole. The breakdown by urbanity of department is shown in Table 4. In general, the more urban the department, the heavier its involvement in collective violence. Yet even the rural departments produced significant numbers of participants—especially during the critical period of reimposition of central control during the last months of 1830.

Collective violence, then, clustered around the cities, but not exclusively in them. Big cities like Lyon and Marseille stand out, as do their surrounding areas. Paris and its department, the Seine, tower over all the rest. Yet very rural departments like Ariège remain in their company. Furthermore, despite the example of Paris, there is no obvious tendency for the fastest-growing cities or the most rapidly urbanizing departments to produce more collective violence than the rest.

To make that fact clearer, we may turn to a correlational analysis of the same data concerning 1830–1832. Table 5 presents correlations of various indicators of crime, malaise, and collective violence with three different measures of urbanism and urbanization: (1) the population in cities of 10,000 or more in 1831, (2) the *change* in that population

Table 4 Urbanization and Violence

Percent of Population in Cities of 10,000 or more	Revolution	Postrevolution	1830 to 1832
0.0	19	54	20
0.1–5.0	42	84	34
5.1–10.0	92	218	66
10.1–15.0	720	136	135
15.1+	2904	412	727
Total	573	175	158

Table 5 Correlations Between Indicators of Urbanization and Indicators of Crime, Individual Malaise, and Collective Violence, Partialed for Total Population, for Departments of France, 1830 to 1832

| | Indicators of Urbanization | | |
1831: Number of persons charged with	Population in cities of 10,000 or more	Increase in urban population 1821–1831	Net Migration into department 1826-1831
Rebellion	0.837	0.613	0.255
Crimes against persons	0.246	0.122	0.236
Crimes against property	0.823	0.626	0.259
Vagrancy	0.771	0.581	0.265
Number of reported			
Illegitimate births	0.771	0.502	0.290
Suicides	0.839	0.693	0.425
Collective violence 1830–1832			
Number of			
Disturbances	0.671	0.673	0.328
Participants	0.913	0.878	0.526
Killed and wounded	0.925	0.840	0.406

Note: Partial correlations of absolute numbers in each category, total population partialed out.

Sources: "Compte de l'administration de la justice criminelle en France, 1831"; Censuses of 1821, 1826, 1831; general sample of disturbances; partial correlations among indicators of urbanization: urban population X urban increase, 0.777; urban population X net migration, 0.465; urban increase X net migration, 0.511.

from 1821 to 1831, (3) the net migration into the department from 1826 to 1831. In general, the measures of crime, malaise, and collective violence are most highly correlated with urban population and least highly correlated with net migration; urban increase regularly occupies the middle position. All the correlations are positive, and some are substantial. As a consequence, a first reading of the table may well produce the impression that crime, individual malaise, and collective violence do, after all, spring from urban growth, and in similar ways. That would be hasty.

The problem, of course, is that urban population, urban increase, and net migration are sufficiently correlated with one another (even when the relationships are partialed for the total population of the department, as they are here) that their separate effects are hard to distinguish. A multiple regression of the same data separates them more sharply. Within a multiple regression incorporating the number of persons in the department charged with "rebellion" (which covered all sorts of resistance to the law) in 1831, the number of suicides, the total population, population in cities of 10,000 or more, increase in urban population 1821–1831, and net migration 1826–1831, the multiple correlation coefficients and standardized regression coefficients for four different indicators of the magnitude of collective violence came out as shown in Table 6. The pattern is the same as we saw with the correlation coefficients, but the differences among the three urbanization variables are now far greater. It now appears there was no relation at all between the volume of recent migration into a department and the extent of collective violence. Whatever the effect of urban increase on collective violence, therefore, it does not operate through the unsettling arrival of uprooted migrants. What is more, the effect of urban population as such appears to be about twice as great as the effect of urban *increase.* The presence of cities made the big difference; their expansion mattered much less.

When looked at more concretely, the distinction is perfectly plausible, and easy to grasp. The segments of the population with sufficient organization to carry on collective action at a scale large enough to bother the authorities—and therefore to lead to violent encounters with troops, police, and others—were concentrated in the larger cities and their vicinities. This is emphatically true of organized workers and is one of the chief reasons for two features of the strike activity of the 1830s and 1840s which our analyses confirm: (1) the considerable correspondence between the geography of strikes and the geography of collective vio-

Table 6   Magnitude of Collective Violence

Dependent Variable	Multiple Correlation	Standardized Regression Coefficient		
		Urban Population	Urban Increase	Net Migration
Number of disturbances	0.785	0.757	0.440	−0.075
Participants	0.960	0.714	0.420	0.042
Killed and wounded	0.959	0.677	0.333	−0.093
Arrested	0.928	0.665	0.307	−0.141

lence, and (2) the tendency of strike activity to come disproportionately from the older, established trades rather than from the expanding factory-based industries. In Aguet's careful enumeration the most strike-prone departments are (in descending order) Seine, Rhône, Seine-Inférieure, Loire, and Bouches-du-Rhône—which is to say, the departments of Paris, Lyon, Rouen, St. Etienne, and Marseille. These same departments ordinarily rank high in tallies of disturbances. In short, strikes and collective violence went together.

Not that they were the same thing. I have already pointed out how many of this period's smaller disturbances were food riots, conflicts with tax collectors, and forcible invasions of rural property. Practically none of them began as strikes. But a significant number of the minor disturbances were simply the violent parts of series of actions pitting workers against employers: demonstrations, political agitation, threats, and property damage, as well as strikes. They grew from the same basic conflicts. And some of the great outbursts (the insurrections of Lyon being the best-known examples) flashed in direct response to strikes.

George Rudé considers the working-class disturbances of the 1830s the start of a great new phase. "For the first time," he concludes, "we find the same workers being engaged in successive political demonstrations, wage demands being put forward at a time of economic depression, and wage earners participating as readily in political as in economic movements" (Rudé 1964: 165). He might have added that the wage earners still came from the older crafts and established industries rather than from the swelling modern factories. To return to Aguet's enumeration of French strikes, the number of strikes reported by industry for five-year intervals are shown in Table 7. The figures drastically underestimate the total number of strikes and give far too much weight to Paris, but they are the best we have so far.

By sheer bulk, the textile industry dominated both the industrial labor force and the strike scene. For their size, however, construction, mining, and, especially, printing seem to have produced exceptional numbers of strikes. As the century wore on, textiles and construction held their own, the mines grew in importance as sources of strikes, the printers lost their force, and the metalworking industries with their factory production came into prominence. The great Parisian series of strikes in 1840 brought out the tailors, papermakers, nailmakers, carters, wainwrights, masons, stonecutters, locksmiths, turners, carpenters, shoemakers, spinners, bookbinders, and bakers—mostly men from the skilled, established crafts.

The same occupations and industries led the Parisian working-class political activity and fed the city's violent confrontations. The city's

Table 7   Number of Strikes in France, by Industry 1830–1844

Industry	1830–1834	1835–1839	1840–1844	Estimated Labor Force in 1840–1845 (in thousands)
Agriculture, forestry, fishing	0	0	1	7,000
Mining and extraction	3	3	8	108
Food products	3	1	3	256
Chemical products	1	0	1	20
Paper and printing	9	2	12	47
Leather products	2	3	3	235
Textiles	32	26	30	1,560
Wood products	10	6	8	502
Metal products	8	2	6	305
Construction	13	6	21	474
Services and professions	0	0	2	3,000
Total	81	49	95	13,507

Sources: Toutain 1963, Aguet 1954.

prefects of police were aware enough of the connection to always have their spies circulating through the workmen's cafes and hiring areas around the Place de Grève and the Place du Châtelet. A prefect's report from July 1831 read like this:

The painters who gathered yesterday at Châtelet said that since the authorities were tolerating recruitment of Legitimist forces for the Vendée, they would take justice into their own hands; and they stated their intention to break into the houses of the Swiss living in the area around Paris and to wreck them.

Those gathered at the Place de Grève started to grumble yesterday; they complained about their poverty, praised the reign of Napoleon and said that in his day there was no shortage of jobs, but since then the working class had always been in bad shape (Archives Nationales F[1c]133, 22 July 1831).

Now, the workers of Grève and Châtelet talked more than they acted politically, and acted peacefully more than they rebelled. But the spies were in the right place, listening to the right things. For the working-class

neighborhoods behind those squares were the breeding grounds of
rebellion after rebellion. And the men who took part were, by and
large, politically alert, organized, integrated into the life of the city.
Not, that is, the uprooted, outcast, dangerous classes.

The studies that have been made of participants in diverse outbreaks
of collective violence in Paris between 1830 and 1860 point in the same
direction. For the Revolution of 1830, Adeline Daumard observes that
"artisans on the border between the common people and the bourgeoisie were at the core of the insurgents" (Daumard 1963: 578); David
Pinkney's careful enumerations agree (Pinkney 1964). The violent days
of April 1834 brought into the action such men as

36-year-old Louis Bertembois, a shoemaker born in St. Framboug (Oise);

Francois Soubrebois, 29, a typographer, originally from Perpignan;

the wagon-painter J. P. Etienne, 17 years old, a Parisian;

caterer Jean Pouchin, 32, from a small town in Calvados, reputed to be
a member of the Society of the Rights of Man;

22-year-old Jean Hallot, a cabinet-maker from Paris, labeled in the
police reports as an "instigator" (Archives de la Préfecture de Police,
Paris, Aa 422).

In the revolution of February 1848, George Rudé points out, the city's
wage earners "left their workshops with their masters and, with them,
jointly manned the barricades; radical journalists, students, *polytechni-
ciens* and National Guards had also played their part; and on the lists of
those decorated for their part in the February events the names of wage
earners appear alongside those of shopkeepers, master craftsmen, and
members of the liberal professions" (Rudé 1964: 168–169).

There is one more Parisian case of special interest: the June Days of
1848. That bloody disturbance deserves our attention both because it
had the most proletarian appearance of any up to its time and because
it left remarkably detailed evidence concerning who took part. Table 8
summarizes the available information on the origins and occupation of
more than 11,000 persons of the probable 15,000 arrested for participation in the June Days. (In order to give a general sense of their relation to the labor force of the time, it also presents the number of
workers in each group of industrial establishments reported by employers to the Chamber of Commerce in 1847 and 1848, and it relates
the arrests to the industries as a series of rates per 10,000 workers.)
While comparisons within the sample display a slight tendency for
construction workers to have been arrested on suspicion, then released,

Table 8 Persons Arrested for Taking Part in June Days of 1848, by Industry and Birthplace

Industry	Birthplace				Total	No. of Workmen Reported in 1848 Survey	Arrests Per 10,000 Workers
	Seine	Other, France	Foreign	Unknown			
Food	53	348	21	42	464	10,428	445
Construction	363	1,511	70	133	2,077	41,603	499
Furniture	214	352	70	44	680	36,184	188
Clothing	160	724	87	74	1,045	90,064	116
Textiles	71	246	11	18	346	36,685	94
Leather	36	113	9	11	169	4,573	370
Carriagemaking, saddlery, etc.	39	135	12	9	195	13,754	142
Chemicals and ceramics	44	76	11	17	148	9,737	152
Ordinary metals	323	886	45	80	1,334	24,894	536
Fine metals	99	109	8	23	239	16,819	142
Basketry	32	93	4	6	135	5,405	250
Novelties, toys, etc.	67	126	12	9	214	35,679	60
Printing	167	217	21	42	447	16,705	268
Transportation	132	336	25	41	534	....	
Services	67	321	30	43	461	....	
Retail trade	168	518	36	69	791	....	
Military	111	272	15	103	501	....	
Liberal professions	81	193	17	37	328	....	
Other	264	770	60	96	1,190	....	
Not reported	65	169	15	197	446	....	
Total	2,556	7,515	579	1,094	11,744		

Sources: Archives Nationales F⁷ 2586, "Liste générale en ordre alphabétique des inculpés de juin 1848"; Chambre de Commerce de Paris, "statistique de l'industrie à Paris résultant de l'enquête faite par la Chambre de Commerce pour les anneés 1847–8" (Paris, 1851).

and a significantly greater tendency for arrested soldiers and persons born in Paris to be finally convicted, this tabulation represents the men and women actually implicated in the rebellion fairly faithfully.*

It does not show a simple cross-section of the Parisian population, but it does show a wide spread across its various categories. The largest single occupational group were the 699 day laborers, who were in the company of 575 stonemasons, 485 cabinetmakers, and 447 shoemakers. Construction, metalworking, and the clothing trades had the largest shares in absolute numbers. Compared with their parts in the working population of the time, men from construction, food production, and metalworking industries seem to have played an exceptional role. Their arrests run around 5 percent of all the men reported in each industry. Mechanics (especially from the railroads), leatherworkers, and printers also appear to have contributed more than their share to the rebellion. Textile workers, it seems fair to say, were underrepresented.

George Duveau's sketch of the June Days has as its principal characters a mechanic of La Chapelle, a hosier of the faubourg Saint-Dénis, and an ébéniste from the faubourg Saint-Antoine (Duveau 1965). If he had added a stonemason from the Hotel de Ville, a day laborer from Popincourt, and a tanner from Saint-Marcel, his cast would have been representative.

The distribution we find is remarkably like the strike activity of the time: an amalgam of the old, politically active trades with a few sections of modern industry. By comparison with previous disturbances, the center of gravity was shifting toward the mass-production industries, gradually, in step with other forms of contention and political activity, not in such a way as to call the miserable outsiders into the streets.

The bulk of the rebels had originally come from outside of Paris. That is most true of construction (as one might expect) and least true of printing. Just under a quarter of those arrested and a little less than a third of those convicted were natives of the Seine. But as it happens, Louis Chevalier's data indicate that about 40 percent of the Paris popu-

*The source of quantitative data is a huge register (Archives Nationales $F^7$2586) containing uniform descriptions of about 12,000 persons arrested for taking part in the June Days; a duplicate of the register resides in the Archives historiques de l'Armée, as do the individual dossiers of the arrestees. Lynn Lees and I have examined a 1% sample of the individual dossiers, which establishes that the registers accurately represent the general characteristics of those apprehended for taking part in the insurrection, but omit a large part of the information actually available concerning the average individual. The register has been drawn on before, by Rémi Gossez (1956), George Rudé (1964) and very likely Georges Duveau (1948); see also Gossez 1967 for background. However, no one has so far reported the sorts of detailed counts and comparisons presented here.

lation of the time, including children, were natives (Chevalier 1950: 45). The adult working population was surely well below that proportion. So there is no clear sign that outsiders were *over*represented. Furthermore, the distribution of departments of origin follows Chevalier's estimates for the Paris of 1833 quite faithfully. In addition to the 2556 born in the Seine, we find 516 from Seine-et-Oise, 335 from Seine-et-Marne, 362 from Moselle, 276 from Nord, 236 from Creuse, 222 from Somme, 220 from Aisne, and so on through the list of regular suppliers of migrants to Paris. While these data do not make the point, Rémi Gossez, who knows the histories of the individual rebels of June far better than anyone else, remarks:

The typical insurgent was an individual who, if a native of the provinces, came to Paris to settle or at least to complete his training and who in general was moving up in the world, a move blocked by economic change and crisis (1956: 449).

Again the violent masses turn out to be those integrated into the setting rather than those at the margins of society.

The findings therefore cast doubt on theories that trace a main link between cities and protest, through a process of disorganization. On the contrary, the whole array of evidence we have been examining suggests a positive connection between *organization* and conflict. The moderate relation discovered earlier between collective violence in 1830–1832 and urban growth from 1821 to 1831, for instance, probably represents the appearance of new contenders for power in the largest industrial centers over the whole decade rather than individual disorientation or malaise at exposure to the modern city.

We are not, in any case, dealing with a constant pattern. Over the long run of the nineteenth and twentieth centuries, collective violence in France drifted away from the countryside and toward the cities faster than the population itself did, as the power and resources that mattered most politically concentrated in the great cities. Politics nationalized and urbanized simultaneously. In the short run, the extent of urban concentration of collective violence depended on the nature of the unresolved political issues at hand. Food riots formed a more dispersed pattern than violent strikes; strikes were more scattered than major struggles for control of the national political apparatus. Since food riots, strikes, and major struggles for control followed different rhythms, the geographic pattern fluctuated. Perhaps the largest alternation went from battles for power at the center (which produced a high urban concentration of collective violence) and resistance to pressures from the center (which produced more disturbances at the periphery).

In the period we are examining here, the revolutionary years 1830 and 1848 concentrated their violence in cities, while years of consolidation of central power like 1832 and 1851—both very turbulent times—spread their violence farther and more evenly.

Some of this alternation comes out in Table 9, which chops up the entire period from 1830 to 1860 into five-year blocks. The table shows the striking contrast in overall participation between a revolutionary period like 1830-1834 and a nonrevolutionary one like 1835-1839. It also shows how much steeper the gradient of collective violence from rural to urban departments was in years of fundamental struggle for control of the state than in years of consolidation of state power; a comparison of 1845-1849 (which includes, of course, the revolution of 1848) with 1850-1854 (whose biggest violent conflict was the resistance to Louis Napoleon's 1851 coup, which eventually permitted him to move from elected president to emperor) makes that point dramatically.

The long trend and the short-term fluctuations both followed the same principle: Nationalization of political conflict produces urbanization of collective violence. The principle has nothing to do with the disorganizing effects of urban life. It has a great deal to do with the location of groups of people mobilized to join different kinds of struggles for power. Explaining the actions of the participants in collective violence as responses to the chaos of the city discounts the reality of their struggle.

That is the general conclusion toward which all our explorations point. The absence of the uprooted, the continuity of different forms

Table 9 Participants in Collective Violence per 100,000 Population, by Urbanity of Department, 1830-1859, Corrected to Annual Rates

Percent of Population in Cities of 10,000 or More	1830-1834	1835-1839	1840-1844	1845-1849	1850-1854	1855-1859
0.0	17	4	40	25	152	0
0.1-5.0	23	22	16	70	70	0
5.1-10.0	53	22	48	68	43	9
10.1-15.0	104	19	10	81	15	2
15.1+	731	57	64	689	86	0
Total	147	22	37	210	56	3
Total participants (thousands)	240	41	64	371	101	5

of conflict, their gradual change in response to shifts in the collective conditions of work and community life, the sheer lack of correlation between rapid urban growth or extensive in-migration and mass violence all challenge the cateclysmic theories of urbanization. And yet our evidence confirms that the distinctive social organization of cities—their hospitality to formal associations, the complexity of their communication systems, their widespread external relations, their gross patterns of segregation—strongly affects the character of the collective conflicts that occur within them. In that sense, urbanization, over the long run, transforms collective violence.

Through the chaos of living cities, what do we see? Certainly not the lawless disorder a romantic notion of urbanization has advertised. Not bucolic bliss, either. We see men held to their routines by commitments and controls, often dismayed by their routines, sometimes articulating and acting on their dismay, mostly singly, mostly in nonviolent ways, but occasionally being trained in another way of understanding and combatting the evils of their present situation and joining with other man to strike out against the situation itself. There is a kind of order to the city's collective disorders, if not the one the forces of order would like to see prevailing.

It takes another poet, Christopher Fry, to state the theme properly: "There's no loosening, since men with men are like the knotted sea. Lift him down from the stone to the grass again, and, even so free, yet he will find the angry cities hold him." Angry cities, but not mad. Violent cities, but not pathological. Living cities, and in the last analysis not nearly so chaotic as widespread sociological ideas imply.

ACKNOWLEDGMENTS

The research reported in the paper received support from the Center of International Studies (Princeton University), the Social Science Research Council, Harvard University, the MIT–Harvard Joint Center for Urban Studies, the Canada Council and the National Science Foundation. The Institute for Advanced Study gave me much-prized leisure to complete the revision. I am especially grateful for research assistance to Karen Ambush, Lutz Berkner, Judy Carter, Priscilla Cheever, James Doty, Ronald Florence, Judy Kammins, Lynn Lees, A. Q. Lodhi, Ted Margadant, Virginia Perkins, Sue Richardson, James Rule, Ann Shorter, Gerald Soliday, Cyrus Stewart, and Sandra Winston

REFERENCES

Arendt, Hannah, *On Revolution,* London: Faber, 1963.
_____, *On Violence,* New York: Harcourt Brace Jovanovich, 1970.

Aguet, Jean-Pierre, *Contribution à l'histoire du mouvement ouvrier français: les grèves sous la Monarchie de Juillet (1830–1847)*, Geneva: Droz, 1954.

Bellanger, Claude, Jacques Godechot, Pierre Guiral, and Fernand Terrou, eds., *Histoire générale de la presse périodique. II. De 1815 à 1871*, Paris: Presses Universitaires de France, 1969.

Belvèze, Claude, "L'Insurrection des 5 et 6 juin 1832," unpublished Diplôme d'Etudes Supérieures, History, Paris, 1959.

Bezucha, Robert, "Association and Insurrection: The Republican Party and the Worker Movement in Lyon, 1831–1835," unpublished doctoral dissertation in History, University of Michigan, 1968.

Bienen, Henry, *Violence and Social Change: A Review of Current Literature*, Chicago: University of Chicago Press, 1968.

Bouvier, Jean, "Mouvement ouvrier et conjonctures économiques," *Mouvement social, 48* (1964), 3–28.

Brode, John, *The Process of Modernization: An Annotated Bibliography on the Sociocultural Aspects of Development*, Cambridge, Mass.: Harvard University Press, 1969.

Chevalier, Louis, *La formation de la population parisienne*, Paris: Presses Universitaires de France, 1950.

_____ , *Classes laborieuses et classes dangéreuses*, Paris: Plon, 1958.

Cobb, Richard, *Les armées revolutionnaires, instrument de la Terreur dans les départements*, Paris: Mouton, 2 vols., 1961–1963.

_____ , *Terreur et subsistances, 1793–1795*, Paris: Clavreuil, 1964.

_____ , *The Police and the People*, Oxford: Clarendon Press, 1970.

Collins, Irene, *The Government and the Newspaper Press in France*, London: Oxford University Press, 1959.

Conant, Ralph W., and Molly Apple Levin, eds., *Problems in Research on Community Violence*, New York: Praeger, 1969.

Connery, Donald, ed., "Urban Riots: Violence and Social Change," *Proceedings of the Academy of Political Science, 29* (1968), entire issue; also published separately.

Cornelius, Wayne A., Jr., "The Political Sociology of Cityward Migration in Latin America: Toward Empirical Theory," in Francine F. Rabinowitz and Felicity M. Trueblood, eds., *Latin American Urban Annual*, Beverly Hills: Sage Publications, 1970.

Daumard, Adeline, *La bourgeoisie parisienne de 1815 à 1848*, Paris: SEVPEN, 1963.

Davies, C. S. L., "Révoltes populaires en Angleterre (1500–1700)," *Annales; Economies, Sociétés, Civilisations, 24* (1969), 24–60.

Duveau, Georges, "L'ouvrier de 1848," *Revue socialiste*, n.s. nos. 17–18 (1948), 73–79.

_____ , *1848*, Paris: Galimard, 1965.

Fischer, Wolfram, "Social Tensions at Early Stages of Industrialization," *Comparative Studies in Society and History, 9* (1966), 64–83.

Fogelson, Robert M., and Robert B. Hill, "Who Riots? A Study of Participation in the 1967 Riots," *Supplemental Studies for the National Advisory Commission on Civil Disorders*, Washington: U.S. Government Printing Office, 1968.

Furet, François, Claude Mazauric, and Louis Bergeron, "Les sans-culottes et la Révolution française," *Annales; Economies, Sociétés, Civilisations, 18* (1963), 1098–1127.

Godechot, Jacques, *The Taking of the Bastille,* New York: Scribner, 1970.

Gossez, Rémi, "Diversité des antagonismes sociaux vers le milieu du XIXe siècle," *Revue économique,* (1956), 439–457.

――――, *Les Ouvriers de Paris. I. L'Organisation, 1848–1851,* La Roche-sur-Yon: Imprimerie Centrale de l'Ouest, 1967.

Graham, Hugh Davis, and Ted Robert Gurr, *Violence in America: Historical and Comparative Perspectives,* Washington: U.S. Government Printing Office, 1969; several other paperback editions.

Gurr, Ted Robert, *Why Men Rebel,* Princeton, N.J.: Princeton University Press, 1969.

Hatin, Eugene, *Histoire politique et littéraire de la presse en France,* Paris: Poulet-Malassis & de Broise, 8 vols., 1859–1861.

Hauser, Philip, "The Social, Economic and Technological Problems of Rapid Urbanization," in Bert Hoselitz and Wilbert Moore, eds., *Industrialization and Society,* The Hague: Mouton for UNESCO, 1963.

Hobsbawm, E. J., *Bandits,* New York: Delacorte, 1969.

Hobsbawm, E. J., and George Rudé, *Captain Swing: A Social History of the Great Agrarian Uprising of 1830,* New York: Pantheon, 1968.

Hofstadter, Richard, "Reflections on Violence in the United States," in Richard Hofstadter and Michael Wallace, eds., *American Violence: A Documentary History,* New York: Knopf, 1970.

Huntington, Samuel P., *Political Order in Changing Societies,* New Haven, Conn.: Yale University Press, 1968.

Kayser, Jacques, *La presse de province sous la Troisième République,* Paris: Colin; Cahiers de la Fondation Nationale des Sciences Politiques, *92* (1958).

――――, *Le quotidien français,* Paris: Colin; Cahiers de la Fondation Nationale des Science Politiques, *122* (1963).

Kirkham, James F., Sheldon G. Levy, and William J. Crotty, *Assassination and Political Violence,* Washington: U.S. Government Printing Office, 1970; also published separately.

Manévy, Raymond, *La presse de la IIIe République,* Paris: Foret, 1955.

Masotti, Louis H., and Don R. Bowen, eds., *Civil Violence in the Urban Community,* Beverly Hills: Sage Publications, 1968.

Mazauric, Claude, *Sur la Révolution française,* Paris: Editions Sociales, 1970.

Meadows, Paul, and Ephraim Mizruchi, eds., *Urbanism, Urbanization and Change: Comparative Perspectives,* Reading, Mass.: Addison-Wesley, 1969.

Mottin, J., *Histoire politique de la presse, 1944–49,* Paris: Bilans Hebdomadaires, 1949.

Mumford, Lewis, *The City in History,* New York: Harcourt Brace Jovanovich, 1961.

Nelson, Joan, "The Urban Poor: Disruption or Political Integration in Third World Cities?" *World Politics, 22* (1970), 393–414.

Peacock, A. J., *Bread or Blood: The Agrarian Riots in East Anglia: 1816,* London: Gollancz, 1965.

Pinkney, David, "The Crowd in the French Revolution of 1830," *American Historical Review, 70* (1964), 1–17.

Rudé, George, *The Crowd in the French Revolution,* London: Oxford University Press, 1958.

_____ , *The Crowd in History,* New York: Wiley, 1964.

_____ , *Paris and London in the 18th Century,* London: Collins, 1970.

Rule, James, and Charles Tilly, "1830 and the Unnatural History of Revolution," *Journal of Social Issues,* 1971.

Sewell, William, "The Working Class of Marseille under the Second Republic: Social Structure and Political Behavior," *Mouvement social,* 1971.

Shorter, Edward, and Charles Tilly, "The Shape of Strikes in France, 1930–1960," *Comparative Studies in Society and History,* 1971.

Skolnick, Jerome H., *The Politics of Protest,* Washington: U.S. Government Printing Office, 1969; also published separately in paperback.

Smelser, Neil J., *Theory of Collective Behavior,* New York: Free Press, 1963.

Soboul, Albert, *Les sans-culottes parisiens en l'an II,* La Roche-sur-Yon: Potier, 1958.

Thompson, E. P., *The Making of the English Working Class,* London: Gallancz, 1963.

Tilly, Charles, "Reflections on the Revolutions of Paris," *Social Problems, 12* (1964), 99–121.

_____ , "Collective Violence in European Perspective," in Graham and Gurr, 1969.

Tilly, Louise, "The Food Riot as a Form of Political Conflict in France," *Journal of Interdisciplinary History* and (in translation) *Annales; Economies, Sociétés, Civilisations,* 1971.

Tilly, Richard, "Popular Disorders in Nineteenth Century Germany: A Preliminary Survey," *Journal of Social History,* 1971.

Tønnesson, Kåre, *La défaite des sans-culottes,* Oslo: University Press, and Paris: Calvreuil, 1959.

Toutain, J. C., *La population de la France de 1700 à 1959,* Paris: Institut de Science Economique Appliquée; Cahiers de l'ISEA, AF 3, 1963.

Vidalou, Huguette, "Les mouvements revolutionnaires d'avril 1834 à Paris," unpublished Diplôme d'Etudes Supérieures, History, Paris, 1959.

Vovelle, M., "From Beggary to Brigandage: The Wanderers in the Beauce during the French Revolution," in Jeffry Kaplow, ed., *New Perspectives on the French Revolution,* New York: Wiley, 1965.

Weill, Georges, *Le journal. Origines, évolution et rôle de la presse périodique,* Paris: Albin Michel, 1934.

Williams, Gwynn, *Artisans and Sans-Culottes,* London: Oxford University Press, 1968.

7

Perspectives on Collective Violence:
A Critical Review

HARLAN HAHN
University of Southern California
JOE R. FEAGIN
University of Texas, Austin

The numerous ghetto revolts of the last decade have accentuated both the complex problems that now confront American cities and the urgent need for solutions to these problems. Thus the urban riots and the plight of urban areas have increasingly been viewed as interrelated. The emphasis on this interrelationship has made it almost impossible to discuss one of these topics without considering the other.

In large measure, an adequate understanding of collective violence in urban areas is dependent on an understanding of the process and consequences of urbanization. The relation between the problems of cities and the problems of collective violence, however, discloses critical theoretical and empirical weaknesses in existing discussions of both subjects. Not only had social scientists failed to devote serious consideration to the role of collective violence in American society prior to the ghetto riots of the 1960s, but they also had acquired a perspective on urbanization that embodied an unusual assortment of misconceptions and questionable assumptions. Since the available literature reveals a paucity of information on collective violence, and since an adequate comprehension of this subject seems contingent on a satisfactory knowledge of urban problems, these deficiencies pose fundamental obstacles to the comprehensive understanding of ghetto riots.

Perhaps one of the most critical errors in prevailing assessments of city life and structure is the general tendency to view the urban scene in pathological terms. Complex social phenomena are seen as symptoms of a basic "sickness in the center of our cities,"[1] just as a fever is one of the symptoms of bodily illness. Thus, ghetto riots have been seen as symptomatic of some deeper malady requiring the immediate invocation of curative, if not surgical, powers. The flaw in this approach does not lie in its rhetorical appeal; such language may be necessary to convince others to initiate constructive action. Yet there is always the danger that people may begin to take the analogy too seriously. Both urban problems in general, and the occurrence of ghetto rioting in particular, have been perceived not only as unhealthy but also as abnormal. Consequently, the belief that urban riots are a manifestation of a pervasive sickness may prompt the conclusion that it can be corrected by strong palliatives, quarantined by repression, or dismissed as atypical.

The purpose of this chapter, therefore, is to review conventional assumptions about the nature of the urbanization and adaptation of black Americans, as well as to examine theories of collective violence that appear to be grounded in these and related assumptions. In addition, an attempt will be made to present an alternative view of urbanization that emphasizes the structural rather than the pathological nature of cities and to develop a different framework for the examination of urban riots.

THE IMPACT OF URBANIZATION

One of the most significant features of the American urbanization process has been the large-scale trek northward by millions of black Southerners, which provoked tensions as early as the second decade of the twentieth century.[2] Pushed by the declining situation in Southern agriculture and pulled by the war-spurred industrialization of Northern and Western cities, large numbers of black Southerners crossed regional borders in one of the most massive migrations in American history. A common view of this urbanization process emphasizes its disorganizing effects on black migrants.[3] In line with much of the literature on migrants in general,[4] black migrants have been viewed as uprooted from the traditional rural milieus to which they had become accustomed. They were suddenly thrust into a strange environment with new obligations and customs; they were cut off from the restraining and integrating effects of traditional social controls, resulting in the troubling phenomenon of social isolation, anonymity, and deviance—developments commonly associated with urban migration.

The influx of black migrants to the destination cities appeared to contribute significantly to the growth of urban problems. As growing numbers entered Northern cities, there were increases in various highly touted indices of social pathology, such as welfare expenditures, family instability, juvenile delinquency, crime rates, radical agitation, and eventually collective violence. All of these problems, therefore, were easily attributable to the wrenching experience that was produced by the translocation from a rural to an urban environment and by the impersonality and malaise that allegedly characterized ghetto life. Since this image of the plight of the black migrant and of the ills of urban America was widely accepted both by the general public and by academic analysts, it seemed to form a natural benchmark for the development of theories of collective violence. The rapidity of the social changes black Americans had endured seemed to be responsible for the instability and pathological conditions that had emerged in cities. Consequently, significant departures from the "normal" order of urban life, even collective violence, seemed to be understandable in this context.[5]

Basic to this account of the process of urbanization and to many existing theories of urban violence, therefore, is the concept of marginality. Thus, the black resident of ghetto areas is often viewed as functioning outside the prevailing normative system of the cities. He is in many ways an unassimilated alien, an outsider, a man whose antisocial behavior could be explained because he had not been able to achieve a niche in the conventional framework of city life. Moreover, his state is frequently pictured as one of normative conflict or anomie; he is caught between the standards of the old rural order and those of the urban scene. In fact, for many explanations of urban problems and of ghetto violence, the characterization of the ghetto dweller as a marginal man appears to be crucial.

Although the theories and explanations that were developed to explain ghetto riots have been so numerous that any effort to catalog them is almost certain to be incomplete, many of the major approaches we have examined seem to have at least one basic concept in common. Explicitly or implicitly, they accept some version of the assumption of marginality: that participants in ghetto riots were uprooted from old social controls and were not fully integrated into the normal or accepted order and processes of city life. As a result, the tension or strain suffered by a people who had migrated from a rural Southern milieu to an urban Northern locale is a distinguishing feature of many theories of collective ghetto violence.

EARLY EXPLANATIONS OF URBAN VIOLENCE

Perhaps the one interpretation that embodied this theme most explicitly was the first explanation offered by public officials after the initial outbreak of violence in major American cities. Immediately after the explosion of riots in New York and Los Angeles in 1964 and 1965, mayors and other public spokesmen advanced the proposition that the rioting had been sparked by the enormous wave of recent black migrants from the South, who had sorely taxed the resources of the city and whose unfamiliarity with urban life had led to a wrenching culture shock.[6] In a more sinister form, a somewhat similar theme was struck by numerous public officials and many private citizens who attributed the rioting to the work of outside agitators, Communists, or other alien radicals who had migrated to the ghetto community with the specific aim of arousing an otherwise contented rank and file to engage in acts of violence against duly constituted civic authorities.[7] The agitator interpretation even received federal recognition in the passage by Congress of riot-related legislation, including the bill prohibiting the interstate travel of persons for the purpose of inciting others to riot.

Although these perspectives differ considerably in characterizations of the motives of the riot instigators and in estimates of the numbers involved, both ascribe the problem to external sources—to outsiders or to persons who are not really assimilated into the predominant norms of the urban community. Such views contain important advantages for incumbent city officials. Although many acknowledged that their own areas had problems that required assistance from other sources for their amelioration, community leaders could preserve the image of an essentially harmonious local community. The basic source of the trouble, therefore, was not to be found among long-standing and well-established residents of the city, an otherwise tranquil and satisfied populace.

While interpretations attributing the blame for violence to recent migrants or to external agitation continued to enjoy widespread popularity, these views were soon joined by yet another individualistic explanation that also focused upon the personal characteristics of the riot participants. This view was what social scientists have termed the "riffraff" theory of rioting.[8] From this perspective, the major groups of people involved in the upheavals were hoodlums, vandals, and other criminal elements.[9] This orientation possessed many similarities to the approaches emphasizing external influences. In each case the instigators and the participants in the riots are described as external to the mainstream of the urban community. Neither recent migrants nor criminals, hoodlums, and similar groups could be described, from this perspective at least, as persons who were fully acculturated to the predominant norms and values of the community. Furthermore, the riffraff explanation had distinct advantages for the civic leaders who widely espoused it. Civic authorities argued that this troublesome fraction of the populace was quite small and did not detract from the "exemplary race relations" and harmony of the general community.[10]

Because they focus specifically upon the individual characteristics of the rioters, the theories of ghetto rioting that attempt to characterize the participants as recent migrants, agitators, or riffraff are the most easily disproved. For example, arrest data indicate that rioters were more likely than the noninvolved to have been born in the North; and available data indicate that long-term residents of ghettos were more likely than recent migrants to participate.[11] In addition, several investigations by government commissions and agencies have failed to uncover any evidence that the riots were instigated by organized conspiracies or by outside agitators from other cities who were imported for the specific purpose of inciting violence.[12] In addition, available studies also suggest that people who were active in the riots were no more likely to have extensive records of criminal convictions than any other young black adults living in the areas where violence exploded.[13] On a wide range of personal attributes or characteristics, the participants in the riots appeared to be generally representative of the ghetto community as a whole, at least of the adult males in their twenties and thirties. The overwhelming weight of the evidence, therefore, has failed to support the interpretations that portrayed the riots as the work of alien, threatening, or atypical elements in the ghetto population.

Yet another popular explanation of ghetto violence, an individualistic one having elements in common with the theories we have just examined, was the "wild youngsters" theory. Some of the first city officials to comment on ghetto riots stressed this argument.[14] The wild youngsters theory was also one of the first explanations of ghetto rioting in the 1960s and set the tone of much that followed.[15] This interpretation generally emphasized two major characteristics of the rioters: their age and their youthful propensity to engage in destructive acts because of their excitable nature or their natural rebellion against the constraining influences of the social order.

One of these contentions was susceptible to relatively direct examination. While some evidence indicated that decreasing age was related to activity in the riots, participation seemed to be most prevalent among men in their twenties and early thirties.[16] The second portion of the wild adolescents theory concerns motivation and thus is less amenable to proof or disproof. Like the theories that stressed the individual traits of the rioters, however, it suggests a purposelessness and a lack of direction to the behavior of rioters. According to this view, the violence was not provoked by specific social, economic, or political grievances; nor did it present a determined effort to ameliorate those conditions. Furthermore, the description of rioting merely as an expression of adolescent rebellion seems to rest also on the assumption that the rioters were not adequately integrated into the prevailing social system. In this case, however, the source of the maladjustment was defined less as a product of social and economic circumstances than as a function of the failure of youth to recognize or respect the need for regulations on social behavior. The description of riots as youthful rampages, therefore, also seemed to contain an implicit premise that the rioters were marginal men—marginal not because of their social and economic circumstances but because of their inadequate socialization into the world of adult responsibilities.

SOCIAL THEORIES OF COLLECTIVE VIOLENCE

The characterization of the rioter as a person who was marginally assimilated or unassimilated into the prevailing norms of the urban scene was not limited to those interpretations that sought to explain the violence in terms of the individual characteristics of the participants. This assumption seemed to permeate a large number of social science theories also. Unlike the earlier accounts, those explanations frequently attempted to interpret the origins of the violence less as the action of specific groups or segments of the population than as the outcome of a social process that had placed the riot participants in a frustrating or tension-producing position from which violent disruptions might be an expected result.

One of the most commonly accepted points of origin for the scholarly investigation of urban violence emerged from certain traditional sociological theories of collective behavior.[17] Although those studies have yielded important, and elaborate, frameworks for investigation of collective action, perhaps the most central concept in many such social science theories is the notion of tension or strain. Participants in collective behavior, including ghetto rioters, are viewed as engaging in violence as a result of their exposure to unusual or highly potent pressures or serious malintegration. Most commonly, some type of social change leads to tension or strain; the change can take a variety of forms, such as urbanization, migration, a shift in unemployment, or economic decline.[18] As a result of these wrenching experiences, and given conducive conditions such as the breakdown of social controls, certain individuals—typically those experiencing the greatest tension—participate in collective action. The resulting behavior has often been seen as deviating from the established norms; consequently, it is often portrayed in terminology suggesting irrationality or inappropriateness, as contrasted with what is regarded as normal or orderly institutionalized behavior.

A variation on this collective behavior theory is related to ideas in what is often termed mass society theory. This approach gives great emphasis to the lack of effective social controls or binding networks, usually combined with the idea of tension or frustration.[19] The social constraints commonly operative in relation to other individuals are thought to be ineffective. Migrating or uprooted individuals, in particular, are viewed as highly susceptible to manipulation because of their presumed lack of local affiliations and group loyalties. Ghetto rioting is thus seen as a hostile outburst by social isolates.[20]

A few perceptive critics have noted that the assumptions implicit in many such theories frequently lead to explanations of collective behavior that portray such activity, implicitly or explicitly, as deviant, abnormal, or irrational.[21] Such theories of collective behavior often appear to be designed to explain forms of conduct that represent a marked departure from the theorist's view of what is normal or ordinary.[22] Yet this view makes the problematical assumption that there is a definable pattern of human conduct that can be classified as orderly and organized and can be contrasted with forms of behavior that are easily classified as disorderly and disorganized.

Even more importantly, the basic presuppositions encompassed by these theories of collective behavior seem to contain many of the root concepts of marginality that are embodied in popular explanations. Merely by definition, an individual subjected to severe social strain inducing him to engage in violent activities is depicted as a marginal man. He is somehow not protected, or not fully protected, by the common social safeguards that would otherwise shield him from disruptive influences. From this point of view, one of the most disturbing sources of tension to which an individual can be exposed is the process of sudden or telescoped social change, such as the transplantation of a person from a placid rural environment to an industrialized urban milieu. In fact, in many descriptions of collective violence, the unsettling effects of rapid urbanization are accorded a prominent role among the forces that may produce the intense tension underlying the development of collective violence. Hence, interpretations of ghetto riots founded upon these sociological appraisals of collective behavior seem to have much in common with popular individualistic assessments of those events. Even though they emanated from different sources and embodied different theoretical aims and concepts, both perspectives seem to be grounded in the assumption that the riots were the products of marginal men who acted outside the normal perimeter of acceptable social or political behavior. To the extent that this assumption is accurate, of course, these theories may provide a useful explanation of the violence. But to the extent that this assumption is inadequate or incomplete, they may not only fail to achieve these goals, but they may also promote serious misconceptions in the existing understanding of violence.

Moreover, a serious misconception about collective violence emerges from the prevailing emphasis in many social science analyses on one side of the collective behavior situation: the focus on the marginal groups and the strain situations in which they find themselves. Yet collective violence, including ghetto riots, inevitably involves at least two sides, two formations of antagonists—one the dispossessed and the other the agents of the state, fronting as it were for the power-holding groups in the society. Political authorities play a much more important role in the recurrent phenomenon of collective violence than many analyses suggest. As a result, emphasis might appropriately be placed also on the strain experienced by groups in power. The role of the civil authorities is not just social control; it also may be one of precipitating collective violence or of channeling violence once it has begun.

Yet another interpretation of ghetto violence that emerged from the social sciences employed the now-common theme of alienation. Although this concept also is derived from a well-established tradition in social thought, it has yet not been fully developed in relation to collective behavior. The idea of alienation has encompassed a variety of meanings and has been used in numerous contexts to explain popular reactions to established authorities, ranging from the defeat of referendum issues to full-scale acts of insurrection. Perhaps the only common element that can be divined from the many conceptions of alienation is again the underlying premise of marginality. A person who is alienated presumably stands apart from others; he feels cut off from society and generally unable to control events around him.[23] His sense of isolation ultimately is transformed into deep and chronic feelings of disaffection that may eventuate in outbursts of violence. Although a much more focused and specific concept of alienation might conceivably be used in the development of a comprehensive political theory of violence, in the vague senses of common usage it seems to obscure the possibility that ghetto rioting arose from a background of specific political grievances. Moreover, documenting the presence of alienation in a given population does not provide an explanation of why those attitudes might result in the outbreak of collective violence rather than in some other form of resistance.

Although interpretations of ghetto rioting based on tension, isolation, and alienation attracted some adherents in the flurry of research interest in the 1960s, perhaps the "easiest and by far the most popular explanation of social violence"[24] emphasized the psychodynamics of frustration and aggression in human beings. Frustration-aggression theories vary greatly in complexity, but the central concepts can be stated in relatively simple terms. Given the requisite conditions, an individual whose basic desires are thwarted and who consequently experiences a profound sense of dissatisfaction and anger is likely to react to his condition by directing aggressive behavior at what is perceived as responsible for thwarting those desires, or at a substitute. The greater the perceived importance of the desires and the more comprehensive the checking, the more vigorous the aggressive response. Recent analysts have given particular emphasis to aggression as a reaction to frustration seen as the blockage of ongoing goal-directed behavior, rather than to aggression seen as an aspect of instinctual human behavior.[25] Arguments grounded in the concepts of frustration and aggression, therefore, attempt not only to examine the process by which frustration induces discontent and anger but also to provide some indication of the likely response of the frustrated. Moreover, an extension of this conceptualization might provide also some indication of the target of aggressive action, presumably those individuals or groups responsible for the frustration.

In many important respects, a well-developed sociopsychological model of frustration–aggression provides a more comprehensive framework for the examination of urban violence than some of the other explanations previously discussed; it certainly provides a more penetrating psychological analysis than the quasi-psychological explanations of some prominent observers of recent turbulence, some of whom like Schlesinger see America's violent way of life as attributable to "the destructive impulse." Explanations in terms of the "darkest strains in our national psyche" do not lead us very far in understanding the origin or nature of collective political violence.[26]

Yet, there are some basic weaknesses in the common frustration-aggression approaches to collective violence. By using terminology connoting instincts or chronic inner conflict and by focusing on the psychodynamic forces that shape human behavior, frustration–aggression theorists frequently divert attention from a thorough examination of the broader forces that shape the situations of individuals and the groups to which they belong. Certainly light can be shed on collective violence, including ghetto rioting, from the frustration–aggression point of view, but major gaps remain. Frustration–aggression theories do not indicate how or why individual dissatisfaction becomes collective and how or why that collective discontent eventuates in collective aggression. Missing too in many frustration–aggression explanations is a discussion of why the aggression is directed outward rather than inward and why it frequently focuses on the real source of the frustration rather than a substitute. Utilizing the sociological approaches, it is at least possible to suggest social forces such as rapid social change, urbanization, or value conflict that may have been responsible for generating group discontent and ultimately collective violence. By concentration on the internal or individual mechanisms, the frustration–aggression approaches tend to discourage the systematic investigation of fundamental questions about the social context.

Yet another problem with frustration–aggression analyses is that anger and resultant aggression can occur without the postulated frustration. For example, a black youth may throw a rock at police because he has just seen a pregnant woman beaten and dragged to a police car, because the situation violates his "learned standards of justice and right," not because of frustration in the sense of blockage of his own goal-directed activity.[27] According to frustration–aggression approaches, the type of frustration endured by an individual participating in collective violence seems to differ from the normal stresses and strains of everyday life; it is frustration that leads to aggressive behavior. While most persons in a society are compelled to endure frustration, the sort of frustration that is implied by the frustration–aggression hypothesis seems to be substantially more intolerable by virtue of its resulting in aggressive conduct; those subjected to this type of frustration are in an unusual position compared with people whose frustrations can be directed to nonaggressive outlets. Although frustration–aggression explanations often do not devote much attention to identifying the social forces responsible for placing people in the frustrating position, they do suggest that individuals subjected to the frustration that produces aggression occupy a somewhat distinctive status. Thus, the model of frustration–aggression is also similar to theories that derive their fundamental assumptions from an image of the marginal man. Presumably persons exposed to the type of frustration leading to aggression are not as fully integrated into prevailing routines of life as those who are not buffeted by this kind of frustration or those who can manage or control such frustration in nonaggressive ways. Furthermore, a serious question might be raised about whether or not frustration–aggression approaches assume the abnormality of the behavior studied. They appear to suggest that those who react to frustration with aggressive behavior are in a separate psychological category from persons who react in other ways.

The basic postulates of the frustration–aggression perspective seem to be closely related to another psychological approach widely used in studying collective violence. This is the relative deprivation perspective. This concept has taken a number of different forms, depending on the particular type of disparities emphasized. In looking at the situation of black Americans in the 1960s, some analysts have emphasized discrepancies in the status of black rioters compared with other reference groups within black communities.[28] Other analysts have stressed the objective deprivation revealed in black socioeconomic levels examined relative to whites, usually noting a decline in the relative position of blacks prior to the ghetto uprisings.[29] Still others have emphasized the "revolution of rising expectations," arguing that the actual socioeconomic gains of blacks have not been accumulating with sufficient rapidity to satisfy rapidly rising expectations.[30] And this approach is often connected with an emphasis on the declining objective socioeconomic situation of blacks relative to whites.[31] A severe reversal after a period of sustained advance, Davies has argued, is particularly conducive to collective violence.[32]

One of the most sophisticated theories of collective violence places heavy emphasis on the concept of relative deprivation, interpreted to mean a state of mind where there is a discrepancy between what men seek and what seems attainable.[33] The greater this discrepancy, the greater their anger and their propensity toward violence. Frustration is no longer seen as the blockage of present goal-directed activity, but as anticipated frustration, frustration engendered by discrepancies between what is realistically attainable, given the social context, and what is sought.[34] Indeed, this perspective opts for a version of the "revolution of rising expectations" argument in explaining the emergence of ghetto riots; that is, although aspirations of black Americans have been increasing dramatically in recent years, their perceived capabilities to secure the goals they desire are increasing less rapidly.[35] The want-gap, therefore, is also increasing, at least as perceived by those who engaged in rioting.

Basic to most theories of relative deprivation is the idea that there is a relation between the willingness of particular groups to engage in violence and their status or position in society. Consequently, this approach not only suggests some of the basic sources of sentiments that lead to collective violence but also hints strongly that the structural features of a society play a role in spawning such sentiments. Yet, while relative deprivation theories seem to offer one of the most sophisticated approaches to explicating ghetto violence, they also reflect some serious deficiencies.

One of the critical problems is the lack of specificity of the referent. Relative to what? The referent used in the measurement of relative deprivation has varied widely in different studies, and the exact nature of the referent or the discrepancy is sometimes only vaguely specified. Relative deprivation theories also share some of the problems of frustration–aggression theories. Again the relation between individual deprivation and collective deprivation is frequently assumed rather than explicated and the linkage between collective deprivation and collective violence is often weakly developed. Furthermore, there is the thought-provoking suggestion that "anger can occur without one's being frustrated or deprived."[36] Persons can react in violent fashion in an affront to their learned values, their sense of what is right and just, without any personal sense of deprivation.

In many relative deprivation arguments, there is also the problem of vaguely specified declining objective conditions. While many have used the argument of declining socioeconomic position of blacks vis-à-vis whites prior to the emergence of ghetto riots to explain collective violence, few have carefully examined the trends in these socioeconomic conditions.[37] Indeed, many available data indicate that, relative to whites, blacks were making significant strides by the 1960s. Particularly difficult to demonstrate would be the sharp reversal in conditions just before riots, postulated by many as significant to the emergence of black violence. While it is impossible to suggest a Pollyanna view of ghetto conditions, particularly in the absolute sense, it is also clear that black Americans generally made socioeconomic gains relative to whites before the emergence of serious riots. To illustrate, nonwhite median income as a percentage of white increased systematically from 53 percent in 1961 to 63 percent in 1968. This measure reflects a relative gain;[38] between 1950 and 1961 the yearly percentage figures fluctuated up and down with no clear declining trend discernible. The period also saw a decrease in the number of black poor and no increase in the relative seriousness of the chronic black unemployment problem.[39] In addition, research on variations in deprivation levels and rioting has so far offered little support for relative deprivation approaches, which stress discrepancies in objective socioeconomic conditions. One careful empirical study of variations in objective relative deprivation found that, when the size of black population in the cities was controlled, there was no association between measures of relative deprivation, such as the ratio of nonwhite median income to white median income, and the number of ghetto riots.[40]

Just as other theories examined previously have imputed a socially marginal position to persons who engage in violence, there may also be a variant of this marginality assumption in some deprivation theories. Persons active in a riot are viewed as materially deprived in relation to some contrasting group; in the case of black rioters the standard is often white urbanites or the white middle class. Their deprivation becomes an indication of their social or cultural marginality, of unique distinctiveness. Rioters are seen as occupying a social or cultural position that is distinguishable from the position of those who do not engage in violence.

ADDITIONAL EXPLANATIONS OF VIOLENCE

Although the relatively general social science theories of strain, alienation, frustration–aggression, and relative deprivation certainly provide
more sophisticated models for interpreting riots than the statements of
public officials, they do not seem to have adequately incorporated an
awareness of the wide-ranging social and political significance of racial
discrimination and segregation, in both its institutional and individual
forms. While some of these theories are certainly broad enough to en-
compass a comprehensive treatment of the pervasiveness of racism in
relation to ghetto violence, they have tended to divert attention from
this issue. Perhaps in recognition of this problem, a number of more
specific interpretations have been developed. Each of these explorations includes a greater awareness of the impact of racial discrimination
and segregation on black Americans living in encapsulated ghettos.

In one of the most widely publicized interpretations of ghetto rioting,
the National Advisory Commission on Civil Disorders concluded that
"white racism is essentially responsible for the explosive mixture that
has been accumulating in our cities since the end of World War II."[41]
By attributing the blame for ghetto violence to the pernicious effects
of an ideology of racial superiority, the Commission succeeded—where
other interpretations seemed to fail—in drawing an explicit relationship
between the external effects of racial bigotry on ghetto communities
and the outbreak of rioting. Yet, while giving attention to problems
of race prejudice and discrimination, the Commission did not probe
many of the interactive implications of their assertions about the causal
role that white racism played in the development of ghetto rioting,
specifically in the political setting of American cities. Moreover, this
causal judgment of the Commission, as well as its sweeping recommendations for programs to alleviate the plight of ghetto residents, did not
appear to result in massive public support for the conclusion or in determined political efforts to implement its proposals. By stressing the
pervasive and insidious effects of attitudinal racism, the Commission
perhaps confronted the white public and governing officials with a
problem that was so overwhelming and so amorphous that it would
have paralyzed the national will for action, even if other restricting
factors had not been present.

There are at least two additional interpretations of ghetto violence—
the "new ghetto man" view and the "riot ideology" perspective—that
also seem illuminating, both of which focus specifically on the American racial situation. According to the first interpretation, the eruption

of riots is related to the emergence of what is called "the new ghetto man"[42]—to the growth of a new set of values and self-perceptions in certain segments of the ghetto population. Although the conduct of most members of society is affected by a normative structure that assigns a higher value to the maintenance of social order than to the venting of aggression or violence, the outbreak of ghetto violence reflects a growing feeling that attaches greater importance to the visible and physical expression of dissatisfaction than to the external constraints that have traditionally inhibited such displays. This shift in attitude toward violence in turn reflects a change in conceptions of black life and potential, increased black consciousness, and a feeling that one can shape one's own destiny, coupled with a rejection of the passive acceptance of ghetto conditions characterizing the past.[43] From this perspective, socialization into black consciousness and militancy has become a distinctive and extraordinarily important characteristic of urban ghetto communities in the United States. Perhaps, too, as a part of this general process, there has been a shift in black political socialization.

According to the "riot ideology" point of view, the outbreak of ghetto violence was inspired and perpetuated by a developing orientation among black Americans, a view of riots as protest, as a legitimate and productive way of making demands on the existing structure of authority. This argument is partially based on several postriot surveys that found that a large proportion of ghetto residents, as well as riot participants, discussed riots in protest terms; a relatively brief development of this intriguing conception has emphasized the view that a riot ideology gradually emerged in the activist segment of the ghetto population and spread easily among less sophisticated ghetto residents.[44] Others have elaborated this approach to include the development of riots from the early 1960s into the 1970s. Perhaps the first riots were both hostile outbursts and crucibles in which the riot ideology was born, an ideology that in turn led to more "creative rioting."[45] Rioting seemed to bring gains, even if they were limited gains. With the spread of the belief that rioting represented a significant and utilitarian instrument of protest ("the demonstration effect") came an increasing likelihood of more riots, given an appropriate riot situation and precipitating event.[46] Consequently, a major advantage of this perspective, in contrast to frustration-aggression or relative deprivation explanations, is that it views riot participants as political dissidents; and it implies an interactive relationship—crucial to the development of ghetto rioting—between the existing authority structure and the black community. Yet the view of rioting as a type of protest may convey the impression that the violence was only designed to attract the attention of public officials and to arouse them to action. Although this intention apparently represented one of the objectives of rioters, it does not appear to exhaust their goals. Ghetto rioting reflected more than a strong hope that the political system would respond peacefully and favorable to black needs and demands. Rioting also appeared to be a desperate and concerted effort not only to compel political authorities to change their policies but also to force alterations in the process by which those decisions are made.

Admittedly, each of these relatively limited and ghetto-specific explanations of collective violence is underdeveloped in comparison with other theories such as the relative deprivation approaches. Yet they do have several advantages over previously discussed perspectives in at least two major ways: (1) They point toward the wide-ranging, perhaps distinctive, significance of racial discrimination and segregation in shaping the development of collective behavior among black Americans; and (2) they point up the interactive character of relationships between black Americans and white authorities in urban ghetto settings.

SOME GENERAL PROBLEMS

Having reviewed a number of theories and perspectives devised to explain collective violence, and before proceeding to some suggestions for an alternative framework for viewing ghetto rioting, it may be appropriate to recapitulate and summarize briefly what are considered the most serious weaknesses in the common approaches to collective violence. Certainly, many of the theories applied to ghetto rioting have important explanatory power; many contribute to understanding ghetto rioting. Yet most contain premises that should, at the very least, be carefully and rigorously investigated, not simply accepted as a matter of conjecture and assumption.

Perhaps one of the basic faults of many approaches to ghetto riots is that they are explicitly or implicitly oriented toward a reactive rather than toward a proactive view of collective actions taken by black Americans.[47] Violence is not viewed as reflecting any specific objective or goal; it is perceived as a response to a set of adverse circumstances and conditions that impel people to engage in what is portrayed as unusual or aberrant conduct. The immediate conditions that produce violent actions often are depicted as a state of social and personal disequilibrium, usually seen as resulting from significant social changes. Although the various theories proposed to interpret urban violence assume different forms, many seem to have several key concepts in common. To oversimplify somewhat, many seem to assume a sequence of events that might be depicted as follows: social change → frustration or tension → aggressive release of frustration or tension. According to this basic formulation, therefore, those who undergo intensive social changes such as rapid urbanization, economic recession, or declining conditions relative to a critical reference group will be subjected to extreme strain or tension, which eventually, perhaps inevitably, is released in a display of aggression such as collective violence. Such a view of disequilibrating events is often coupled with the notion of a breakdown in traditional social controls or the weakening of traditional normative restraints. In some perspectives, this pattern is only implicit. In other explanations, only part of the sequence is emphasized and other parts may be lacking entirely. But the sequence does seem to be a common feature of both general theories of collective behavior and of explanations focusing specifically on ghetto rioting.[48]

Moreover, frequently underlying many existing explanations of ghetto riots, particularly popular explanations, is the idea that the persons who engaged in rioting can be found at the edge of society; they are not fully assimilated into the norms of the prevailing social system, or their aberrant behavior is not as strongly influenced by commonly accepted social values as is the conduct of others. Such assumptions facilitate the interpretation of events of collective violence as marked deviations from "normal" forms of political expression. As a result, these assumptions have permitted the maintenance of an image of a social order that has excluded the use of collective violence as a legitimate tactic and that might be disrupted only by a small segment of the population located on the fringe of that order.

As a result of these various assumptions, ghetto violence has frequently been viewed as nonpurposive, meaningless, or a temporary outburst of aggressive impulses. Perhaps this is a natural consequence of the dominant assumptions and orientations of many theories. Since the principal origins of the violence are ascribed to situations that produce psychodynamic tensions or frustrations, the fundamental assumptions of the theories seem to exclude the possibility that the riots were purposeful or rationally related to relatively well-defined aims or objectives. The major targets of the violence, or the effects that many rioters apparently sought to accomplish, do not appear to form a crucial feature of many theories of violence. Nor is the crucial role of authorities, interacting with those challenging their authority, given much attention in those theories, especially prior to the stage of riot control and suppression. As a result, it has been easy for many to conclude that the riots represent random, generally unintentional, or apolitical behavior rather than purposive and political activity.

TOWARD AN ALTERNATIVE THEORY OF GHETTO VIOLENCE

Hence, there appears to be a need for a thorough reexamination of existing theories of collective violence in general and ghetto riots in particular. An appropriate point of departure for such a reexamination might be the environmental context within which ghetto rioting occurred.

Much of the literature on black urbanization seems to distort this process by devoting undue emphasis to the impersonal, dehumanizing, and disorganizing aspects of the movement of rural settlers to an industrialized urban milieu. There are other features of this process that are equally deserving of attention and that may have contributed to the eventual outbreak of ghetto violence. As increasing numbers of black migrants from the South entered urban areas in the North, they congregated in relatively confined and tightly bounded sectors of the cities.[49] Newly arrived black residents in a Northern city were not free to locate at just any place in the community; their choices were severely limited by the prevailing discrimination, both individual and institutional, that divided the city into distinctive black and white areas.[50] Thus, geographic residential segregation became one of the most crucial and continuing social facts both for black residents and for cities in which they reside.

The separation of black and white inhabitants into sharply divided sectors, therefore, had important consequences for the subsequent social and political development of metropolitan areas and eventually for the outbreak of urban violence. Initially, the migration resulted in the concentration, for the first time, of very large numbers of black Americans in tightly bounded areas. At least as important was the fact that the concentration of black urbanites promoted a degree of informal and formal interaction. Confronted with similar problems, faced with omnipresent prejudice and discrimination, and drawing on previous social ties, ghetto residents developed extensive social networks and patterns that were restricted primarily to the black community. In contrast to the widely circulated and accepted image of disorganized and atomized black migrants set adrift in an alien urban setting, much evidence indicates that a protective web of kinship and friendship envelopes most black migrants in the destination cities, actually influencing the pattern of migration and facilitating the integration of black Southerners into the urban milieu.[51]

According to available evidence, the interdependence and relationships that emerged in urban ghettos continued and prompted a substantial degree of social cohesion in most ghetto neighborhoods, conventional pathological theories notwithstanding.[52] As a result of the circumscribed nature of their associations, their relatively infrequent interpersonal ties with whites on an equal-status basis, and the omnipresent discrimination they faced, black urbanites tended to develop common perspectives. This solidarity provided the basis for substantial organization to advance the collective interests of the black ghetto, or significant segments thereof. Unlike the white segment of the population, which was frequently divided by sharp socioeconomic, ethnic, and other cleavages, as well as by diverse problems and interests, many black communities seem to have generated a growing sense of unity and purpose.

Furthermore, this urbanizing situation of black Americans might be viewed as a general process of group mobilization.[53] Moving from the traditionalism of the rural milieu, ghetto blacks have become part of a broad process, the underlying goal of which is to break into the American system. Increasing the number of black persons in encapsulated urban areas increases the number of available participants in civil rights and other group activities, accelerates the growth of material resources such as money and weapons, develops important formal organizations and leadership, strengthens old social and communication networks and builds new ones, and enhances black solidarity and consciousness. While these processes can produce phenomena that work at cross purposes, they have generally increased the resources available to urban black communities and to subgroups within those communities. Thus, it is important to view black migration as a process that was primarily responsible for the generation of large encapsulated ghetto communities.

The mounting numbers of black migrants segregated in numerous cities in the North and South, coupled with growing cohesion and organization, thrust them into urban politics, into the ongoing competition between various competing groups.[54] (Unless the meaning is otherwise clear from the context, the terms "politics" and "political" may be construed in the broadest sense as referring to competition for power and influence between different organized or informal groups representing diverse social, economic, and political interests.)[55] At a relatively late stage in the development of American cities, black citizens were thrown into contention with other important segments of the urban community for the rewards and benefits that could be provided by full political participation. With growth in numbers and the stirrings of mobilization of resources, the black community emerged as a force to be reckoned with.

However, in pursuing their political interests, including attempts to move government to meet their needs, black urbanites confronted major obstacles, including some important barriers not encountered by earlier white ethnic groups with similar aspirations and goals. The migration and encapsulation of black Americans not only resulted in a framework for potential and actual group mobilization, but it also presented an unusual opportunity for previously established white groups to exploit black urbanites in what might be termed a neocolonial fashion. Black migrants and their descendants in subsequent generations faced the handicaps of traditional racism and discrimination, as well as other attempts by whites to exploit encapsulated ghetto residents for their own purposes. There was the raid on the ghetto pocketbook in the form of exploitative ghetto merchants, including many whites who operated ghetto businesses long after their own families had moved out; these whites profited from the restricted consumer alternatives of an encapsulated people.[56] White landlords and other real estate groups intent on taking advantage of profits in a restricted situation moved into ghettos or expanded their operations.[57] Moreover, ghetto land was sometimes coveted by city authorities who by the process called urban renewal removed black urbanites from valuable land, profiting as a result.[58] In addition, black progress was hampered by a declining supply of low-skilled jobs, work that had greatly facilitated the emergence of earlier ethnic groups.[59] Important too was the fact that many governmental resources and benefits remained in the hands of white-dominated politicians and machines; these nonresidents of ghettos controlled, to cite one important example, many jobs important on the ghetto scene, including the positions of policemen, postman, school officials, and teachers.[60]

Such restrictions, however, were not the only obstacles black urbanites faced. City officials reacted to rising ghetto crime rates by introducing new police invasions of ghetto life—for example, in the form of preventive patrolling.[61] Indeed, some analysts would argue that the ghetto situation has parallels to that of many underdeveloped countries caught in the vise of colonialism.[62] Critical aspects of colonialism have been economic and governmental subjugation; in both cases the black residents of urban ghettos found themselves and their movement to political self-determination hemmed in by influential white groups.

Moreover, particularly because the racial distinctions were more visible and more salient to large masses of white voters and leaders than other community cleavages, the efforts of black Americans to achieve their objectives by means of traditional electoral and party politics frequently enhanced the unity of opposing white groups.[63] When a particular issue gained recognition as a "civil rights issue" or as a proposal of primary interest to the black community, heterogeneous forces in the city—such as the Irish, Italians, the business community, and unions—often abandoned their internecine squabbles and united against the

black community.[64]   The conventional process of coalition formation
in electoral struggles commonly collapsed when the race question was
injected. Indeed, a clear sign of the significance of a new or emerging
group in urban politics was the response of incumbent or entrenched
groups. Unified resistance of antagonistic groups to black demands
signified the emergence of a real threat by blacks to seize a share of
urban power.[65]

Significantly, the white immigrant groups that entered the cities between the Civil War and World War II came at a time when the economic
system required much unskilled labor. Coupled with other factors such
as the development of urban machine politics, those economic resources
enabled white immigrant groups to become, together with big business
and earlier groups, power holders within the framework of the urban
political system. It was this coalition that resisted so vigorously the
claims for power by the millions of blacks establishing communities in
cities a few decades later. Because of opposition of entrenched interest
groups, black citizens usually failed to achieve either representation in
city government proportionate to their numbers or the enactment of
major programs to alleviate their most pressing problems; nor were they
able to penetrate in a significant way the economic and welfare institutions of the cities.

It is not surprising that existing power-holding groups resisted the entrance of a new group of have-nots into the system. Acceptance of
black Americans into the power arena would have meant a significant
reallocation of certain basic economic resources available. In addition,
the admission of black Americans would have meant a change in the
rules for admission to the ruling coalition, providing a precedent for
the entry of other powerless nonwhite minorities into the power-holding
arena.

Given this background, the prospects of attaining more than token
racial progress through traditional party and machine politics increasingly seemed remote to the growing numbers of black urbanites. Black
citizens in the North as well as the South were forced to utilize other
methods in promoting their objectives. One such tactic involved the
use of the legal process. By seeking to obtain redress of grievances
through the courts, black Americans gained a number of significant,
if in several ways limited, judicial victories in such areas as residential covenants and public accommodations.[66]   But the victories were
frequently hollow. The implementation of judicial decrees required
administrative or economic support that was often absent, and court
decisions often exerted little pressure on the distribution of political
benefits in cities. Changing the allocation of major urban resources, so

that they would be used to the advantage of black Americans, seemed to require alternative tactics.

Another technique widely employed by black citizens was verbal persuasion. For several decades blacks attempted to demonstrate, through the sheer force of argument, the debilitating effects of racial discrimination and to arouse the conscience of the white public. Yet such efforts were not very successful. A principal problem was the refusal of white groups to recognize the distinctive effects of racial bigotry and discrimination; or, if they did recognize discrimination, to propose renewed individual efforts as the preferred remedy.

As a result, black citizens began to make increasing use of techniques designed not only to gain increased prominence for black grievances but also to force white groups into a negotiating situation. Black protest activity, North and South, began to take the form of mass marches, picketing, sit-ins, and other civil disobedience tactics. The civil rights movement escalated in the late 1950s and early 1960s, marking an important new direction in the black struggle for power. The sit-in movement in Greensboro, North Carolina, was organized and aggressive, was outside party politics, and was focused directly on the economic camp of the enemy. As such tactics yielded modest successes, the movement increased in size and significance in the urban North and South.[67]

The result was often a type of bargaining process: demonstration; coercive government response coupled with some type of negotiations; on occasion, significant gains from the negotiations; then, demonstration again. Indeed, the avowed intent of nonviolent demonstrations and their leaders was to force whites into negotiations directed at altering the distribution of power and resources. Martin Luther King, Jr., for example, emphasized that the intent of demonstrations was to force a community that "constantly refused to negotiate" to face the issue and bargain with the demonstrators, "to create a situation so crisis-packed it will inevitably open the door to negotiation."[68] The shock and threat of disruption generated by black actions began to force established interests, which valued civic tranquility, to negotiate and even to begin to show signs of a willingness to relinquish some power. Such nonviolent tactics were by no means limited to the South.[69] Nevertheless, the increasing use of civil disobedience and other nonviolent tactics did not produce a total amelioration of conditions in ghetto communities. Black urbanites continued to suffer from significant underrepresentation in important decision-making councils. And even though the movement-prompted passage of civil rights legislation began to establish a legal basis for black equality, such legislation could do little to precipitate a redistribution of resources and power.

Thus, the collective violence that began to occur in cities in the early 1960s occurred against a backdrop of various politically motivated activities on the part of black Americans. Indeed, as the forms of nonviolent expression increased in number and intensity, they were increasingly referred to as "violent" demonstrations rather than as nonviolent or protest demonstrations. Underlying much of the thought during this period was the notion that these events contained a potential for violent confrontation.

Seen from the point of view of a minority attempting to advance in a political system, collective violence historically appears to be one of the last alternatives adopted in their struggle for power. However, if one were to conclude an analysis of collective violence with such a statement, it would be quite inadequate. Collective violence involves more than a dissident minority that was exhausted alternatives to violence. Other questions must be raised. For example, where does collective political violence typically occur? It occurs where major shifts in power are occurring, or where there is increasing pressure for such shifts. Indeed, the differential and unequal distribution of power and authority in a society form a basic source of social conflicts, including collective violence.[70] Historically, collective violence has been part of the regular and normal political life of all nations, part of the process by which competing interest groups maintain power, gain power, or lose power in the process of jockeying for influence and control over governmental and other social institutions.[71] Consequently, collective political violence may be defined as an instance of mutual and collective coercion within an autonomous political system; it includes violence to persons or property and threatens the existing control over the organized means of coercion within the system.[72] This definition points up the problematical nature of focusing only on emergent or challenging political minorities. The emphasis on mutual coercion points to the involvement of other interest groups—or governmental agencies that represent them, commonly in the form of police forces—in collective violence. Moreover, critical to the development of mutual and collective violence is the threat that the actions of the emergent minority pose to the control of existing power-holding groups, particularly with reference to the means and use of coercion.

In contrast, many recent popular and scholarly analyses of collective violence, including assessments of ghetto rioting, have been "violence" in the actions of those trying to alter the existing structure of power rather than in the activities of those defending established order.[73] Terms like "order," "disorder," and "violence" have usually been defined in the political process itself; the definitions of those in power tend to prevail in determining which actions represent order and which disorder. From the alternative perspective, however, the police forces that suppressed ghetto rioting were also engaged in collective violence as governmental agents for those authorities attempting to maintain their power and control in American cities.

Moreover, the question of why this type of collective behavior occurs might be answered both in terms of the emerging minority and in terms of the existing power holders and governmental agents. On the one hand, collective action on the part of an emerging group trying to progress in a political system is certainly not uncommon in the histories of nations, taking a variety of forms ranging from electoral politics, to the politics of civil disobedience, to the politics of violence. American history is replete with examples of emerging groups that have engaged in collective violence in the struggle for power. On the other hand, both the development and timing of collective violence are greatly affected by the actions of power-holding groups and governmental authorities, particularly in their responses to alternative political tactics and their willingness to relinquish power. Moreover, collective violence also occurs at the behest of those in power, usually through the means of governmental agents such as the police or armed forces, in an attempt to recapture a monopoly over the means of coercion and force.

In many respects, therefore, the rioting that erupted in America's black ghettos represents what can be termed the "politics of violence." Such a perspective helps explain the timing of collective political violence at the end of decades of civil rights struggle. Black Americans had not been successful in achieving their principal objectives through the political processes of voting, parties, or machine politics. Nor had they fulfilled their goals through rhetoric or nonviolent activities such as sit-ins and demonstrations. Given the presence of a white society unwilling to restructure the extant pattern of racial subordination, to growing numbers of black Americans the prospects of achieving major advances through nonviolent tactics must have seemed increasingly dim. As a result, violence emerged as the ultimate alternative for many, to be engaged in regardless of the personal consequences. The ghetto rioting that erupted in hundreds of cities represented a concerted attempt to achieve political objectives that had not been accomplished through other means. Such rioting does not represent simply random and senseless destruction lacking meaning or purpose (as some would define "riot"), nor does it represent a full-scale rebellion or revolution seeking to overthrow the national government. If the urban violence of the 1960s fits any of the neat categorizations evolved in the historical analyses of collective violence, it might best be seen as insurgency, or perhaps as insurrection against local political arrangements and authorities by those lacking the status of a formal belligerent.

In one sense, ghetto rioting might be perceived as a continuation of the type of collective bargaining that developed in earlier nonviolent efforts, as a way of disrupting the affairs of the existing political system in the hope that negotiations would result.[74] Viewed as a method of redressing popular grievances, of influencing governmental authorities, and of forcing a shift in the distribution of power and resources, rioting has a long history. During the eighteenth and early nineteenth centuries, urban areas in England and elsewhere were in some cases nearly governed by a type of collective bargaining by riots that continued for many years before these areas were placed under the surveillance of organized police forces.[75] "Politics" often has been portrayed as though its essence were peaceful negotiation and interaction, while violence frequently has created the situation in which those in power were forced to take political dissidents seriously and therefore were pressed to negotiate.[76]

From this perspective, ghetto rioting means a new group is acting for itself to achieve its primary objectives. On the other hand, counterviolence by civic authorities indicates a clear recognition of the seriousness of the black threat to the political status quo. Mutual and peaceful influence may be most typical of interaction between stabilized groups or coalitions of relatively equal powers. In a political system where it is difficult or impossible for an emerging group to secure a place in the sun, to secure a nonviolent transfer of power from existing groups, significant negotiation may well be "unlikely unless the weak can threaten to disrupt and therefore damage the social order which the powerful value."[77] At the very least, ghetto rioting generates a situation where those in power are forced to take black America seriously. Significantly, negotiations on a variety of matters actually occurred during and after a number of major ghetto riots.[78] Subsequent to the riots, notable concessions also were won from existing authorities in some cities.

The characterization of ghetto violence as an act of political disruption, however, is not intended to imply that it was viewed as such by all those who rioted. The motives of black riot participants were doubtless varied. To some extent, the violence may have encompassed the motives of some in the earlier nonviolent protest demonstrations, in focusing public attention upon ghetto problems in the hope that ameliorative action would be forthcoming from conscience-stricken whites. For some, the rioting may have been viewed as an attempt to seize authority and control over an area, even for the brief period of time before the law enforcement arm of the government restored complete control. For others, it reflected the hope of forcing local authorities to bargain, to participate in negotiations. And for many more, it meant expropriation of economic goods and property, or the destruction of the property of those guilty of expropriation. Taken singly or in concert, such motives or objectives influenced the behavior of the rioters, even though some of the participants may have been only dimly aware of these objectives, caught up as they were in the indignation and exhilaration of a moment of political assertion. Yet all of these motives are consistent with the basic goal of seeking the fulfillment of broadly political aspirations. Moreover, the interpretation of rioting as the politics of violence and disruption does not preclude the possibility that there was a widespread recognition among rioters that the rioting was an act of desperation, which might not succeed in attaining lasting goals.

Does this approach imply that ghetto riots were political from the point of view of the rioters, from the point of view of powerholding groups the rioters were challenging, or from the point of view of observing social scientists trying to assess the importance of rioting? Perhaps riots were political from all three perspectives. Although it is difficult to assess directly the motives of ghetto rioters, available survey evidence indicates that they were quite critical of the existing arrangements of power in ghetto areas, particularly economic and governmental structures. Furthermore, their motivation can be inferred in part from the groups they challenged and the targets they commonly attacked: ghetto merchants and the police.[79] Their attack was on accessible representatives of the existing centers of power that controlled their destinies. Their actions may not have been as focused on government buildings and higher level government officials as other recent demonstrations in America, but they were intensely political in the targets attacked and in their attempt to remove hated examples of outside oppression and exploitation. In addition, black rioting was political in that it was perceived by white groups and civic authorities as a serious threat to their power and control in cities, including control over the means of coercion. The magnitude of the coercive reactions of authorities clearly reflected the importance attached to ghetto rioting in contrast to, for example, the apparent significance of violent rioting after a sports event. From the point of view of social scientists, ghetto riots seemed intensely political primarily as a result of their occurrence and role in the recent struggle of black Americans to progress in the American structure of power. Moreover, ghetto riots seemed political in terms of their consequences. After the rioting, significant political developments took place, ranging from the local and national response of study commissions and general legislative action to specific economic relief programs, which came to ghettos as a result of the rioting.

SUMMARY

Viewing ghetto riots as politically disruptive acts in a continuing politically motivated struggle between competing interests on the urban scene, therefore, seems the most promising and suggestive framework for a comprehensive understanding of recent shifts in the direction of collective violence. Instead of treating the prevailing social and political system as a given that cannot be altered, or as an irrelevant context, this orientation makes that structure accountable as an integral feature of the circumstances that precipitated collective violence. Violence did not result primarily from the failure of ghetto residents to adjust satisfactorily or normally to the tensions and strains imposed on them in an urban context to which they were unaccustomed; in the main, collective violence was occasioned by the failure of the existing urban political system to respond adequately to their desires and aspirations, to allow them a proportionate role in the urban structure of power. Ghetto rioting, therefore, reflected an attempted reclamation of political authority over ghetto areas and a type of political recall, not necessarily of specific public officeholders, but of the entire political apparatus that had failed to grant a reasonable share of political resources to ghetto residents. Collective political violence may well represent the ultimate act of popular sovereignty. In a tradition that dates back in this country to the revolutionary period, and, even before, in the lengthy English tradition of popular violence, collective violence is one of the ultimate weapons of any people whose political aspirations remain significantly unfulfilled after other alternatives have been exhausted.

Whether or not these actions represented an effective method of promoting black goals over the long term remains difficult to assess. Yet it seems clear that ghetto rioting did at least produce a momentary retrieval of significant power for those engaged in the rioting; for a brief period of time, until the authority of external coercive agencies was restored, the perspectives and policies sanctioned by the groups on the streets constituted the ruling majority opinion in ghetto areas. As a result, the political emergence of black Americans on the urban scene was made conspicuously evident. This collective violence did not emerge as a sweeping revolution, for a number of reasons, but it did mean revolutionary home rule for a moment. Ultimately, as it became clear, the forces of suppression available to the white authorities would make any attempt to wrest permanent political control from existing authorities by force extraordinarily difficult.

Unlike many alternative theories of violence, therefore, the politics of violence perspective emphasizes that the rioting of ghetto residents represented a demand to change both the outcomes of day-to-day decisions and the overall decision-making process itself. The dissidence generated by the failure of the processes of city government and electoral politics to satisfy the demands of black Americans yielded a growing recognition that this failure was not produced solely by the intransigence of those public officials in office at any one point in time. There is also a critical flaw in any political structure, including governmental arrangements, that prevents an emergent minority within its midst from securing the political goals they seek. Thus, the outbreak of ghetto violence and the subsequent growth of demands for self-determination, community control, and the decentralization of political authority were more than coincidental. Both during the ghetto riots themselves and in the movement for community control that accompanied later riots, black Americans seemed to be pressing a demand for significant powers of self-goverance and for the right to control their own lives and destinies.

NOTES

1. The phrase is from one of the first governmental reports on a ghetto riot. Governor's Commission on the Los Angeles Riots, *Violence in the City—An End or a Beginning?* Los Angeles, 1965, p. 2.
2. Elliott M. Rudwick, *Race Riot at East St. Louis,* Carbondale, Ill.: Southern Illinois Press, 1964.
3. See, for example, Governor's Commission on the Los Angeles Riots; U.S. Department of Labor, Office of Planning and Research, *The Negro Family: The Case for National Action,* Washington: U.S. Government Printing Office, 1965; E. Franklin Frazier, *The Negro Family in the United States,* Chicago: University of Chicago Press, 1939.
4. See William Kornhauser, *The Politics of Mass Society,* New York: Free Press, 1959, especially pp. 145–150; Philip Hauser, "The Social, Economic, and Technological Problems of Rapid Urbanization," in *Industrialization and Society,* ed. by Wilbert E. Moore and Bert F. Hoselitz, The Hague: Mouton, 1963, pp. 210ff; Clark Kerr et al., *Industrialism and Industrial Man,* Cambridge, Mass.: Harvard University Press, 1960.
5. For discussion of research indicating that black migrants are less likely than natives to participate in crime, see Charles Tilly, "Race and Migration to an American City," in *The Metropolitan Enigma,* ed. by James Q. Wilson, Cambridge, Mass.: Harvard University Press, 1968.
6. Governor's Commission on the Los Angeles Riots, p. 3.
7. *New York Times,* July 22, 1964, p. 18. For similar comments on extremists made by the Los Angeles police chief and the Attorney General of California after the 1965 Watts riots, see the *Los Angeles Times,* August 17, 1964, p. 15.

152   *Institutional Determinants of Political Violence*

8. Joe R. Feagin, "Negro Riot Participants: 'Rotten Apples' or Otherwise Law-
    abiding Citizens?" Riverside, California, May 1967 (typewritten); Robert
    M. Fogelson and Robert B. Hill, "Who Riots? A Study of Participation in
    the 1967 Riots," in *Supplemental Studies for the National Advisory Com-
    mission on Civil Disorders,* Washington: U.S. Government Printing Office,
    1968, pp. 217–244.
9. Quotes from this hard-to-get FBI report can be found in John D. Morris,
    "FBI Says Riots Had No Pattern or Single Leader," *New York Times,* Sep-
    tember 27, 1964.
10. The phrase in quotes is from a statement of Mayor Sam Yorty after the 1965
    Los Angeles riot. *Los Angeles Times,* August 18, 1965, p. 16.
11. Feagin; Fogelson and Hill; Nathan S. Caplan and Jeffrey M. Paige, "A Study
    of Ghetto Rioters," *Scientific American, 219* (August 1968), 15–21.
12. *Report of the President's Advisory Commission on Civil Disorders,* New
    York: Bantam, 1968, pp. 210–202; Governor's Select Commission on Civil
    Disorder, *Report for Action,* State of New Jersey, 1968, p. 142; Morris.
13. Cf. Fogelson and Hill; Feagin.
14. *New York Times,* July 22, 1964, p. 18; see also, Edward C. Banfield, *The Un-
    heavenly City,* Boston: Little, Brown, 1970.
15. Morris.
16. The data are not broken down so that this can be precisely assessed; but from
    our review of the available data this appears to be true for most serious riots.
    Fogelson and Hill, pp. 234–235; Feagin.
17. Neil J. Smelser, *Theory of Collective Behavior,* New York: Free Press, 1963.
18. Cf. *Ibid.,* pp. 1, 74ff.
19. On social isolation and ghetto riots, see James A. Geschwender, Benjamin D.
    Singer, and Richard D. Osborn, "Social Isolation and Riot Participation," an
    unpublished manuscript, University of Western Ontario, n.d., p. 14; for gen-
    eral mass society views, see Clark Kerr *et al., Industrialism and Industrial Man,*
    Cambridge, Mass.: Harvard University Press, 1960, pp. 200ff; William Korn-
    hauser, pp. 74ff; Eric Hoffer, *The True Believer,* New York: Mentor Books,
    1951, pp. 44ff.
20. Other theorists have emphasized the breakdown of social control, not in the
    sense of social isolation or the lack of social networks, but in the sense of
    the inability of local authorities to handle the collective disorder. This ele-
    ment has been given emphasis in traditional collective behavior discussions
    as well as in recent treatments of ghetto riots. See Morris Janowitz, *Social
    Control of Escalated Riots,* Chicago: University of Chicago Center for
    Policy Study, 1968.
21. Elliott Currie and Jerome Skolnick, "A Critical Note on Conceptions of Col-
    lective Behavior," *The Annals, 391* (September 1970) 34–45; cf. Smelser's
    reply in Neil J. Smelser, "Two Critics in Search of a Bias: A Reply to Currie
    and Skolnick," *The Annals, 391* (September 1970), 46–55.
22. One of the best discussions of social science theories can be found in Jerome
    H. Skolnick, *The Politics of Protest,* New York: Simon & Schuster, 1969,
    pp. 329–339. For an example of this tension approach applied to ghetto
    riots, see Morris Janowitz, "Patterns of Collective Racial Violence," in *The
    History of Violence in America,* ed. by Hugh D. Graham and Ted. R. Gurr,
    New York: Bantam, 1969.
23. See H. Edward Ransford, "Isolation, Powerlessness, and Violence: A Study
    of Attitudes and Participation in the Watts Riots," in *Racial Violence in the
    United States,* Chicago: Aldine, 1969, pp. 434–446.

24. Leonard Berkowitz, "The Study of Urban Violence," in *Riots and Rebellion,* ed. by Louis H. Masotti and Don R. Bowen, Beverly Hills, Calif.: Sage Publications, 1968, p. 39.

25. *Ibid.*

26. Arthur Schlesinger, Jr., *Violence: America in the Sixties,* New York: Signet Books, 1968, p. 31.

27. Peter A. Lupsha, "On Theories of Urban Violence," *Urban Affairs Quarterly, 4* (March 1969), 289.

28. Caplan and Paige, 20.

29. James C. Davies, "The J-Curve of Rising and Declining Satisfactions as a Cause of Some Great Revolutions and a Contained Rebellion," in *The History of Violence in America*, ed. by Graham and Gurr, pp. 716-725.

30. Thomas F. Pettigrew, *Racially Separate or Together?* New York: McGraw-Hill Paperback, 1971, pp. 148-152. Cf. also Thomas F. Pettigrew, *A Profile of the Negro American,* New York: Van Nostrand Reinhold, 1964, pp. 192-193.

31. Pettigrew, *Racially Separate or Together?* pp. 147-149.

32. Davies, pp. 690ff.

33. Ted Gurr, "A Causal Model of Strife," in *When Men Revolt and Why,* ed. by James C. Davies, New York: Free Press, 1971, pp. 293-313.

34. Lupsha, 288.

35. Ted Gurr, "Urban Disorder: Perspectives from the Comparative Study of Civil Strife," in *Riots and Rebellion*, ed. by Masotti and Bowen, pp. 51-67.

36. Lupsha, 288-289.

37. Cf. Ted R. Gurr, *Why Men Rebel,* Princeton, N.J.: Princeton University Press, 1970, p. 54; Pettigrew, *Racially Separate or Together?* p. 148; Davies' evidence on this point is quite weak. Davies, pp. 772-725.

38. Bureau of Labor Statistics, *The Social and Economic Status of Negroes in the United States, 1969,* Washington: U.S. Government Printing Office, 1970, pp. 14-15.

39. *Ibid.*

40. Seymour Spilerman, "The Causes of Racial Disturbances: A Comparison of Alternative Explanations," *American Sociological Review, 35* (August 1970), 627-649; Seymour Spilerman, "The Causes of Racial Disturbances: Tests of an Explanation," *American Sociological Review, 36* (June 1971), 427-442.

41. *Report of the National Advisory Commission on Civil Disorders,* p. 203.

42. Nathan Caplan, "The New Ghetto Man: A Review of Recent Empirical Studies," *The Journal of Social Issues, 26* (Winter 1970), 59-74.

43. *Ibid.*, 70-71. This argument meshes well with recent data on system-blame perspectives among blacks. See John R. Forward and Jay R. Williams, "Internal-External Control and Black Militancy," *The Journal of Social Issues, 26* (Winter 1970), 74-92.

44. T. M. Tomlinson, "The Development of a Riot Ideology among Urban Negroes," in *Racial Violence in the United States,* ed. by Allen D. Grimshaw, Chicago: Aldine, 1969, pp. 226-235.

45. James A. Geschwender, "Civil Rights Protests and Riots: A Disappearing Distinction," in *Blacks in the United States,* Scranton, Pa.: Chandler, 1969, p. 407. This point is emphasized in regard to the historical spread of rioting in Lupsha, 292. See also George Rudé, *The Crowd in History*, New York:

Wiley, 1964; E. J. Hobsbawm, *Primitive Rebels,* New York: Norton Paperback, 1965.

46.   Cf. Gurr, *Why Men Rebel,* p. 173; Ulf Hannerz, *Soulside,* New York: Columbia University Press, 1969, p. 170.

47.   A similar argument is made with regard to opposition to police violence by William A. Gamson and James McEvoy, "Police Violence and Its Public Support," *The Annals, 391* (September 1970), 97–110.

48.   An example of a general theory of collective political violence which emphasizes this sequence of events is Chalmers Johnson, *Revolutionary Change,* Boston: Little, Brown Paperback, 1966, especially pp. 59–82.

49.   Evidence on the extreme segregation of black Americans can be found in Karl E. Taeuber and Alma F. Taeuber, *Negroes in Cities,* Chicago: Aldine, 1964.

50.   On the important role of institutional racism, including banking and real estate patterns of discrimination, see John H. Denton, *Apartheid American Style,* Berkeley, Calif.: Diablo Press Paperback, 1967.

51.   Tilly, "Race and Migration to an American City," pp. 147ff; cf. also Charles Tilly, *Migration to an American City,* Newark, Del.: University of Delaware Division of Urban Affairs and School of Agriculture, 1965.

52.   Joe R. Feagin, "The Kinship Ties of Negro Urbanites," *Social Science Quarterly, 49* (December 1968), 660–665; Joe R. Feagin, "A Note on the Friendship Ties of Black Urbanites," *Social Forces, 49* (December 1970), pp. 303–308; Joe R. Feagin, *The Social Ties of Negroes in an Urban Environment: Structure and Variation,* unpublished Ph.D. dissertation, Harvard University, 1966; Leonard Blumberg and Robert R. Bell, "Urban Migration and Kinship Ties," *Social Problems, 6* (Spring 1959), 328–333; Nicholas Babchuk and Ralph V. Thompson, "The Voluntary Associations of Negroes," *American Sociological Review, 27* (October 1962), 647–655; Kathryn P. Meadow, "Negro–White Differences among Newcomers to a Transitional Urban Area," *The Journal of Intergroup Relations, 3* (Autumn 1962) 320–330.

53.   We are here extrapolating on the basis of provocative ideas on mobilization in Amitai Etzioni, *The Active Society,* New York: Free Press, 1968; and Charles Tilly, "Revolutions and Collective Violence," multilith, Ann Arbor, Mich.: University of Michigan, 1970.

54.   Hereafter we will use the term "interest group" broadly to refer to the various class, ethnic, and other groups with common interests jockeying for power and legitimate authority in urban settings, similar to Gamson's use of the term "solidary group." Cf. William A. Gamson, *Power and Discontent,* Homewood, Ill.: Dorsey Press, 1968, pp. 34–35.

55.   We have been influenced in our image of the urban political situation by Gamson, *Power and Discontent* and Tilly, "Revolutions and Collective Violence."

56.   *Report of the National Advisory Commission on Civil Disorders,* pp. 274–277; Richard E. Rubenstein, *Rebels in Eden,* Boston: Little, Brown, 1970, p. 124.

57.   Rubenstein, p. 122; William K. Tabb, *The Political Economy of the Ghetto,* New York: Norton paperback, 1970, pp. 12–20.

58.   Chester W. Hartman, "The Housing of Relocated Families," in *Urban Renewal: People, Politics, and Planning,* ed. by Jewel Bellush and Murray Hauaknecht, Garden City, N.Y.: Doubleday Anchor Books, 1967, pp. 315–353.

59. See *Report of the National Advisory Commission on Civil Disorders,* p. 278.
60. Rubenstein, p. 125.
61. President's Commission on Law Enforcement and Administration of Justice, *Task Force Report: The Police,* Washington: U.S. Government Printing Office, 1967,
62. See Tabb, pp. 23–24.
63. See *Report of the National Advisory Commission on Civil Disorders,* pp. 279–280.
64. Rubenstein, pp. 91–92.
65. Cf. the discussion in Chuck Stone, *Black Political Power in America*, rev. ed., New York: Delta Books, 1970, pp. 116ff.
66. Inge P. Bell, *CORE and the Strategy of Nonviolence,* New York: Random House Paperback, 1968, pp. 6–7; Richard Bardolph, ed., *The Civil Rights Record,* New York: T. Y. Crowell, 1970, especially pp. 233ff.
67. St. Clair Drake and Horace R. Cayton, *Black Metropolis,* New York: Harper Torch Books, 1962, Vol. I, pp. 88–113; Bell, pp. 12–17; John Hope Franklin, *From Slavery to Freedom,* New York: Vintage Books, 1969, pp. 623–634; Arthur I. Waskow, *From Race Riot to Sit-In,* Garden City, N.Y.: Doubleday, 1966, pp. 225–234.
68. Martin Luther King, Jr., *Why We Can't Wait,* New York: Signet Books, 1964, especially pp. 79–80.
69. Bell, pp. 13–15; Waskow, pp. 236–246.
70. Ralf Dahrendorf, *Class and Class Conflict in Industrial Society,* Stanford, Calif.: Stanford University Press, 1959, pp. 165, 210–217.
71. Charles Tilly, "Collective Violence in European Perspective," in *The History of Violence in America,* ed. by Graham and Gurr, pp. 1–3, 37–41.
72. This definition has been formulated by Charles Tilly.
73. Skolnick is one of the few to give some emphasis to this point. *The Politics of Protest,* pp. 4–5.
74. Cf. the discussion of political bargaining in H. L. Nieburg, *Political Violence,* New York: St. Martin, 1969, pp. 56–61.
75. Hobsbawm, *Primitive Rebels.*
76. Matthew Stolz, "A Speculation Concerning Politics and Violence," unpublished paper presented at the annual meeting of the Western Political Science Association, Seattle, Washington, March 1968.
77. *Ibid.,* p. 13.
78. See *Report of the National Advisory Commission on Civil Disorders,* p. 112.
79. *Ibid.,* pp. 112–116.

Institutional Reactions to Political Violence

Kent State, Jackson State, and Chicago all pointed to the importance of the "system's" reaction to civil disorders. Yet observers of violence have been loathe to brand as "violent" the behavior of systemic agencies. Violent activity has, most typically, been viewed as the action of actors other than the legitimate authorities.

In Part Three the first two essays examine the consequences of two forms of institutional reaction. In the first essay, Lipsky and Olson inquire into the means through which society interprets the urban riots. They note that the "political meaning of events may depend as much on the reception as on the generation of stimuli." In order to determine the nature of the "system's" reception of the stimuli presented by the riots, they note three ways in which established institutions might respond to the grievances posed by the rioters: "(1) by increasing the costs of rioting beyond tolerable limits; (2) by reducing the extent to which events are perceived as related to real grievances and as strategies designed to achieve redress; and (3) by reducing the sense of grievance over the distribution of values or the process by which such values are distributed." They then examine riot commissions as a case study of elite response to violence and conclude that the ritual involved in the appointment and operation of the riot commissions "serves to divert attention from the problem to the play," and thereby reduces interest in positive action. Certain ultimate consequences follow: "The elaborate procedures through which black frustrations are processed in the United States thus ultimately yield a remarkable product. No individual, no institution, no particular group is responsible for the conditions perpetuating black grievances. Black concerns are legitimized while they are deprived of their political content. The riots are credited with calling attention to deprivation while they are simultaneously declared to have been, and are regarded as if they were, entirely unjustified. Official bodies charged with investigating disorder and making appropriate recommendations systematically operate in response to prevailing political arrangements, tend to moderate insistence upon major reforms, and contribute to the restabilizing of the political order in line with the status quo ante."

In the second essay, Ivo and Rosalind Feierabend examine the nature of another institutional reaction. Inquiring into the "violent consequences of violence" their cross-national analysis concludes that "under some conditions" the use of force "is a stimulus for further violence, but under other circumstances it provides a deterent, diminishing outbursts of political instability." What is ultimately important, according to the Feierabends' analysis, is that the use of force must be consistent; for "the surest way to provoke others is to treat them alternately with great force and with no force. Fluctuation between weakness and brutaility is the deadliest of combinations."

The last essay in Part Three is by James Bill. It is both a critique of some of the earlier papers and an attempt to improve our conceptualization of polical change. Using the Davies essay as a foundation, Bill constructs a "system scheme of power relationships" that he believes will "enable us to analyze the related issues of political violence and political change." Building on this, and adding to it through the introduction of Halpern's conceptualization of "transformation," he distinguishes between "transformation" and "modification." Noting how the literature on development "reveals a one-sided emphasis upon modifying change," he critizes this focus and then moves on to examine the role of violence in bringing about political change. Violence, according to Bill, may erupt from above or below. He concludes by noting that the most difficult task is the transformation of existing sociopolitical relationships.

Part Three thus demonstrates that the institutions of an ongoing political system tend to move somewhat ambiguously in responding to violence. The response of appointing a commission to study the phenomenon is most often used as a method to defuse important issues. That "violence breeds violence" has long been a popular cliché and the Feierabends find, in their cross-national analysis, empirical evidence to demonstrate that this is at least partially true. Ultimately, however, the important question when one is discussing violence of any sort is whether violent responses are becoming institutionalized means for dealing with life problems. That we live in a period of intense violence is known by all observers. That we do not fully comprehend the nature of the phenomenon of violence is almost equally obvious. Until we are more fully able to understand the nature of the behavior with which we deal, we will remain unable to answer the important questions posed above. With this in mind, the concluding essay in this volume (Part Four) notes ways in which we might go about "improving the state of research on violence."

8

Civil Disorders and the American Political Process: The Meaning of Recent Urban Riots

MICHAEL LIPSKY
Massachusetts Institute of Technology
DAVID J. OLSON
Indiana University

INTRODUCTION

A central question in the analysis of civil disorders of the 1960s has been: To what extent were the riots *political*? Considerable debate has developed over whether the riots should be viewed as expressive of political demands. Were these events implicitly expressive of demands for changes in the authoritative allocation of values, or for changes in the established authority structures of the society? Answers to these questions are fundamental to understanding the meaning of recent civil disorders.[1]

In one sense the question is fatuous. It is easily demonstrated that the state forcefully intervened to stop the riots; that political leaders styled their public images around fears generated by riots; that legislatures passed laws seeking to control riotous behavior; and that politicians responded to the disorders with proclamations of varying content. In short, as in the case of oil spills, mining accidents, and natural disasters, political institutions were engaged by the disorders and responded to them in some way. Political content may be read into any event that makes more than minimal impact on the system.

In another sense, however, the question is more complicated and endowed with profound implications. Public officials in whose jurisdictions riots occurred expressed the view again and again that the riots were meaningless acts engaged in by unrepresentative members of the community.[2] They repeatedly proclaimed that riotous behavior would not be rewarded. If the riots consisted of meaningless outbursts against the law, conducted in a carnival spirit without instrumental implications and unrelated to furthering black community interests, then the riots might be effectively ignored once they had been suppressed. However, if the riots were in some sense rebellions against ghetto conditions and were engaged in or supported by a substantial portion of the black community, then they cannot be so easily dismissed. In such a case, the implicit black demands arising from ghetto revolts require serious consideration for reasons of both social justice and domestic tranquility.

The view that riots may be understood as expressive of political demands has been advanced by black leaders and by scholars of both races in analyzing the events subsequently.[3] This view has some plausibility. It is based upon evidence that the rioters were a large and representative minority of the young adults in the ghetto; that during some of the riots and notably after they were over, blacks often stated explicitly that they were rioting to arouse white concern; that during the riots clear patterns were observable in the targets of the rioters—the police, and stores that charged excessive prices or sold shoddy merchandise; that in some cities stores displaying "soul brother" signs were spared; and, perhaps most important, that an extremely large majority of blacks, when interviewed subsequently, considered the riots to be at least partly a protest against their condition. Needless to say, motivation for such behavior and attitudes may be found in the history of blacks in America.[4]

Perhaps the most prominent proponent of the view that recent riots were politically "meaningless" is Edward Banfield in his essay, "Rioting Mainly for Fun and Profit."[5] Banfield ignores much of the evidence suggested above, or regards it as inappropriate to the question.[6] He is particularly critical of utilizing survey data obtained *after* the event to attach meaning to observers' and participants' actions *during* the riots.

For our purposes, however, this criticism is either incorrect or unimportant. If survey evidence obtained after the event does provide valid indicators, Banfield is incorrect. On the other hand, if survey evidence cannot be used in this way (and obviously Banfield has an undeniable epistemological point), it still remains that the ways in which people reconstruct events may be as important as their attitudes during the events themselves. We may argue that people caught up in complex and confusing events search for meaning[7] and that an event is likely to "become" what people later rationalize it to be. To deny the importance of meanings of political events attached after the fact would be to reduce political life to the most antiseptic of caricatures, where only statements clearly labeled as "demands" and composed in fully rational and instrumental fashion would be permitted to engage our attention.

How may we come to grips with our concern for assessing the political content of recent civil disorders, particularly in light of continued controversy along the lines suggested above? We suggest that the issue is unresolvable as usually posed, because conventional approaches fail to consider the *entire political process* in which civil disorders occur. We propose that the question of interpreting riot events is as much a problem of the way the society interprets the events as it is a problem of determining rioters' motivations. Like the tree falling unheard in the forest (to use a familiar image), the political meaning of events may depend as much on the reception as on the generation of stimuli. Robert Fogelson, after reviewing the evidence suggesting that indeed the riots might be considered political in demands, is in accord with this approach. "The blacks delivered a protest," he concludes, "but most whites did not receive it."[8]

Let us review American elite responses to recent disorders. Recent riots have threatened widely shared social values of order, security, and property, and have been engaged in by people representative of groups with long-standing grievances. In response to such grievances or to the threat to shared values, or in order to reduce the jeopardy to such values in the future, public officials have acted to reduce the likelihood that the rioting groups will repeat this activity, or to reduce the perception of threat imposed by riots. Schematically, these ends may be accomplished in three ways: (1) by increasing the costs of rioting beyond tolerable limits; (2) by reducing the extent to which events are perceived as related to real grievances and as strategies designed to achieve redress; and (3) by reducing the sense of grievance over the distribution of values or the process by which such values are distributed.

The first way involves suppression of groups during periods of rioting, surveillance in anticipation of possible reoccurrences, and postures on the part of public officials that convey the message that riotous behavior will be neither condoned nor rewarded.

Elements of this mode of response clearly have been evident in American elite reactions to civil disorders. Since the race riots of 1917, public officials with highest responsibility have indicated that riots would not be rewarded and continued riotous behavior would not be tolerated.[9] They have also placed primary emphasis in initial stages of riot development on utilizing available military and paramilitary forces to suppress disturbances.

However, continuous surveillance and repression of aggrieved groups involve great costs to the society as a whole. They imply denial of civil liberties to some citizens, indiscriminate attitudes toward members of the aggrieved group, considerable expense for a nonproductive activity, and a reduction in liberty for the society as a whole. For these and other reasons, these measures have generally been rejected in the recent period.[10]

Following termination of civil disorders, however, official reactions have been characterized by the initiation of processes related to the second and third modes of response. They have consistently maintained that racial violence was of no political significance, that only a small and unrepresentative fraction of the community engaged in it, and that participants came from the criminal element of society.[11] Further, while not directly recognizing the legitimacy of the grievances of the group represented by the rioters, public officials have responded to civil disorders almost invariably by appointing a commission or its equivalent (task force, review team, study group) to explain the episodes, study the issues, and make recommendations for future official action.[12]

These bodies have had license to confer legitimacy on the complaints of rioters, and to make authoritative recommendations for the amelioration of conditions associated with grievances. The high status of the commission and the ostensibly representative nature of its membership hold out at least the possibility that its recommendations will be adopted and its findings accepted by both the group of whom the rioters are members and the rest of society, toward which threats and appeals are directed.

Most recent authoritative riot commissions have concluded that black grievances were legitimate, that the riots were approved by a wide segment of the black community (certainly a wider segment than had been originally supposed), and that major public policy adjustments were called for, involving considerable alteration of priorities and attendant redistribution of resources. We dwell on riot commission responses for several reasons. While the commissions by no means represent the totality of elite responses, they clearly represent the modal official response to civil disorders. Indeed, it is difficult to discover any significant instance of racial disorder in this century that was not quickly followed by the appointment of a commission or study group to investigate the incident.[13]

Given the plausibility of viewing riots as expressive of political demands, the creation of public bodies with opportunities to legitimate those demands, and the relative sympathy of recent riot commissions to black claims,[14] how do we account for the continued denial that the riots themselves were political (however legitimate black grievances) and the continued failure of the political system to act positively on those demands? As suggested earlier, the answer may lie in the structure of responses to riots, rather than in the content or intentions of the rioters themselves. In a provocative essay Allan Silver has suggested one reason why riots in the United States are not considered to have political content.[15] He asserts that compared with the traditional response to mob action in Western society, typified by the mob of preindustrial eighteenth-century Europe, American society has lost the capacity to view collective violence as expressive of political demands. Whereas elites understood that the preindustrial mobs in Europe rioted for redress of grievances, in the United States a number of developments have reduced the prevalence of and capacity for this understanding; expectations of public order have generally increased, and police forces have been introduced to protect property and the personal security of the expanding middle classes. These developments, Silver argues, result in the tendency to define behavior directed against property, or against privileges of the middle and upper classes, as antipolice; hence, such behavior is "criminal"; hence, it is nonpolitical. The mythology that riots are caused by the "riffraff" is consistent with such developments.[16]

Silver's essay attempts to provide theoretical linkages between one form of collective violence and its political impact. In this paper we are also interested in aspects of the American political system that may account for tendencies to minimize views of collective violence as political in origin. We attempt to describe some of the factors that intervene in the relation between the possible political content of riots and their reception as political demands, and to explain these developments by examining aspects of the political system conducive to such intervention. We generally hope to illuminate the debate on the putative "political" content of recent civil disorders, as well as shed light on the much discussed but rarely researched subject of the impact of riot commission recommendations.[17]

Finally, this analysis may contribute to better understanding of a critical consideration in the internal politics of nations—their response to, and manipulation of, domestic crises.[18]

RIOT COMMISSIONS

The remarkable consistency with which American public officials have appointed riot commissions or their equivalents after racial violence over a period spanning more than half a century suggests that this development represents a primary response of political leaders to race-related civil disorders. Typically, men and women of high status, representative of dominant political and economic institutions are charged with studying the events in question, describing and explaining what took place, and prescribing measures to prevent their reoccurrence.[19] Although the nature of collective race-related violence has changed,[20] the nature of leadership response has remained relatively consistent (with the possible exception that the flagrant propolice positions of some early riot commissions has been more muted in recent times).

We have described elsewhere the outlines of riot commission political and organizational behavior.[21] Rather than repeating that discussion here, we will focus on aspects of riot commission politics that may decrease systemic capacity to perceive collective violence as reflective of political demands and to translate demands perceived as such into public policy.

Commissions and Urgency

In confused or emotionally provocative times, when public anxiety may be heightened by threatening images of public disorder, people seek decisive action from leaders, reassurance that events are under control, and explanations of the events that they can assimilate into their world view. Sometimes these needs, which may also be understood as demands on political leadership, result in a readiness to accept simplistic explanations of causality.[22] This may help explain the tendency of some politicians to attribute riots to the riffraff or to left-wing conspiracies. It also may explain the desirability of establishing high-status commissions to puncture these notions and to impede the simplistic and reactionary policy proposals that are derived from such assumptions.

The establishment of a riot commission provides a symbolic response to these pressures. There is an appearance of action, yet political executives are not required to develop any but suppressive policies during the turbulent period. Indeed, they can effectively postpone action until the commission reports,[23] at which time the pressures surrounding their responses will have changed, and in any event will more resemble the normal pressures of office than do those that develop just after the rioting. Thus riot commissions may be said to perform the *latent function* of reassuring an aroused public, while continuing their *manifest function* of attempting to study the riot events and make recommendations. The latent function of riot commissions is enhanced during the period between establishment and reporting by deliberate commission efforts to alert various publics that they are at work and developing findings in a balanced way.

In view of the fate of a majority of the recommendations proposed by riot commissions (of which more later), the latent function of assuring anxious citizens that racial problems are being looked into may be more important than the manifest function of investigating causes of the disorder and prescribing corrective reforms. Successful performance of the latent function may, in fact, impair the ability of riot commissions to perform the manifest function. In fact, the more thorough riot commissions are in investigating causes of disorder, the less successful they may be in achieving implementation of their recommendations. By reducing citizen demands for action (the latent function), riot commissions may remove the necessary condition of mass support for costly and innovative reforms that prove difficult to implement. This may partially explain why so few riot commission recommendations are adopted, even though civil disorders are directly relevant to processes of change within urban political systems. In support of the social scientists who view conflict and violence as politically relevant, it also explains how civil disorders have simultaneously a direct impact on urban political attitudes but only marginal influence in altering public policy.

If this explanation of the impact of establishing riot commissions has validity, we may also ask which concerned publics the formation of riot commissions may be thought to reassure. Clearly it is not the rioters themselves, since participants in and supporters of collective violence are invariably omitted from commissioners' ranks, and the degree of rioters' cynicism and distrust of white society precludes assumptions that this group may be reassured by the appointment of relatively conservative white and black commissioners. Indeed, appointments to recent riot commissions have been heavily criticized by a fairly broad spectrum of black spokesmen.

Although the black public that is relatively unsupportive of riots may be thought to gain some comfort from knowing that white politicians will address these problems, it seems more persuasive to assume that it is the concerned white publics of various political leanings to which the symbol of commission formation is directed. While there is evidence that some recent commissions have been motivated by a desire to maintain faith with the black community,[24] the genesis of commissions in reassuring white publics that events are under control should help explain subsequent concern with the direction and strength of recommendations.

Commissions and Representation

Presidential commissions and special commissions developed at other levels of government partly derive their legitimacy from the high status of their members and their "representative" quality. Commission reports are presumed to command respect and attention because they are produced by individuals who represent a spectrum of viewpoints. However, examination of commission rolls reveals that members actually represent a limited spectrum and the variety is somewhat constrained. Rioters and their militant supporters are unrepresented on such boards. More importantly, the presence of members representative of dominant community interests results in commission reports notable for their failure to challenge these same interests in concrete ways. One might suggest that the more the specific, dominant interests are represented, the greater the potential for diluting concrete criticisms. An apparent exception to this rule in fact seems to confirm the generalization. The New Jersey Governor's Commission on Civil Disorders was extremely critical of various aspects of Newark politics. The Commission went so far as to recommend general investigations of corruption in the city and a state takeover of the public schools.[25] But, notably, this commission was appointed at the state, not the city, level; thus members were not necessarily recruited to protect city interests.

Anticipating the Appointing Executive

In developing their reports, riot commissions confront inevitable tensions between their "objective" study and the recognition that goals may be advanced by tailoring recommendations to maximize their potential for acceptance. Thus some findings may be eliminated or toned down, and some proposals altered, in anticipation of the reactions of the executive who appointed the commission and on whom implementation of recommendations depends. This tactic may backfire, as in the case of the housing recommendations of the Kerner Commission. By precisely doubling the President's recommendation, Kerner Commission staff members hoped to provide President Johnson with an endorsement of his basic proposals, while permitting him to appear more conservative than the Commission. Unfortunately, by the time the Commission reported, the President was not receptive to large-scale spending programs.

Anticipating the political needs of the appointing executive also influences the posture riot commissions assume toward the riot-related behavior of the appointing executives immediately before, during, and after racial violence. To the extent that the appointing executives exercise discretion over which established institutions are represented on commissions, the composition of riot commissions incorporates a built-in tendency to "whitewash" the behavior of the appointing executive. The silence of riot commissions on the conduct of political executives who appoint them manifests this tendency. In each of the three cities we have analyzed intensively, the official commissions withheld critical analysis and commentary on the appointing executive. While ignoring the performance of the appointing executive, riot commissions often single out other public officials (usually from jurisdictions other than the one in which the commission was created) for critical review. Thus the New Jersey Commission pointed to what it considered numerous shortcomings of the Addonizio administration in Newark, but failed to mention the inflamatory rhetoric during the civil disorder by Governor Hughes, the appointing executive.

Commissions may also help "take the heat off" chief executives by directing recommendations to other jurisdictions. This inference is supported by examining the jurisdictions toward which some recent riot commissions have addressed their recommendations. Of the 99 recommendations developed by the New Jersey Commission, less than a third (29) were directed toward state action. Significantly, recommendations directed toward the primary jurisdiction received much more favorable responses than those directed toward others (see Table 10).[26] Somewhat supportive of this point, of the 39 points of Milwaukee's Mayor Henry Maier, which formed the core of the city's authoritative response to disorders, more than 80 percent were directed toward jurisdictions outside the city. Again, the likelihood of implementation was much greater when recommendations were directed toward the

Table 10 New Jersey Commission's Recommendations, by Jurisdiction Targeted for Reform and Number Receiving Favorable Action

Governmental Jurisdiction Targeted for Reform	Number of Recommendations	Percent of Recommendations	Number with Some Favorable Action	Percent Recommendations Receiving Favorable Action
Newark	33	33.0	7	21.0
Essex County	6	6.0	1	16.6
State of New Jersey (Primary Jurisdiction)	29	29.0	14	48.2
Federal Government	4	4.0	1	25.0
Combined or no jurisdiction specified	22	22.0	3	13.6
Englewood	2	2.0	?	...
Plainfield	3	3.0	?	...
Total	99		26	26.0

jurisdiction presided over by the executive originally appointing the commission (see Table 11).[27]

Sources of Commission Legitimacy

Commissions in theory derive their legitimacy from two sources: the high status and representative nature of members, and the authority conveyed by the appointing executive. Whatever their precise titles, they are always "official" commissions, and therefore may claim that their findings will be received with greater interest and attention than those of similar groups lacking "official" designation.

Curiously, among recent commissions there seems to have been an inverse relation between their representative character and the extent to which their findings were accepted by primary jurisdictions. The narrower the base from which commissioners are drawn, the more have commission recommendations been endorsed by appointing executives. This hypothesis is suggested by the experiences of some recent riot commissions we have studied in detail. In Detroit and Milwaukee, Mayors Jerome Cavanaugh and Henry Maier made little effort to secure "representative" panels. Mayor Cavanaugh appointed agency heads and other

Table 11 Milwaukee's 39-Point Program, by Jurisdiction Targeted for Reform and Number Receiving Favorable Action

Governmental Jurisdiction Targeted for Reform	Number of Recommendations	Percent of Recommendations	Percent with Some Favorable Action	Percent Recommendations Receiving Favorable Action
Federal	13	33.3	1	7.6
State	14	35.8	2	14.2
Federal and State	2	5.1	1	50.0
County	3	7.6	0	0.0
City of Milwaukee (Primary Jurisdiction)	7	17.9	3	42.8
Total	39		7	17.9

officials loyal to him to a Mayor's Development Team to prepare recommendations for postriot policies. Mayor Maier, in developing his postriot program, incorporated the suggestions of two organizations that he considered friendly to his interests. Thus when chief executives have not emphasized the representative nature of commission members in studying riots and developing recommendations, they have controlled or shortcut the appointment process and have been receptive to recommendations. However, when executives have emphasized the representative aspects of commissions, as in the Kerner and the New Jersey Commissions, executives have ignored or tried to ignore salient recommendations.

Competing Commissions and the Interest-Group Process
We have suggested elsewhere that as commissions develop "commission identities" and assume group interests distinct from the interests of individual members, they may be simultaneously disowned by executives who are not anxious to respond to commissions bringing in reports of an unwelcome character.[28] Although we have previously said that the appointment of commissions permits executives to suspend action and thus avoid the immediate pressures of tumultuous periods, they must still respond to commission reports some months later. Despite the fact that riot commissions are appointed as "official" bodies in the United States, there is no reason to think that chief executives suffer any penalties of office if they are faithless to the recommendations or interpretations. It is this point that Kenneth Clark dramatized so well in his frequently quoted testimony to the Kerner Commission that riot commission reports were rarely, if ever, implemented.[29] Riot commissions, rather than retaining the authoritative status with which they are originally launched, instead must compete politically like other interest groups, enjoying as much or as little influence as they can muster without the aid of the executive branch.

   As they lose authoritative status, riot commissions also relinquish their monopoly over the processes of investigation and recommendation. "Competing riot commissions" arise to promote interests that either their sponsors consider neglected in the final report or that they *anticipate* will be neglected. Thus riot commissions are additionally circumscribed by competing commissions. These groups not only challenge the legitimacy and appropriateness of the findings and recommendations of commissions; by arousing public opinion to the continued uncertainty of conclusions and interpretations, they dilute the impact of the latent functioning of commissions as well.

The Destruction of Spurious Explanations

One of the most important functions played by recent riot commissions
has been to explode false interpretations of the causes of the disorders.
Initially it was widely believed among public officials and mass publics
that the recent disorders were caused by either the riffraff of the ghetto,
or a conspiracy (black militant or left-wing). The Kerner Commission
contributed substantially to refuting these beliefs.[30] The Commission
could find no evidence of conspiracy and endorsed Fogelson and Hill's
refutation of the riffraff theory.[31] But here, too, we may raise questions concerning the relation of these findings to the perception of the
riots as expressive of political demands. On the one hand, the continued
prevalence of these myths present major barriers to interpretations of
collective violence as politically expressive. Yet, on the other hand,
their prevalence may so concern blacks and white sympathizers that
the very refutation of the myths may satisfy these groups that the commission has been "sympathetic" and may deflect attention away from
programs for vigorous action. This would be reinforced by the tendency
to pay most attention to the report on the day of issuance, with correspondingly less attention to the process of implementation.[32]

IMPLEMENTATION OF RIOT COMMISSION RECOMMENDATIONS

As in other areas of political inquiry, we are not content with reviewing
the formation of riot commissions and analysing their subsequent reports. To understand their significance in the political process we must
appreciate the extent to which their recommendations in fact tend to
be accepted and implemented. Studies of the implementation of riot
commission recommendations should assist us in determining the extent
to which (1) riots were efficacious, (2) riot commissions play a critical
role in the policy process, and (3) the American political system has a
capacity to perceive potentially politically expressive demands articulated in recent civil disorders. On these questions the following points
seem particularly pertinent.

Degree of Compliance

Most observers concede that the implementation of Kerner Commission
recommendations has been dismal.[33] While it is surely hazardous to
attribute the inspiration for national policy making to a single document, nonetheless the hopes of Kerner Commission members and staff,
and sympathetic publics, that Commission efforts would signal a new
tone in national priorities have not materialized. It is, of course, difficult to relate this observation to a single set of causes. Yet it is none-

theless noteworthy since, despite the much-remarked liberality of the report, it confirms previous assumptions about riot commission efficacy.

Bleak pictures also emerge when we examine the degree to which local riot commission recommendations were implemented. As Tables 10 and 11 suggested, in Newark and Milwaukee a distinct minority of recommendations received some favorable action. In Detroit, the Mayor's Development Team, with the clear support of the chief executive, received considerable assistance from city agencies in alleviating riot-related problems, but wholly failed to influence the municipal bureaucracies in implementing organizational reform proposals. City agencies complied with directives from the Mayor's Development Team in providing emergency relief and restoring vital public services after the riot, but these same agencies successfully resisted implementation of a comprehensive set of recommendations designed by the Mayor's Development Team to remove existing agency autonomy through consolidation of the municipal bureaucracy.[34]

Compliance and Jurisdiction
The degree of compliance may be related to the relationship between the jurisdiction in which the commission or its equivalent is appointed and the jurisdiction to which recommendations are targeted. The jurisdiction targeted in commission recommendations is usually not the same as that within which riot commissions are appointed, as the data in Tables 10 and 11 suggest. The New Jersey Commission, with the State of New Jersey as its primary jurisdiction, thus issued a large number of recommendations aimed at the local jurisdiction—of Newark (33 percent, the largest of the jurisdictional categories). Milwaukee's 39-point program similarly sought reform of the state jurisdiction (35.8 percent of the recommendations were aimed at the State of Wisconsin, the largest of the jurisdictional categories). Even the Kerner Commission, generally regarded as promulgating a *national* agenda, paid equal attention to the responsibilities of local governmental and police officials.[35]

While recommendations emerging from riot studies are likely to be directed away from the jurisdiction in which the commission is appointed, these same recommendations are more likely to be implemented, if at all, when they are addressed to the primary jurisdiction. Thus 48.2 percent of the recommendations aimed at the primary jurisdiction by the New Jersey Commission, as reported in Table 10, received favorable action. Similarly, in the Milwaukee case, as shown in Table 11, 42.8 percent of the recommendations aimed at the primary jurisdiction were implemented. This pattern may be contrasted with the relatively few recommendations receiving favorable action from secondary jurisdictions. The relatively high degree of recommendation implementation within primary jurisdictions stems from at least two factors. First, riot commission members reflect dominant interests in the primary jurisdiction. In turn, they tend to formulate programmatic recommendations coincident with the aims of public officials in the primary jurisdiction. This may be because they tend to share attitudes toward regime interests and policy orientations with the executive. Or it may be because they attempt to anticipate the executive agenda, as discussed immediately below. Second, the tendency of riot commissions to aim reform proposals *away* from the primary jurisdiction, particularly on controversial issues, increases the likelihood of a higher implementation rate at that level.

One important consequence of riot commissions' tendency to deflect the target for reform away from primary jurisdictions is to create the potential for stalemate between governmental jurisdictions. An *ad hoc* group in one governmental jurisdiction calls upon public officials in another jurisdiction to adopt reforms. The degree of authority commanded by commissions is at best tenuous in the jurisdictions within which they are created, as we have suggested above. Their authority is even more tenuous in prescribing reform programs for alternative governmental jurisdictions. Thus the tendency of riot commissions to recommend a large number of reforms for secondary jurisdictions reduces the likelihood that commission recommendations will be implemented.

Compliance and Executive Agendas

Much of the support provided by political executives for commission recommendations may be explained by their previous general political agendas. Over three-fourths of the 39 points promulgated by Milwaukee's Mayor Maier had been included in policy proposals he had made previously.[36] Detroit Mayor Jerome Cavanaugh's support of proposals to reorganize the bureaucracy derived from his previous frustrations at holding office in a strong civil service city where the municipal bureaucracy is relatively independent of City Hall control. Even Mayor Hugh Addonizio's support of proposals highly critical of education in Newark may be understood as an extension of the Mayor's previously unsuccessful attempt to dramatize the financial difficulties encountered by the city.

Riot commissions may have some impact on the political process by identifying certain issues as salient, or by proposing that some salient issues deserve higher priority than others. By so doing they influence the grounds of future political struggles. It may also make sense for riot commissions to try to anticipate the agendas of public officials in order to further their proposals on specific issues. The implications of this approach, however, are consistent with our previous arguments. The agendas of public officials who have appointed riot commissions in the first place are not likely to be directed toward fundamental changes, particularly given the rhetoric with which recent executives who have appointed commissions have greeted riots. (Additionally, such a strategy may backfire, as pointed out above in the case of the Kerner Commission and the anticipation of President Johnson's agenda.)

Commissions and Direct Intervention

Riot commissions have had some visible impact when they have undertaken to develop specific policies and utilized personal and organizational resources to implement them. The intervention of individual members of the New Jersey Commission was critical in inducing Governor Richard Hughes to develop special urban budget proposals of particular benefit to Newark. The Kerner Commission's special meetings with police and media officials have been widely recognized as contributing substantially to the improved control and coverage techniques displayed by these professions during the April 1968 disorders associated with the assassination of Martin Luther King, Jr. In Detroit, the Mayor's Development Team easily implemented plans to mobilize agencies to clean up riot areas, because it consisted of key city officials. Although the New Jersey example seems to be a possible or limited exception, it would seem that this kind of intervention is most successful in obtaining concrete, relatively limited goals.

Compliance and Conflict

Because commissions are composed of individuals who are in positions to protect major interests or dominant social values, the more divisive and the more specific are recommendations, the less are they likely to be adopted. To the extent that divisive recommendations are adopted, these developments sometimes may be explained by the fact that the commission was not appointed in the jurisdiction to which the recommendation was addressed. This was the case when the New Jersey Commission identified the issue of corruption in Newark, and when Milwaukee Mayor Maier's 39 points seemed to require a special session of the legislature. They may also be explained by the fact that the commission was not representative of the interests targeted for major reform. The above examples fit this condition, as does the attempt of the (Detroit) Mayor's Development Team to consolidate and reorganize the city bureaucracy.[37]

Clearly the nature of each recommendation will affect the probabilities of implementation. Two dimensions seem particularly pertinent in understanding the probabilities of implementation: the cost, and the divisiveness of the recommendation. This may be clarified by distributing riot commission recommendations into one of four cells as in the matrix presented in Figure 16 (with the usual ambiguity in some cases). The horizontal axis distinguishes between those recommendations that may be implemented by rewarding individual actors or discrete groups without inflicting deprivations on other actors or groups (pluralistic) as opposed to recommendations that, when implemented, reward some actors or discrete groups and simultaneously deny benefits to other actors or groups they might otherwise receive (divisive).[38] Pluralistic recommendations thus potentially allocate recognition, goods, or services to discrete political interests at no cost to other interests while divisive recommendations potentially dispense rewards in a manner essentially involving zero-sum calculations; that is, if recognition, goods, or services are allocated to one political interest they are at the same time denied, at some cost, to other interests. The vertical axis in Figure 16 distinguishes between recommendations that would, if implemented, have tangible impacts (material) and those that would have primarily psychological impacts (symbolic).[39]

	Symbolic	Material
Pluralistic	1	2
Divisive	3	4

Figure 16

It may be useful to provide examples of recommendations from riot commissions to illustrate the kinds of implementation politics associated with each cell. (1) The appointment of a black administrative assistant in the mayor's office in Milwaukee represents a pluralistic-symbolic recommendation. The appointment is symbolic to the degree that it involved recognition of black interests in the city without transferring sizeable goods or services to black people. It is pluralistic by virtue of the mayor's having more than one assistant and the discretion of award-ing remaining positions to alternative interest groupings in the commu-nity. (2) The charge to the Mayor's Development Team in Detroit to restore vital services in the riot areas and clean them up represents a pluralistic-material recommendation. The charge dealt with the provi-sion of tangible goods and services (therefore material) and affected particular neighborhoods without disadvantaging other neighborhoods (therefore pluralistic). (3) The proposal of the New Jersey Commission to introduce a police civilian review board may be regarded as a recom-mendation with divisive-symbolic implications. We consider this re-commendation as symbolic to the extent that police review boards in the past have been widely regarded as ineffectual in redressing citizen grievances against police behavior, even in the rare cases when they have been introduced. And given the manner in which demands for such review boards have pitted whites against blacks, the recommenda-tion is divisive. (4) The Detroit proposal to reorganize thoroughly the municipal bureaucracy may be regarded as divisive and material in its orientation. It related directly to the provision of goods and services (material) and involved significant deprivations to existing, autonomous city agencies and their personnel.

The last two illustrations are divisive also because the reorganization of either police or city agencies was proposed in a manner that meant they could not be organized in any other way—the issue posed a zero-sum game. Divisive recommendations may also, of course, be more or less conflictual. But for our analytic scheme the degree of conflict *engendered* by a proposed reform is another dimension to the politics surrounding implementation of riot commission recommendations (the more conflict engendered, the less the likelihood of implementation).

What we have suggested is that the classification of recommendations along the two dimensions provided in Figure 16 facilitates understanding the likelihood of implementation and may, by itself, help us to under-stand which issues will be more conflictual. While we have not completed analysis of city riot commission recommendations in terms of these di-mensions, we hypothesize that probabilities of implementation are inversely associated with the suggested ordering of the cells and that the intensity of conflict is similarly inversely related to the cell ordering.

Analysts of American politics have observed that the system runs smoothly so long as demands may be regarded as incremental and not divisive.[40] In the case of riots and riot commissions, when highly divisive issues concerning the distribution of material goods and services emerge and the society encounters demands for significant change, the political system functions to reduce the pressures for change directed toward political executives; to minimize the surfacing of divisive, authoritative proposals for change; and to minimize the extent to which such proposals may be adopted. These observations are consistent with Robert Dahl's more general point:

> Even in the face of proposals for far-reaching changes, and even in the presence of increasingly severe conflict, the tendency of the political institutions is to handle severe conflicts along the same lines as moderate conflicts.[41]

CONCLUSIONS

This study was initiated with an interest in examining the political content of recent civil disorders and the extent to which they may be considered efficacious. We have concluded that judgments concerning the political nature of the riots are not separable from analysis of elite responses to the disorders that may have contributed to minimization of the political content of riots and to weak responses to the putative implicit demands as interpreted by riot commissions to the society.

We conclude with the following observations, which have not received extensive treatment above.

The process of dealing with riots may have an independent impact of considerable importance. From the first grave speeches and official proclamations, through the appointments process and speculation over findings, to the final report, the riot commission process seems to serve the society as a safe surrogate for the racial conflict that has been recently experienced. Here the terms of the conflict are benign, the actors sanitized, and the results, like good drama, engaging but ultimately not really consequential. We would suggest that the ritual itself serves to divert attention from the problem to the play, with consequent reduction in interest in positive action.

It may be that the drama and the delay protect groups of which rioters are a part from the wrath of an indignant and brutal majority. Surely the atmosphere in which the commissions of 1967 were established was anything but sympathetic. This argument has some force, although it is difficult to know how much weight to give it. In any event, two additional points in this connection should be made. First, there is something circular about attitude formation among the alleged unsympathetic majority, since the majority is constantly assured by its leaders that the rioters are worthless and should not and will not be given respectability. These messages contribute to reducing the extent to which the rioting group will have its actions interpreted in a political context.

Second, significantly, it is the black, historically oppressed minority that has been involved in the rioting. While the riot commission process may protect the blacks from backlash, it remains evident that this potential mechanism for drawing attention to grievances has been shown to be unavailable to the group. The riot commission process is not "neutral" because the propensity to riot is not evenly distributed throughout the society.

One aspect of the American political system that accounts for some of the problems noted here is its decentralization. One specific manifestation of this arrangement is the propensity to interpret riot occurrences as essentially local phenomena. Riots, of course, take place in cities. Local police forces have responsibility for suppressing riots, and, to a large extent, it falls to local officials to develop programs for improving conditions. For complex and diverse reasons, there seems to be great reluctance to consider riots national phenomena and to accept national responsibility for preventing their reoccurrence. Perhaps symptomatic of the reluctance to involve national institutions in riot control are the elaborate procedures that local governments must follow to receive assistance from U.S. Army units, as Governor Romney discovered during the Detroit disturbances.[42]

Assumptions of local responsibility for riot occurrences are also manifest in the way riots are conceived by intellectuals. The Kerner Commission staff encountered severe conceptual difficulties in setting out to explain the degree of riot severity as a function of city characteristics. Evidence of their relative failure may be read in the implicit rejection of this analysis in the Kerner Commission report, and in the evaporation of nonriot "control" cities as the rioting spread. Various scholars have undertaken aggregate analyses of riot causation using the city as the unit of analysis, with most modest theoretical benefits.[43] This is the structural equivalent of the problem associated with identifying "white racism" as "essentially responsible" for the social problems leading to the disorders.[44] When all are to blame, none can be found guilty, or more culpable, than others.

In the decentralized political system, it is difficult to fix blame and perhaps still more difficult to fix responsibility for change. The idea that riots are somehow a function of city characteristics represents only part of the problem. Federal, state, and local jurisdictions are variously considered responsible in commission reports, but when everyone is eligible for responsibility, difficulties of resting responsibility on a single individual or office are formidable. This is particularly true when pressures for action have been reduced by the creation of the organizations charged with fixing responsibility in the first place.

The fragmentation of power within cities also contributes to the difficulties in fixing responsibilities. In Detroit, Mayor Cavanaugh despaired of obtaining a more responsive bureaucratic machinery. In Milwaukee, Mayor Maier refused to accept city responsibility for open occupancy, while suburban jurisdictions in the same housing market refused to enact comparable legislation. In New Jersey, five out of ten commissioners concluded that proposals for change were only meaningful if the city could take advantage of the potential resources of the suburbs through some form of metropolitan government, despite the fact that this would imply diminishing black strength in Newark.

Where public officials have been willing to accept responsibility for recommendations, it has most often been when the recommendations fit their previous program priorities. Wherever one reviews riot commission politics at the local level, one encounters the textbook problems of accountability and resources that have traditionally beleaguered American cities.

These problems of responsibility are system related, and they supplement other difficulties in identifying responsibility for riot occurrences. These difficulties include the protection of dominant interests through "representative" commissions and the tendency of some commissions to broadcast responsibility so widely that everyone is touched and therefore none is accountable. So it was with "white racism" and the Kerner Report.[45]

The elaborate procedures through which black frustrations are processed in the United States thus ultimately yield a remarkable product. No individual, no institution, no particular group, is responsible for the conditions perpetuating black grievances. Black concerns are legitimized while they are deprived of their political content. The riots are credited with calling attention to deprivation while they are simultaneously declared to have been, and are regarded as if they were, entirely unjustified. Official bodies charged with investigating disorders and making appropriate recommendations systematically operate in response to prevailing political arrangements, tend to moderate insistence upon major reforms, and contribute to the restabilizing of the political order in line with the status quo ante.

In our view, the problem of assessing the political content of the riots rests as much in the process of responding to riots as in the character of the riots themselves.

NOTES

1. This essay is based upon the authors' study of the political impact of riots in American cities. In a forthcoming book we will report in detail our investigations of the operation and impact of the National Advisory Commission on Civil Disorders (Kerner Commission) and riot commissions or their equivalents appointed in response to disorders in Newark, Detroit, and Milwaukee in the summer of 1967. We have also studied, where appropriate, other American riot commissions, reaching back to the race riots that occurred around the time of the First World War, and reaching out geographically to other riot cities in the current era of racial violence. Space limitations prevent us from presenting detailed accounts of all of our findings here. Instead we have attempted to summarize our results as they relate to our interest in the ways this form of collective violence is "processed" by the legitimate political institutions.

    We have previously reported on this research in Michael Lipsky and David J. Olson, "Riot Commission Politics," *Trans-action, 6* (July–August 1969), 9–21, and elsewhere, as indicated in notes below. For detailed accounts of the formation and impact of riot commissions and their equivalents in Detroit, Newark, and Milwaukee, see David J. Olson, "Racial Violence and City Politics: The Political Response to Civil Disorders in Three American Cities," unpublished Ph.D. dissertation, University of Wisconsin, 1971.

    For assistance in various phases of this research we would like to acknowledge the support of *Trans-action* magazine, the Institute for Research on Poverty of the University of Wisconsin, the M.I.T.–Harvard Joint Center for Urban Studies, and The Brookings Society.

2. "The violence of this summer raised up a new and serious threat to local law enforcement. It spawned a group of men whose interest lay in provoking—in provoking—others to destruction, while they fled its consequences. These wretched, vulgar men, these poisonous propagandists, posed as spokesmen for the underprivileged and capitalized on the real grievances of suffering people." Remarks of Lyndon B. Johnson on September 14, 1967, before the International Association of Chiefs of Police. See, *Public Papers of the Presidents of the United States, Lyndon B. Johnson, Containing the Public Messages, Speeches, and Statements of the President, 1967,* Book II, July 1 to December 31, 1967, Washington: U.S. Government Printing Office, 1968, p. 835.

    "The criminal participants in the riots in Newark—the ambushers of firemen, the killers of children, the mass looters—amount to approximately 1% of the Negro population of that city." Speech by Governor Richard J. Hughes of New Jersey before The 75th Anniversary Convention of the International Longshoremen's Association, Hotel Di Lido, Miami Beach, Florida, July 20, 1967, p. 2.

    "Don't let anyone tell you this terrible thing is the result of the lack of social planning. This was done by the criminal element." Remarks of Governor George Romney of Michigan. Quoted in *The Detroit News,* July 26, 1967.

"We cannot and shall not condone the wanton acts of a criminal few such as our city experienced during the night. There will be no coddling of criminals . . . no excusing of criminal acts." Remarks of Mayor Henry W. Maier of Milwaukee. Quoted in *The Milwaukee Journal,* August 1, 1967.

3. See Detroit Urban League, "A Survey of Attitudes of Detroit Negroes After the Riot of 1967," Detroit, 1967; Opinion Research Corporation, "Negro and White Attitudes Toward Problems and Progress in Race Relations: A Study Among Residents of Newark and Adjacent Communities," Governor's Select Commission to Study Civil Disorders, January 1968; Jonathan A. Slesinger, "Study of Community Opinions Concerning the Summer 1967 Civil Disturbance in Milwaukee," University of Wisconsin–Milwaukee, April 1, 1968; Lemberg Center for the Study of Violence, "A Survey of Racial Attitudes in Six Northern Cities: Preliminary Findings," Waltham, Mass., 1967.

4. For a discussion of this evidence, see Robert Fogelson, *Violence as Protest,* Garden City, N.Y.: Doubleday, 1971, Chapter 1. It may be of some interest in the context of this paper that the social scientists on the staff of the Kerner Commission concluded in a report never fully incorporated into the final *Report,* that at least one of the major disturbances of 1967 was a "political rebellion." See Michael Lipsky, "Social Scientists and the Riot Commission," *The Annals, 394* (March 1971), 75.

5. Edward C. Banfield, *The Unheavenly City,* Boston: Little, Brown, 1970, Chapter 9.

6. The adequacy of the data utilized by Banfield in constructing the "meaningless" view of recent riots is critically assessed in David J. Olson, "Interpreting Recent Civil Disorders: An Alternative To Banfield's 'Rioting Mainly For Fun and Profit'," unpublished paper delivered at the 1971 Annual Meeting of the American Political Science Association, Chicago, Illinois, September 7–11, 1971.

7. See Murray Edelman, *The Symbolic Uses of Politics,* Urbana, Ill.: University of Illinois Press, 1964, pp. 30–31.

8. Fogelson, p. 16.

9. This observation is supported by an extensive analysis of more than 20 riot commissions appointed after racial violence between 1917 and 1943. See Olson, "Racial Violence and City Politics," Chapter 2. While it is generally true that public officials exhibited responses to rioting that signaled intolerance toward this form of behavior, a conspicuous and important exception is the part played by law enforcement personnel during race riots from 1917 through 1943. Police officers and national guardsmen often proved lax in suppressing the violence when rioting featured white mobs attacking black people. In fact, law enforcement officers periodically joined with white mobs in the attacks against blacks. See Allen D. Grimshaw, "Actions of Police and the Military in American Race Riots," in Allen D. Grimshaw, ed., *Racial Violence in the United States,* Chicago: Aldine, 1969, pp. 269–287.

10. See, H. L. Nieburg, *Political Violence, The Behavioral Approach,* New York: St. Martin, 1969, p. 135. Illustrative of the fact that many people at least feared that this alternative was one that might prevail was the statement of Kerner Commission social scientists on "The Garrison State" in their unpublished document, "The Harvest of American Racism."

11. Platt surveys the extensive use public officials make of the "riff-raff" stereotype to explain racial violence and concludes: "These kinds of inference

serve to dramatize the criminal character of riots, to undermine their political implications, and to uphold the argument that social change is only possible through lawful and peaceful means. If riots can be partly explained as the work of a few agitators or hoodlums, it is then much easier to engage wide support in repudiating violent methods of social protest. Official investigations generally publicize the fact that normal, ordinary, law-abiding persons do not instigate riots." Anthony M. Platt, *The Politics of Riot Commissions,* New York: Collier, 1971, p. 34.

12. Olson has previously documented the appointment of over 20 riot commissions following race riots from 1917 through 1943 and more than 30 riot commissions following civil disorders from 1964 through 1968. See Olson, "Racial Violence and City Politics," Chapters 2 and 3. Platt similarly concludes, "The commission is becoming a permanent feature of the political response to riots." Platt, p. 6.

13. The appointment of the Kerner Commission in the summer of 1967 raised the problem of racial violence to the level of a national issue and thereby preempted, in important ways, the creation of riot commissions in localities experiencing racial violence. While the generalization in the text holds, therefore, for racial disorders up to 1967, there have been several important exceptions to this pattern following the Kerner Commission's activities.

14. See Allan Silver, "Official Interpretations of Racial Riots," in Robert Connery, ed., *Urban Riots: Violence and Social Change,* Proceedings of the Academy of Political Science, *29,* No. 1 (New York, 1968), pp. 150–151. Platt suggests this recent identification of riot commissions with black claims results from the commissions' need to account for extensive participation in and support for riots by blacks while continuing to deny the legitimacy of this form of political behavior: "While commissions generally deplore the violence of 'rioters' (but minimize or ignore the significance of official violence) and attribute rioting to the 'riffraff' element, they are still faced with the problem of explaining why riots are participated in by a cross section of the ghetto communities, and given wide support by those communities. Given these facts, few serious official treatments of riots now attempt to explain the resulting violence purely in terms of a 'riffraff' theory. . . . Most commissions resolve this dilemma by arguing that riots are invariably aggravated or instigated by the criminal activities of a small group of provocateurs who take advantage of human weakness and transform basically nonviolent individuals into an irrational mob. Thus, riots are widely characterized as outlets for pent-up frustrations and grievances sparked by a few." See Platt, pp. 36–37.

15. Allan Silver, "The Demand for Order in Civil Society: A Review of Some Themes in the History of Urban Crime, Police and Riot," in David Bordua, ed., *The Police: Six Sociological Essays,* New York: Wiley, 1967, pp. 1–24.

16. A review of riot commission reports since 1917 suggests the continuity of this theme. See Olson, "Racial Violence and City Politics," Chapter 2.

17. Two dramatic statements expressing scepticism concerning the impact of commission recommendations are those of Dr. Kenneth Clark before the Kerner Commission, National Advisory Commission on Civil Disorders, *Report,* New York: Bantam, 1968, p. 483; and Judge Leon Higginbotham, dissenting from the report of the National Commission on the Causes and Prevention of Violence, *To Establish Justice, To Insure Domestic Tranquility,* New York: Award Books, 1969, pp. 119–120.

18. Generalizations concerning the American response to civil disorders must be evaluated in a comparative context to assess their validity, but we are not able to do this in the present context.

Nonetheless, we may hypothesize that the modal response of political elites in most political systems is to dismiss collective violence initially as the work of the riffraff, criminal elements, conspirators, and unreconcilable small minorities with minimum systemic importance. For example, responsibility for the March 1968 student riots in Poland, which lasted about seven days, were variously attributed by authoritative Polish sources to "utterly irresponsible" political elements, "a conspiracy group linked with Zionist centers," and "Zionists, liberal intellectuals and discredited Stalinists" (Foreign Broadcast Information Service Daily Report, March 12, 1968, SS5; March 25, 1968, SS2; *New York Times,* March 18, 1968, p. 11). Similarly, authoritative explanations of the widespread rioting in December 1970 precipitated by the Gdansk shipyard workers focused on "hooligans and inciting elements" (*New York Times,* December 16, 1970, p. 7) and on "unpredictable adventurers recruited among the outcasts of society" (Foreign Broadcast Information Service Daily Report, December 29, 1970, G5). However, it should be noted that, as in the United States following the riots of 1967, riffraff and associated explanations of the violence were later mixed with discussions of legitimate grievances as the rioting spread throughout the country.

It is of further interest that elites in various countries readily seem to attribute collective violence in *other* countries to political factors. The communist press has regularly explained black collective violence as motivated by black political and economic conditions. Similarly, the American press regularly explains domestic violence in the socialist countries in terms of political demands. For example, the above-mentioned short-lived Polish student riots in 1968 were editorially explained by the *New York Times* as expressive of demands for civil liberties, less Russian influence in foreign policy, and greater economic prosperity and security (March 15, 1968, p. 32). It attributed the larger-scale violence two years later as testimony "to the discontent of a misgoverned nation and the bankruptcy of a politico-economic system" (December 20, 1970, p. IV, 10).

Similar observations could be made for the rioting accompanying the initial stages of domestic violence in Czechoslovakia in 1968 and in Northern Ireland (presently continuing), with respect to both domestic and foreign elite reaction. We may speculate that elites in modern industrial societies generally tend to dismiss antielite riotous behavior as political and criminal when it occurs domestically, but to regard it as expressive of political demands and socially useful when such events occur in societies with opposing regime values. Whether or not these hypotheses and speculations eventually would be sustained, these are the kinds of questions that would emerge from a comparative, cross-national analysis of elite response to civil disorders.

19. For the composition of riot commissions see Platt, pp. 10–22; Olson, "Racial Violence and City Politics," Chapter 3; and Lipsky and Olson; and on the composition of presidential commissions more generally, see Frank Popper, *The President's Commissions,* New York: Twentieth Century, 1970, pp. 15–20, 66–73.

20. In this century collective race-related violence has changed from white-initiated violence directed against blacks, with black defense or retaliation (in the

period 1917 through 1943), to black-initiated violence directed against the police and various forms of property (in the 1960s). Masotti distinguishes between the two forms of racial violence by calling the earlier form "white-dominated person-oriented" and the later form "Negro-dominated property-oriented." See, Louis H. Masotti, "Violent Protest in Urban Society: A Conceptual Framework," unpublished paper presented at the 1967 annual meeting of the American Association for the Advancement of Science, New York City, p. 4. Janowitz similarly refers to the two forms respectively as "communal" and "commodity" riots. See Morris Janowitz, *Social Control of Escalated Riots,* Chicago: University of Chicago Press, 1968.

21. Lipsky and Olson.
22. See Lipsky, p. 73.
23. For several recent riot commissions, the times between appointment and release of final reports were as follows: Kerner Commission—eight months; New Jersey Commission—seven months; (Detroit) Mayor's Development Team—three months; and Governor's Commission (McCone) on Los Angeles riot—three months. This lag-time from appointment of commission until release of report assists the postponement of action by public officials. Public officials often use the existence of a riot commission, in fact, as justification for not doing anything so long as the deliberations of the commission are in process.
24. This is revealed in the transcripts of the Kerner Commission proceedings, as well as in interviews with members of the New Jersey Commission.
25. Governor's Select Commission on Civil Disorder, *Report For Action,* State of New Jersey, February 1968.
26. The governmental jurisdiction toward which recommendations were aimed and the impact each recommendation had are presented in detail in Olson, "Racial Violence and City Politics," Chapter 4.
27. *Ibid.*
28. Lipsky and Olson.
29. See Clark's testimony before the Commission, Transcripts of the Proceedings (unpublished), pp. 1224–1288, especially p. 1228; exerpted, National Advisory Commission on Civil Disorders, *Report,* p. 483.
30. See Lipsky.
31. Robert Fogelson and Robert B. Hill, "Who Riots? A Study of Participation in the 1967 Riots," *Supplemental Studies for the National Advisory Commission on Civil Disorders,* Washington, D.C.: U.S. Government Printing Office, 1968, pp. 217–248.
32. One might speculate that statements that recent commissions are about to issue conservative reports may function to alarm groups sympathetic to the black position, and thus encourage a degree of relief when the report turns out to be more favorable than expected.
33. Urban America and the Urban Coalition, *One Year Later,* Washington, D.C.: Urban America, Inc., and the Urban Coalition, 1969; and Philip Meranto, ed., "The Kerner Report Revisited, *University of Illinois Bulletin, 67* (June 1, 1970).
34. Reasons for the failure of commission recommendations to be implemented in Newark, Detroit, and Milwaukee are examined in detail in Olson, "Racial Violence and City Politics," Chapter 4.
35. See, e.g., National Advisory Commission on Civil Disorders, *Report,* pp. 283–299, 410.

36. Before the 1967 riot, the policy proposals were part of Mayor Maier's "Campaign For Resources" for Milwaukee. These were incorporated into the postriot 39-point program. See Olson, "Racial Violence and City Politics," Chapter 4.

37. In each of these three cases, the interests commissions represented stood to benefit from a sizeable majority of the recommendations for change while the same recommendations threatened to inflict deprivations on political interests that either were not formally represented on the commission or were antagonistic to the interests represented by commissioners. For elaboration of this point see *ibid.,* pp. 306–308. Here we are suggesting that controversial recommendations tend to be introduced when they do not affect the primary jurisdiction in which the riot commission was appointed and when the interests affected by the recommendations are not represented on the commissions. The interests of Mayor Addonizio and his Italian-based political machine were not represented on the New Jersey Commission; Mayor Maier's "39 Points" were calculated in many respects to allocate responsibility to jurisdictions other than the City of Milwaukee; and the Mayor's Development Team in Detroit, while advocating bureaucratic reform, was not representative of old-line civil servants, civil service unions, or other interests affected by the recommended municipal bureaucratic reorganization.

38. Lowi's distinction between "distributive" and "redistributive" policies resembles closely the distinction being drawn here between "pluralistic" and "divisive" recommendations. See Theodore J. Lowi, "American Business, Public Policy, Case Studies and Political Theory," *World Politics, 16* (1964), pp. 676–715.

39. See, Edelman.

40. See, Theodore Lowi, *The End of Liberalism,* New York: Norton, 1969.

41. Robert Dahl, *Pluralist Democracy in the United States,* Skokie, Ill.: Rand McNally, 1967, p. 291.

42. See National Advisory Commission on Civil Disorders, *Report,* p. 95.

43. See, Lemberg Center for the Study of Violence, *Survey;* Stanley Lieberson and Arnold R. Silverman, "The Precipitants and Underlying Conditions of Race Riots," *American Sociological Review, 30* (December 1965), 887–898; Milton Bloombaum, "The Conditions Underlying Race Riots as Portrayed by Multidimensional Scalogram Analysis: A Re-analysis of Lieberson and Silverman's Data," *American Sociological Review, 33* (February 1968), 76–91; John G. White, "Riots and Theory Building," in Louis Masotti and Don Bowen, eds., *Riots and Rebellion: Civil Violence in the Urban Community,* Beverly Hills, Calif.: Sage Publications, 1968; and Bryan Downes, "Social and Political Characteristics of Riot Cities: A Comparative Study," *Social Science Quarterly, 49* (December 1968).

44. National Advisory Commission on Civil Disorders, *Report,* p. 203.

45. See, Michael Lipsky, "Review Symposium," *American Political Science Review, 63* (December 1969), 1278–1281.

9

Violent Consequences of Violence

IVO K. FEIERABEND
ROSALIND L. FEIERABEND
California State University, San Diego

The consequences of actions and events are always difficult to determine. Part of the problem lies in the bewildering lack of structure that a look into the future entails. We do not know what consequences we wish to study, when they might occur, in what social settings, under what circumstances, or to whom. The task of inquiry into such an ambiguous topic immediately seems forbidding. And yet a knowledge of consequences has important utilitarian value for the avoidance of error and the maximization of benefits. If men of affairs, whether statesmen or revolutionaries, could know the outcomes of alternative plans of action, their decision-making powers would be enhanced a hundredfold.

In order to study the empirical world systematically, the scientific approach makes use of a structure that relates antecedent conditions to their hypothesized consequences. We usually formulate a question in such terms that the consequence (the dependent variable) is specified, as are the precedent conditions (the independent variables). The goal of empirical inquiry is to discover whether these sets of conditions are, in fact, related as proposed in our hypotheses. We intend to follow that general structure in this presentation. Moreover, we shall simplify our query; not all of the possible consequences of political violence will be pursued. Rather, we shall ask the following specific and relatively narrow questions:

1. What consequences has political violence for the further occurrence of violence within the same political system? Does the use of force breed counterforce or can it quell civil turmoil, disorder, and violence?
2. What is the impact of violence on violence in the short run and in the long run?

3. Of what consequence is a great or a small amount of violence?
4. Of what consequence is the legitimate or the illegitimate use of force?
5. What is the consequence of a consistent or an inconsistent use of force?

To inquire into these questions, we must first define political violence and aggression. Aggression entails the infliction of intentional injury on others, and political aggression consists of aggressive behaviors perpetrated within the boundaries of political systems. Aggressive behaviors involving the use of force we term violence, but not all political aggression needs to be violent. Coerciveness of political regimes includes aggressive behaviors involving the use of force, or other severe sanctions, by the officeholders. However, in our usage the term also involves the threat of force, or the anticipated use of force. Coerciveness of political regimes, then, refers not only to actual aggressive behaviors but also to a disposition to engage in such behaviors.

Internal political aggression can be dispensed by the government (that is, the officeholders), by the incumbents (the loyalists), or by the people (the dissidents, insurgents, rebels, or protestors). And the target of aggression, again, can be either the government or the people. In terms of the initiator and the target of political aggression, this concept can be classified as (1) Aggression perpetrated by the people and directed against the government—insurrections, revolts, assassinations, strikes, and demonstrations are concrete examples. We shall call these aggressive behaviors *political instability* for lack of a better term. *Political stability,* on the other hand, connotes the relative lack of these behaviors—that is, relative quiescence on the part of the people. (2) Aggression perpetrated by the government and directed against the people—arrests, imprisonments, martial law, and censorship are some such events. These we identify with the notion of *coerciveness of political regime.* The opposite state is *permissiveness of political regime.* Again this is a relative term. All political systems in fact rely on some measure of coercion. The role of the policeman or the soldier is present in all states. (3) Political aggression perpetrated by some people or groups against other people or groups—racial unrest or religious riots would be examples of what we shall call *intergroup conflict.* The opposite term is *intergroup conciliation.*

Our presentation, then, has to do with the impact of political instability, coerciveness of regime, and intergroup conflict on the further occurrence of these same forms of political aggression. However, the opposite consequences also interest us—that is, the quieting of tension, producing political stability; permissiveness of regime; and intergroup conciliation.

Our present inquiry into these questions combines a speculative, theoretical approach with an empirical, quantitative one. After formulating and discussing several theoretical propositions concerning the impact of aggression or force on counterforce (in abbreviated fashion), we shall attempt to find some empirical support, not for all of the propositions, but for some of their aspects. The empirical analyses are cross-national in scope and correlational in method, comparing aggregate data for as many as 77 nations, for periods ranging up to 22 years.

THEORETICAL CONSIDERATIONS

A very old insight regarding the consequences of violence is that it simply breeds more violence. The biblical "eye for an eye" or the warning "he who lives by the sword, dies by the sword" are testimony to the antiquity of this view. Force seems to stimulate counterforce as the response, and a wrong is often rectified through revenge. This insight is contained in the following theoretical proposition, which we wish to investigate.

Proposition 1. The higher (lower) the level of political aggression and violence (that is, of political instability, coerciveness of regime, and intergroup conflict) within a political system, the higher the probability for a further high (low) level of political aggression and violence (that is, political instability, coerciveness, and intergroup conflict).

This proposition should be interpreted as postulating that popular violence (political instability) tends to evoke governmental repression (coerciveness), or vice versa. In fact, one could argue that whichever actor initiates the first set of aggressive behaviors, the sequence will continue and perhaps even spiral. Thus a response of government coercion will in turn stimulate further popular aggression, which will in turn stimulate further governmental coercion, and so on. Intergroup conflict can also be included in the picture, either singly or in combination with the other two types of aggression. In this case, aggression and the use of force become a triangular affair in which officeholders and warring group members are all involved in the conflict. The situation in Northern Ireland is a case in point.

There is ample theoretical support for this proposition and it could be justified in terms of every major theory of aggression. Let us begin with the view of aggression as an instinct (Lorenz 1966). This theory points to an attack as an obvious stimulus for an innate reaction of counter-attack. A violent reflex to violence may be as natural as withdrawing one's hand from a hot stove. The frustration-aggression approach also supports the proposition (Dollard *et al.* 1939). This theory postulates frustration—that is, interference with goals, needs, values, aspirations, and expectations—as the fundamental precondition for aggressive behavior and violence (Berkowitz 1962, Gurr 1970). The use of force, violence, aggression, and coercion are injurious by definition. And injury constitutes an interference with some individual or social values and goals. Violence typically interferes with very important welfare values. When physical injury is directed against persons and property, the values of well-being and wealth are injured or impaired. Force and violence, then, may be interpreted as frusrtation that angers men, leading them to retaliate in kind, engaging in their own acts of political violence. This is not a tautological use of the terms frustration and aggression, provided a distinction is maintained between the actor and the target in each behavior sequence. The aggression perpetrated by the aggressor is not at the same time his own frustration. Rather, it is the frustration of the victim of his aggression, who at that moment is not an aggressor within the sequence. Only later may the victim engage in his own retaliatory acts of violence, given the basic insight of the theory. At that time, the roles of aggressor and target are reversed.

Yet another theoretical insight suggests that if threatened by force, men, as rational beings, protect what they value. Here violence is judged as rational and instrumental, not as an angry response (Nieburg 1969). Cost-benefit or value-maximization calculations apply (Boulding 1962, Schelling 1963, Leites and Wolf 1970). To this listing we may add further ramifications of the strategic approach to violence. Notions of rational calculation lead to analyses of spiraling conflicts, such as arms races, as well as of equilibrium points. The view that behavior involves reciprocity, a calculation that matches one party's response to that of the other party, again would support the proposition. Finally, to all of these theories we could add learning. If violence is successful, its further use is reinforced. In addition, it may serve as a model for others to imitate (Bandura and Walters 1963). We do not propose to elaborate any of these theories but only to suggest their applicability to the first proposition.

Let us turn to a second insight, which postulates that violence has the opposite effect on the occurrence of further violence. Force is said to have a deterrent effect; it can control human behavior and inhibit volume. Accordingly, the consequence of violence is not further violence but quiescence. This is as ancient an insight as the one expressed in the first proposition. The ideas of law, or political order, or the state, are based on this recognition. It is rare to find a definition of these three complex concepts that does not invoke the notion of force or coercion. This insight also can find support in the previously mentioned theories, perhaps with the exception of reciprocity. Withdrawal rather than attack can be seen as instinctual behavior, and frustration can lead to fear and withdrawal, as well as to anger and aggression. Given the ratio of cost to benefit, sometimes it is a better strategy to give in to force than to counterattack. Furthermore, the lesson that violence does not pay may be learned from coercion. Let us then formulate a second proposition, which embodies this second insight.

Proposition 2. The higher the level of aggression and violence (that is, of political instability, coerciveness of regime, and intergroup conflict) in a political system, the lower the probability for further high levels of internal political aggression and violence (political instability, coerciveness, and intergroup conflict).

In other words, this proposition, in contradiction to the first one, maintains that regime coerciveness, for example, can inhibit the expression of popular violence, that is, political instability. The higher its intensity, the more effective its deterrent power. Similarly, popular violence may inhibit the use of force (coerciveness) on the part of frightened officeholders and even wring concessions from them. And this may also be true in the relations among various ethnic and racial groups within society.

At first sight, it may appear that the first and second propositions contradict each other and hence that they cannot both be true at the same time. This contradiction is only apparent. It disappears when one points out the possible dual role of aggression as it is viewed, for example, in the frustration–aggression approach: aggression in its role of frustration, and aggression in its role of inhibition (Buss 1962). Violence and aggression, in the role of frustration, only instigate further aggression and violence. A violent potential is created but not necessarily released in violent expression. Secondly, if violence is postulated as an inhibitor, it may prevent such violent expression but will not diminish the violent potential. These two distinct functions of aggression can be present either singly or simultaneously in various situations. It is perfectly possible, then, that the insights of the first and second propositions are both true. And this is the reason why both the first and the second propositions seem to find ample illustration in individual and collective systemic behavior. Sometimes the inhibitory function of aggression is weak and the first proposition finds support. Sometimes the frustration function of aggression may be lessened and the dynamics of the second proposition apply.

For example, a sudden drop in regime coerciveness will cancel the deterrence factor but leave untouched the potential for violence that has been building up under the persistent frustrations of the previous highly coercive regime. Hence political instability is more likely under the new permissive regime than it was previously under the coercive one. The Hungarian Revolution or the demise of Trujillo in the Dominican Republic give dramatic illustration of this point. In the case of the Hungarian Revolution, it was the relaxation of tyrannical totalitarian controls during the period of "thaw" or de-Stalinization that preceded the violent events of 1956. This flare-up of violence should be expected in the short run. In the long run, political quiescence and order will ensue if no additional instigation to violence is created through coercion, or if coercion is again intensified to bring on its deterrent effect.

The opposite situation also will produce violence. If, for example, an habitually permissive regime becomes suddenly repressive, this coerciveness should be experienced mainly as frustration. The deterrent effect of coerciveness might not as yet have been sufficiently demonstrated to the populace. Genuine fear of the regime will develop later. In the short run, increased violence will be experienced, while in the long run political stability will be established through the deterrent effect of coercion. Let us formulate this into a third proposition.

Proposition 3. With a sudden and sharp reversal in an otherwise persistent trend in political aggression and violence (that is, political instability/stability, coerciveness/permissiveness of regime, and intergroup conflict/conciliation), the probability of political aggression will increase in the short run and decrease in the long run.

Reversals in the prevailing trend of a set of aggressive behaviors can be characterized as inconsistency. Such inconsistency, especially if it becomes a matter of frequent fluctuations, may be considered as a further powerful stimulant to political aggression and violence. This is due not only to the two distinct roles of aggression discussed above: aggression as frustration, on the one hand, and as inhibition, on the other. Two additional reasons can be offered. First, perceived inconsistency or fluctuation in important social circumstances and behaviors gives rise to uncertainty of expectations, and this uncertainty may be interpreted as a separate source of frustration. Without going into the underlying psychological mechanisms, let us imagine a polity in which the citizens experience a wildly fluctuating social environment. Sometimes they earn fortune and reward; at other times, disaster and punishment. At no time can the outcome of their actions be calculated or foreseen. The strain and tension of such a situation is not difficult to apprehend, and it may well vent itself eventually in acts of political aggression. Hence, fluctuations in political aggression, whether coerciveness, instability, or intergroup conflict, will also breed even more political aggression and violence.

Secondly, this inconsistent use of force is very likely to be perceived as arbitrary: as the caprice, depravity, arrogance, or incompetence of the perpetrators, be they officeholders, rebels, or minority groups. If this is the case, the exercise of force may then also be perceived by that stratum of the populace as unjustified and illegitimate. And it is the illegitimacy of the aggression, violence, and coerciveness that must be considered a source of frustration. The legitimate exercise of force provides only a minimal sense of frustration, while its deterrent power remains unimpaired (Gurr 1970). By legitimate or illegitimate force, we mean the subjective positive or negative evaluation given to the occurrence and to the use of force and violence. If the use of force is welcomed as "right" by members of the political system, then it is viewed as legitimate. If it is abhorred as wrong and evil, then it is illegitimate. Perhaps the first, as well as the second, proposition should be read in light of the concept of legitimacy. If this is done, the apparent contradiction between them is resolved.

Proposition 1a. Force or aggression that is perceived as illegitimate (legitimate), whether political instability, coerciveness of regime, or intergroup conflict, is the most (least) likely to result in counterforce or further acts of aggression (political instability, coerciveness, and intergroup conflict).

Proposition 2a. Force or aggression (political instability, coerciveness of regime, and intergroup conflict) that is perceived as legitimate (illegitimate) is more (less) likely to deter the overt expression of aggression and force (political instability, coerciveness, intergroup conflict).

This distinction between legitimate and illegitimate force is a crucial one. Present usage of these terms is not markedly different from the usual discussions found in the literature of political science. It is sometimes argued that all political systems must, to some degree, rely on legitimate authority rather than on purely naked force and violence. One could dispute whether this is true by virtue of the definition of the political system. Undoubtedly, in concrete existing systems it is the exceptional state and government that can persist with no support whatsoever, with negative affect from all strata of its citizenry. Perhaps only the completely ruthless dictatorship of a foreign military occupation could so qualify.

If we probe deeper into the notion of legitimacy, we find that illegitimate force is not only unwanted, rejected, and abhorred, but also that its occurrence is apt to be unexpected. An exercise of force that is perceived as legitimate, on the other hand, is not only valued and appreciated, but often it is also expected. This certainly is the case within stable and permissive political systems. The notion of expectation helps to define the sense of frustration (Berkowitz 1962). Strength of frustration is a function of both (1) the intensity of social values, needs, desires, and aspirations and (2) the degree to which the satisfaction of these values is anticipated or expected. The more we expect something desirable to happen, the more we shall be disappointed if, in fact, it does not occur. With lower expectations, our disappointment would be less crushing.

An additional consideration is that the illegitimate use of force not only injures our physical welfare values, such as life and property; this is equally true of a legitimate use of force. Illegitimate force also violates our ideal values, such as freedom, justice, and equality, or some value combination that may represent a shared identity among citizens. No wonder then that the illegitimate use of force is a source of frustration, resulting in anger and indignation, while we may patiently bear or even submit to just punishment and penance. These considerations justify an additional proposition that partially subsumes the dynamics expressed in the third proposition.

Proposition 3a. Fluctuation in the level of political aggression and violence (political instability, regime coerciveness, and intergroup conflict) is likely to lead to high levels of political aggression and violence (political instability, regime coerciveness, and intergroup conflict).

Let us return once again to the dual role of political aggression: aggression as the instigation to violence, and aggression as the deterrent to violence. In light of what has been said, it lends itself to the formulation of yet another proposition, which, without denying the validity of either role, combines them in a new fashion. And for the purposes of our discussion, let us think specifically of the use of force and violence associated with the officeholders (that is, regime coerciveness) and the counterforce and violence of the insurgents, rebels, or protestors (political instability). However, the insight can be generalised and should be seen as applicable to all types of political aggression and violence.

Predominantly permissive regimes must be presumed to give little impulse to political aggressiveness. Minimally engaged in coercive practices, they give minimal offense, and perhaps none at all, if their mild coercive practices are condoned as legitimate. Extremely coercive regimes, although they must be presumed to frustrate the populace maximally, are nonetheless maximally able to inhibit the expression of violence. This is certainly true if such violence is judged as legitimate. And it may be true even if the exercise of force is judged to be illegitimate. A sufficiently brutal, complete, and terroristic use of force may be seen as impossible to combat or resist. The situation in some totalitarian states and concentration camps comes to mind as examples of extreme use of violence. It is regimes at the median level of coerciveness that probably bear the brunt of internal turmoil. Although instigating violence by being coercive, they are not sufficiently coercive to inhibit it. This is especially true if the exercise of force is judged to be illegitimate. The validity of this conclusion, however, is problematic if force is seen as legitimate. On the basis of this analysis, let us formulate a final proposition, which incorporates Propositions 1 and 2. It is plausible mainly because of specific assumptions about the effect of legitimacy at different levels of coercion.

Proposition 4. Very low levels of political aggression—that is, political stability, regime permissiveness, and intergroup conciliation—are likely to maintain such low levels of stability, permissiveness, and intergroup conciliation. Median levels of political aggression and violence (political instability, regime coerciveness, and intergroup conflict) are likely to intensify the level of political aggression and violence (political instability, regime coerciveness, intergroup conflict). High levels of political violence are likely to result in low levels of political aggression and violence (political instability, regime coerciveness, intergroup conflict).

This proposition, too, must be interpreted in light of some of the reasoning justifying the third proposition. For example, high levels of coerciveness, in order to deter popular violence, must persist for some time. A short duration or inconsistent application of coerciveness simply creates a "credibility gap," or uncertainty, impairing the deterrent value of punishment while further instigating an impulse to political unrest. Also, the predominantly low levels of political aggression should persist for some time to sustain the logic of this proposition.

In summary of these theoretical considerations, and using for the sake of brevity and simplicity the term force only, the following may be said. A linear and positive relationship is postulated between the use of political force and counterforce (Proposition 1). However, it would seem that it is mainly the illegitimate use of force that breeds counterforce (Proposition 1a). If legitimate force is exercised, it is the deterrent consequence of force that becomes salient (Proposition 2a). Under these conditions, it is a linear, but negative, relationship that is more likely to obtain between force and counterforce (Proposition 2). The relationship between force and counterforce could furthermore be postulated as curvilinear. This is possible only if force at lower levels is considered to be mostly a source of frustration, while at high levels it is considered as mostly a deterrent (Proposition 4). In addition, fluctuation in the level of force is very likely to stimulate counterforce (Proposition 3a). And sharp and sudden reversals in force levels, where the prior trend was persisting for considerable periods of time, are likely to produce an immediate rise in counterforce. In the long run, however, such political systems should maintain stable levels of force and counterforce (Proposition 3).

Before leaving these considerations, at least two points should be made to put the propositions into proper theoretical perspective. First, we hardly touch upon the central question as to why societies engage in violence and aggression in the first place. To begin one's explanation with the presence of violence is the price paid for addressing the consequences rather than the antecedents of aggression. In our previous studies we postulate systemic frustration and politicized discontent as the main sources of aggression within political systems (Feierabend and Feierabend 1966). The present essay assumes but only hints at this important theoretical domain. Secondly, the expression of political violence, aggression, coerciveness, and political instability must assume some level of aggressive capability on the part of the incumbents, insurgents, and minority groups. Again, without such capability the expression of political aggression would be absent within the political system. This complex variable of capability is also assumed but not discussed in this presentation.

Finally, before turning to the empirical sections, let us note that there is always some gap between theoretical constructs and empirical analyses; this study is no exception. In this section, we have suggested that empirical theory can be constructed with reference to the consequences of political violence. The following section demonstrates that it is also possible to explore the empirical evidence for such a theory, and even to find bits and pieces of support. Such demonstration, however, should not be mistaken for validation. Only some of the propositions are examined, in some but not all of their aspects.

MEASUREMENT OF VARIABLES

In order to explore the empirical world referenced by the theoretical propositions, it is first necessary to find ways of measuring political instability, regime coercion, and intergroup conflict. Our existing research project, Systemic Conditions of Political Aggression, is designed to study the relationships among these variables in all nations and territorial units of the world. The three studies reported in this paper have used different cross-national, aggregate data bases and different samples of nations, but all proceed from the same research project and utilize the same basic definitions of variables.

Event Data: Political Instability, Government
Coercion, Intergroup Conflict

In our research, the level of political unrest within a country is indexed in terms of events, which may range in intensity from such acts as a strike or a peaceful demonstration, to a revolt or civil war. We have completed one data bank of political instability events and are embarked on a more comprehensive one. The first bank covers 84 nations for 18 years of the post-World War II period, 1948–1965. These nations were all independent states in 1945–1950. Twenty-eight nonoverlapping types of events are defined and every instance of the occurrence of these events reported in the news media is incorporated in the data collection. The 28 event categories are election, dissolution of legislature, resignation, dismissal, fall of cabinet, significant change of law, plebescite, appointment, organization of new government, reshuffle of cabinet, severe trouble within a nongovernmental organizaton, organization of opposition party, governmental action against specific groups, strike, demonstration, boycott, arrest, suicide of significant political persons, martial law, execution, assassination, terrorism, sabotage, guerrilla warfare, *coup d'état,* civil war, revolt, and exile. For this particular data bank, the source of information is *Deadline Data on World Affairs* supplemented by the *Yearbooks* of the *Encyclopedia Britannica.* The former is a news service that draws on a variety of papers throughout the world. The reporting, however, is very abridged. The book contains approximately 7000 political instability events that occurred in the 84 countries in the 18 years.

For the measurement of political instability, it is necessary not only to have the data, but also to assess the amount of aggression or violence denoted by each event. For this purpose, we developed a 7-point intensity scale for rating events. Scaling criteria involve the type of event, the number of people participating or affected, the extent of violence or lack of it, the duration, the political prominence of the participants, and the general impact of the event on the society (Feierabend and Feierabend 1965). With each event weighted for intensity, it is possible to profile countries for different periods of time for their general level of political unrest. Different profiling techniques have been used in our research, ranging from a simple summation of event scale scores to a grouped scoring method that weights the intensity of events over their frequency (Feierabend and Feierabend 1966).

The second data bank of political aggression, which we are presently engaged in collecting, uses a more detailed coding format. Seventy-one discrete conflict events are distinguished. Furthermore, the dimension of conciliation is introduced; 25 conciliatory behaviors are defined, ranging from a discussion or conference, to amnesty, repeal of martial law, the granting of independence and regional autonomy. In addition, the coding format distinguishes the initiator of an event, the target, and the issue (as well as a large set of other qualifying information). By coding the initiator and the target, it is possible to distinguish government-initiated aggressive acts (that is, coercive acts) from acts of popular turmoil. These acts can also be distinguished by their event names (arrests, imprisonments, on the one hand; strikes, demonstrations, guerrilla warfare, on the other). Furthermore, this bank identifies the specific groups and issues involved in each event. In this way, events involving ethnic/racial/religious/linguistic/cultural/geographic minority groups can be identified.

Information for this bank is drawn from daily issues of the *New York Times.* The time period is, again, the post-World War II era. To date, however, only some years for some countries are available for use. Data are being collected for 130 countries and territorial units.

These event data are scaled in the same way and on the same 7-point intensity scale described above. Events may be grouped into three types: events of political instability, government coercion events, and minority-related events. Each set of events is scaled separately. In this way, based on *event data,* countries may be profiled for levels of *political instability, government coercion,* and *intergroup conflict,* for differing periods of time.

Rating Scales: Political Structures
The data described above are event data; profile scores of countries are based on the number and intensity of events experienced. Another ap-

proach, however, is also necessary in assessing the level of coerciveness of a political regime. Characterizing a regime as permissive or coercive depends upon the way in which the political system is organized and operates, as well as on the number of coercive acts in which the regime engages. In fact, the acts and the structures are independent dimensions. If a regime is structurally highly coercive, it may hold the populace in check so that overt acts of coercion (such as arrests and executions) occur relatively infrequently.

To determine the structural dimension of permissiveness–coerciveness of political regimes, a separate data bank was formed (Feierabend, Nesvold, and Feierabend 1970). It covers the basic sample of 84 nations represented in most of our research for the post-World War II period, 1945–1966. Countries are rated yearly on a variety of political structures, using a 6-point coerciveness scale (1 = extreme permissiveness; 6 = extreme coerciveness). The information gathered covers the following 21 variables: freedom of speech, of religion, of assembly, academic freedom, and freedom of the arts and sciences; civil rights; freedom of minority groups; freedom from internal and external press censorship and from radio censorship; freedom of labor, of landed interests, and of business; freedom of churches, of universities, and of associational groups; opposition in the lower house; permissiveness of the executive; party opposition; absence of government participation in the economy; and suffrage. In general, ratings answer questions as to whether civil rights are protected, whether there are opposition parties, whether trade unions are allowed to organize independently, and so on.

A mean score on these variables, ranging from 1 to 6, gives a measure of the overall level of permissiveness or coerciveness of each political system. Countries can be scored for different time periods or for the whole 22 years, and for different aspects of the political system or for the system as a whole.

In addition to scoring countries for the *level* of coerciveness of regime, the data bank makes it possible to score countries for *fluctuations* in level of coerciveness. For this purpose, the absolute difference in scores on all variables can be added from year to year; the final score indicates the number and degree of changes in policy characterizing the nation. For example, if a country increases its level of press censorship from 1950 to 1951, and then decreases it again between 1951 and 1952, the differences between yearly press censorship ratings will be added to obtain a measure of fluctuation on this variable. The final fluctuation score for a country is obtained by averaging the degree of fluctuation over the 22 years on all measures.

RESULTS

In seeking empirical support for some of the propositions stated in the first section of this paper, the specific hypotheses are restated in each separate study. These hypotheses explore primarily the relationship between two types of political aggression: regime coerciveness and political instability. In one study, the interaction between regime coerciveness and intergroup conflict is scrutinized.

Study 1. The Effect of Level and Fluctuation in Regime Coerciveness on Political Instability

This study (Feierabend, Nesvold, and Feierabend 1970) is addressed to one application of Propositions 4 and 3a, regarding the consequences of both the level of force and the consistency with which it is applied. The propositions are restated in more limited fashion and more specific terms, with particular application to regime coerciveness and political instability.

Hypothesis A: Very permissive and very coercive political regimes are likely to be politically stable. Regimes at medium levels of coerciveness are likely to be politically unstable.

Hypothesis B: Fluctuation in the level of coerciveness (permissiveness) of political regimes results in a high probability of political instability.

Level and fluctuation in regime coerciveness is assessed by means of the data bank of political structures. This bank measures the level and degree of fluctuation in coerciveness of regime of 73 nations from 1945 to 1966. Political instability is scored on the basis of the events amassed in our first data bank of political instability events drawn from *Deadline Data on World Affairs*. The nations are profiled on level of political instability for the time period 1948–1965. Tables 12, 13, and 14 give the country profile scores on level of coerciveness, fluctuation in coerciveness, and level of political instability.

In Table 12, a value of 1.00 reflects consistently permissive behavior for each of the years 1945–1966; a score of 6.00 reflects consistently coercive conditions during that time. These scores are based on 5 of the 21 measures: suffrage, internal press censorship, party opposition, general civil rights, and permissiveness of the executive. No nation was scored at the extreme level of coerciveness (6.00), but Albania and East Germany come close to this limit. The Communist nations occupy the

Table 12   Level of Coercion Map, 1945–1966 (*n* = 73)

Country	Score	Country	Score
Iceland	1.00	Lebanon	3.26
Luxembourg	1.00	Ethiopia	3.34
New Zealand	1.00	Morocco	3.34
Norway	1.00	Honduras	3.42
Sweden	1.00	Colombia	3.46
Finland	1.02	Venezuela	3.46
Ireland	1.02	Peru	3.48
United States	1.02	Argentina	3.72
Netherlands	1.04	Jordan	3.82
Belgium	1.08	Pakistan	3.84
Canada	1.08	Poland	3.88
United Kingdom	1.14	Thailand	3.98
Italy	1.20	Sudan	4.07
Costa Rica	1.22	Union of S. Africa	4.10
Uruguay	1.28	Tunisia	4.18
Israel	1.36	Egypt	4.24
Australia	1.40	U.S.S.R.	4.38
France	1.40	Indonesia	4.44
Austria	1.44	Syria	4.50
Japan	1.44	Dominican Republic	4.52
Philippines	1.48	Nicaragua	4.54
Switzerland	1.54	Cuba	4.60
Mexico	1.60	Paraguay	4.62
West Germany	1.66	Cambodia	4.66
Chile	2.08	Afghanistan	4.68
Ceylon	2.26	Iraq	4.74
India	2.34	Portugal	4.96
Panama	2.52	Haiti	4.98
Brazil	2.72	Saudi Arabia	4.98
El Salvador	2.86	Spain	5.00
Cyprus	2.92	Czechoslovakia	5.26
Liberia	2.92	Romania	5.28
Bolivia	2.94	Hungary	5.30
Libya	3.00	Bulgaria	5.36
Laos	3.10	East Germany	5.76
Ecuador	3.12	Albania	5.98
Turkey	3.12		

top 6 positions at the coercive end of the scale, and the highly permissive nations are all polities of the Western European type. This is not a surprising finding, and it lends initial face validity to the scoring endeavor.

Table 13 reports the profiles of consistency or inconsistency in coerciveness–permissiveness. There is a considerable range of values, from 0, indicating no change in regime coerciveness, to 14, indicating frequent reversals of policy. The countries lowest in fluctuations are the highly permissive regimes. The countries exhibiting the most fluctuations are principally Latin American states. The Communist nations are scattered throughout the table. Some, such as Albania and East Germany, show very little evidence of regime change. Others, such as Czechoslovakia and especially Poland, indicate considerable change in policy over time.

Table 14 shows the political instability profile of each nation. We see in this table that Indonesia was the most unstable country in the world during these 18 years. Latin American and Middle Eastern countries also show high levels of political unrest. At the opposite end of the continuum, among the highly stable countries, we find primarily modern industrialized democracies, as well as some very traditional states such as Saudi Arabia and Afghanistan. Countries of the Communist bloc are fairly well spread throughout the table. Albania shows the highest level of political stability and East Germany the highest level of unrest in this bloc of nations. The United States is close to the center of the distribution, as is the USSR. Of all the modern Western-style democracies, France is the most unstable.

To test the two propositions, correlational methods were used. A product-moment correlation, which assumes linearity of relationship, and an *eta*, which makes no assumption of linearity, were both calculated. The results are given in Table 15. We find a relatively strong linear relationship ($r = 0.67$) between fluctuation of coercion and political instability. Thus 44 percent of the variance in instability is accounted for in its relationship to fluctuations in coerciveness. Furthermore, this level of relationship stays essentially the same when the *eta* calculation (0.66) is performed. Turning to the level rather than the fluctuation of coercion, we find a more complex association with instability. A sizeable amount of variance in instability (33 percent) is accounted for by making assumptions of linearity in the relationship with level of coercion ($r = 0.58$). Furthermore, the joint relationship between fluctuation and level of coercion accounts for 58 percent of the variance in political instability, an unusually strong association for this type of

Table 13   Fluctuation of Coercion Map, 1945–1966 (*n* = 73)

Country	Score	Country	Score
Iceland	0	Union of S. Africa	2.80
Luxembourg	0	Tunisia	3.00
New Zealand	0	Romania	3.20
Norway	0	Iraq	3.60
Sweden	0	West Germany	3.60
Finland	0.20	Nicaragua	3.80
Italy	0.20	Hungary	4.00
Philippines	0.20	India	4.60
Ireland	0.25	Pakistan	4.60
Albania	0.40	Czechoslovakia	4.80
Netherlands	0.40	Ceylon	4.90
Switzerland	0.40	Bolivia	5.20
United States	0.40	Egypt	5.20
Belgium	0.60	Haiti	5.80
Canada	0.60	Poland	5.80
Israel	0.80	Chile	6.00
Saudi Arabia	0.80	Dominican Republic	6.50
Australia	1.00	Panama	6.50
Cambodia	1.00	Cuba	7.20
U.S.S.R.	1.00	Brazil	7.60
Uruguay	1.00	Jordan	7.60
Austria	1.20	Colombia	7.80
Portugal	1.20	Lebanon	8.20
Afghanistan	1.40	Paraguay	8.20
East Germany	1.40	Syria	8.20
United Kingdom	1.40	Sudan	8.25
Cyprus	1.80	Thailand	8.60
Ethiopia	2.00	Argentina	9.20
Japan	2.00	Indonesia	9.80
Morocco	2.00	Laos	10.20
Bulgaria	2.20	Turkey	10.20
France	2.20	Honduras	10.40
Spain	2.20	Peru	10.40
Liberia	2.25	Ecuador	11.00
Libya	2.25	El Salvador	11.20
Costa Rica	2.60	Venezuela	14.20
Mexico	2.80		

Table 14 Political Instability Map, 1948–1965 (*n* = 73)

Country	Score	Country	Score
Luxembourg	03012	Sudan	12189
Netherlands	04021	Pakistan	12231
New Zealand	05015	India	12360
Saudi Arabia	05018	Cambodia	13071
Ireland	05031	Czechoslovakia	13100
Sweden	06020	Philippines	13105
Australia	06026	Hungary	13113
Finland	06056	Cyprus	13123
West Germany	06087	Jordan	13145
Iceland	07026	Thailand	13152
Austria	07057	Poland	13179
United Kingdom	07112	Turkey	13189
Norway	08034	Portugal	13190
Switzerland	08042	Morocco	13194
Canada	08084	Brazil	13209
Afghanistan	09029	Union of S. Africa	13422
Costa Rica	09058	France	13435
Romania	09060	El Salvador	14079
Libya	09069	Panama	14101
Italy	09192	Honduras	14105
Ethiopia	10034	Tunisia	14126
Liberia	10036	Laos	14129
Israel	10064	East Germany	14138
Uruguay	10100	Paraguay	14141
Mexico	10111	Egypt	14152
Chile	10156	Lebanon	14212
Belgium	10162	Peru	15196
Albania	11067	Haiti	15205
Bulgaria	11071	Syria	15329
Japan	11123	Venezuela	15429
Ceylon	11152	Colombia	16244
Dominican Republic	11195	Iraq	16274
Spain	11284	Cuba	16283
United States	11318	Bolivia	16318
Nicaragua	12096	Argentina	16445
Ecuador	12117	Indonesia	18416
U.S.S.R.	12165		

Table 15 Relationships Among Measures of Coerciveness and
Political Instability

A. Product–Moment Correlation Coefficients

		1	2	3
1.	Fluctuation of coercion	–		
2.	Level of coercion	0.36	–	
3.	Political instability	0.67	0.58	–

$$R_{3 \cdot 12} = 0.76$$

B. Eta Coefficients

		1	2	3
1.	Fluctuation of coercion	–		
2.	Level of coercion	0.78	–	
3.	Political instability	0.66	0.69	–

complex cross-national study ($r = 0.76$). Nevertheless, the *eta* coeffi-
cient between instability and level of coercion (0.69) exceeds the linear
value, a finding that brings support to our proposition suggesting a curvilinear patterning between these two variables.

Figure 17 plots the relationship between fluctuation of coercion and
instability, and Figure 18, level of coercion and instability. It is possible
to see the linear patterning in Figure 17, in which increasing fluctuation
is accompanied by increasing political instability. In Figure 18, however, the most unstable countries are at medium levels of coerciveness.
No countries at the highest levels of coerciveness fall into the highest
scale position on instability. On the other hand, only one highly coercive country falls at the most stable end of the political violence scale.
In these plots we can see that the strong tendency for permissive nations
to be peaceful has an overriding effect on the correlational analyses. If
these permissive nations are removed from the plot, linearity is still
noticed between inconsistency in coercion and political instability, but
a tendency toward curvilinearity appears in the relationship between
level of coercion and political unrest.

We find, then, in this study of 73 nations, covering approximately a
20-year period, considerable support for Hypotheses A and B.

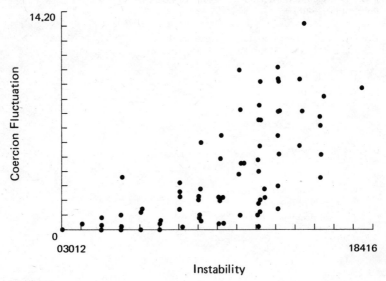

Figure 17

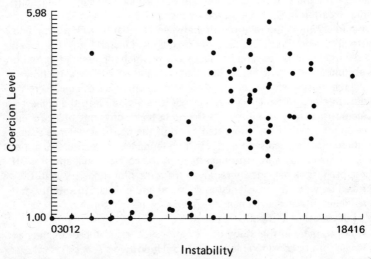

Figure 18

206

**Study 2. Governmental Coerciveness and
Political Instability: Time Trends**

This study (Markus and Nesvold 1972) deals with the interrelationship
between acts of government coercion and acts of political instability.
Both are looked at within a relatively short time period, but a distinction is drawn between acts that occur more or less simultaneously (within the same month) and acts that are separated by a one-month time
interval. Interest lies in determining when government coercion stimu-
lates political instability and when, on the contrary, it serves to deter it.
This analysis differs from the previous one since the emphasis is on coercive events rather than on coercive structures. The day-to-day coercive actions of the government are explored in relation to the actions
of the citizens. The coercive structure of the government is introduced
as a controlling variable, suggesting that coercive acts may have a different impact when they proceed from governments that are normally
permissive or normally coercive.

The study tests the relationships postulated in Propositions 1 and 2,
which are now restated as follows:

Hypothesis C: The higher (lower) the level of coercive behavior by a
                  regime, the higher (lower) the level of political insta-
                  bility within the society, in the short run.
Hypothesis D: The higher the level of coercive behavior by a regime,
                  the lower the level of political instability within the
                  society, in the long run.

In order to test these hypotheses, coercive acts of government were
compared to acts of political instability in ten countries for a three-year
period, 1959–1961. Both sets of events were drawn from our more
comprehensive and most recent data collection, based on daily issues
of the *New York Times.* The ten countries are: Argentina, Haiti, Italy,
Japan, Laos, Mexico, Poland, South Korea, Spain, and the Union of
South Africa. They were selected to avoid any particular geographical
bias and because of the relatively large amount of information available
on them.

The data for the three years were broken into monthly periods. Each
country received a coerciveness score and an instability score for each
month, based on the summed scale values of instability and coercive
events for the month. Event scores were first squared before summing
to give relatively more weight to more intense events. Two analyses
were performed. One, a simultaneous time analysis, related coerciveness and instability scores for the same month. The second, a lagged
time analysis, related coerciveness scores for one month to instability

scores for the following month. This one-month time lag made it possible to observe the consequences of coercive acts on political instability.

The simultaneous time analysis supports Hypothesis C. The intensity of acts of governmental coercion and the intensity of acts of political turmoil show a positive linear relationship. This may be seen in Table 16, which presents the frequency and percentage of low, medium, and high monthly scores of both coerciveness and instability for the 10 countries. With 36 monthly scores for each of 10 countries, 360 instability scores and 360 coerciveness scores are generated. It is clear that over half of the scores indicate a low level of intensity of both instability and coercion. This shows that the most common tendency is for a low level of both forms of political aggression to prevail within any particular short time period. Another way to say this is that violence does not occur every day, on the part of either the people or the government.

It is also evident that, within the same month, there is a strong linear relationship between coercive and instability behaviors. This positive linear trend is also brought out in Figure 19, which plots the mean monthly coercive event score against the mean monthly instability score for countries at low, medium, and high levels of coerciveness. This linear trend supports Hypothesis C, indicating that coercive and instability behaviors are fairly evenly matched in intensity in the very short run.

The one-month, time-lagged analysis indicates the deterrent effect of coercion, at least when it is practiced at a high level of intensity. This is in support of Hypothesis D. Actually, a curvilinear relationship emerges between government coercion and political instability, if all three levels of intensity of government coercion are considered (see

Table 16 Relationship Between Monthly Levels of Coerciveness and Instability for Ten Countries, 1959–1961

Instability Level	Coerciveness Level			
	Low	Medium	High	Total
Low	73% (157)	40% (50)	10% (2)	58% (209)
Medium	23% (50)	40% (49)	33% (7)	29% (106)
High	4% (9)	20% (24)	57% (12)	13% (45)
Total	100% (216)	100% (123)	100% (21)	100% (360)

Gamma = 0.62
Z = 7.64 $p < 0.01$

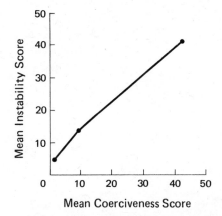

Figure 19   Mean Coerciveness Score Versus Mean Instability Score for Countries at the Three Levels of Coerciveness

Table 17 and Figure 20). A low level of government coercion leads to a low level of political instability one month later. Medium levels of government coercion lead to higher levels of political instability one month later. And high levels of government coercion lead to a reduction in political instability the following month. The upward trend in Figure 20 between low and medium levels of coercion supports Proposition 1. The downward trend in the same figure between medium and high levels of coercion supports Proposition 2. In combination, they give additional support to Proposition 4.

Table 17   Relationship Between the Level of Coerciveness for Each Month and the Level of Instability for the Following Month, 10 Countries, 1959–1961

| Instability Level | Coerciveness Level | | | |
	Low	Medium	High	Total
Low	65% (136)	46% (56)	62% (13)	59% (205)
Medium	30% (62)	34% (41)	29% (6)	31% (109)
High	5% (10)	20% (24)	10% (2)	10% (36)
Total	100% (208)	100% (121)	100% (21)	100% (350)

Gamma = 0.31
Gamma (low–high–medium) = 0.65
Z = 3.79 $p < 0.01$

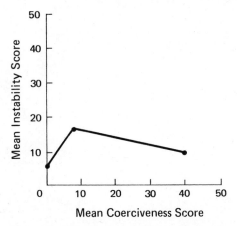

Figure 20   Mean Coerciveness Score Versus Mean Instability Score for Countries at the Three Levels of Coerciveness (Time Lag of One Month)

Study 3. Minority Group Conflict and Conciliation

The final study to be reported (Mullick and Feierabend 1971) deals exclusively with conflicts involving minority groups (intergroup conflict). Minority, for the purposes of this study, is used in the sense of a group's having ethnic/racial/linguistic/cultural/geographic characteristics that set the members apart from the rest of society (Feierabend, Feierabend, and Nesvold 1969). The study is directed to the relative merits of frustration and deterrence views of aggression; thus Propositions 1 and 2 are again the focus of attention. In this case, the hypothesis formulated favors Proposition 1, based on notions of reciprocity in conflict behaviors. The analysis examines the violent behaviors of three actors in society: the government, the ethnic/racial minority, and the dominant ethnic/racial group, called the "majority." The majority group consists of persons distinguishable from the minority along the same ethnic/racial dimensions that give the minority its identity. It need not represent an actual numerical majority within the population, but is the group that enjoys a more favored or dominant status over the minority.

Time is not a dimension in this analysis; comparisons were made without exploring the effect of a time lag. In this respect, the study differs from the previous one. It is the complement of Study 2, however, exploring the same type of simultaneous relationship between coercion and instability, but extending the analysis to the variable of intergroup conflict. The specific hypothesis formulated in this study is the following:

Hypothesis E: The higher (lower) the level of coercive behavior by a regime, the higher (lower) the level of political instability engaged in by ethnic/racial minority groups.

    The study looks at countries, for which event data on minority-related conflict were available from the *New York Times* collection, for a 5-year period, 1955–1959.

    These event data were divided into coercive acts, initiated by the government and directed against the minority group; minority-initiated acts of political instability, directed against the government; and acts initiated by nonminority groups (majority groups) and directed against the minority or the government. In addition, conciliatory behaviors were included in the analysis. These tend to be primarily government initiated by their very definition: It takes considerable power to grant concessions (amnesty, repeal of laws, autonomy). Minority groups tend to be in the position of trying to wring concessions and conciliatory behavior from the government, rather than performing conciliatory acts.

    As in the previous analysis, data were scored on a monthly basis, yielding 60 scores for each country for the 5-year period, or 1500 scores in all. Furthermore, these 1500 scores were calculated for each of 6 types of behavior: minority-initiated aggression (instability); minority-initiated conciliation; majority-initiated aggression (instability); majority-initiated conciliation; government-initiated aggression (coercion); government-initiated conciliation. A correlational analysis was performed using the same month's scores on all 6 variables.

    Results of this simultaneous time analysis are the same as in the previous study by Markus and Nesvold. A strong positive linear association emerges between the intensity of minority hostility and the intensity of government coercion. Table 18 gives the correlation matrix among measures. The strongest relationship is a correlation of 0.71 between level of minority hostility and level of government hostility. The next highest relationship is a correlation of 0.44 between levels of majority hostility and conciliation. The import of this correlation is questionable, since majority-group members initiated acts (whether hostile or conciliatory) in only 12 of the 25 countries. The correlation appears to tell us, however, that where majority groups are active, they tend to engage in both hostile and conciliatory behavior. The remaining correlations are low, especially those involving government.

    A second analysis of these same data also supports the positive association between minority hostility and government coercion. In this case, following a procedure used by McClelland (1967), events were classified into four categories: amicable (conciliatory behavior), mildly

Table 18 Relationships Among Behaviors Initiated by Different Participants: Twenty-Five Nations (Product–Moment Correlations) (*n* = 1500)

	Government Hostility	Government Conciliation	Majority Hostility	Majority Conciliation	Minority Hostility	Minority Conciliation
Government Hostility						
Government Conciliation	0.06					
Majority Hostility	0.22	0.13				
Majority Conciliation	0.17	0.09	0.44			
Minority Hostility	0.71	0.03	0.03	0.01		
Minority Conciliation	0.09	0.03	0.08	0.12	.10	

hostile, moderately hostile, and severely hostile. Then the events initiated by each actor in each country during the 5-year period were categorized in terms of the predominant tendency—that is, the category containing the highest frequency of events. Table 19 classifies countries in terms of the predominant type of behavior of both the government and the minority. Again a strong positive linear trend is apparent. If the government engages primarily in conciliatory behavior, the behaviors of minority groups range from mildly hostile to severely hostile. If the government engages in moderately hostile acts, the actions of minorities are moderately to severely hostile. If the government engages in severely hostile acts, the minority behaviors show the same high level of hostility.

Results of this study seem in support of Proposition 1. They reinforce the view that, in the very short run, behaviors between participants in the political arena appear to be reciprocal in character and intensity.

SUMMARY AND DISCUSSION

What can be said regarding the violent consequences of violence? Can we answer the five questions formulated at the outset of this paper? The first question addressed itself directly to the consequences of violence. It asked whether force breeds counterforce or whether it serves to quell civil turmoil and disorder. The particular domain used to explore these relationships is the interplay between government coercion and political instability, including the instability created by ethnic/racial conflicts. The findings indicate that violence can produce both outcomes. Under some conditions it is a stimulus for further violence, but under other circumstances it provides a deterrent, diminishing outbursts of political instability. In the empirical studies, two factors influence the type of outcome: the intensity or level with which force is applied and the time elapsing between the use of force and the assessment of consequences. Thus, in order to answer the first question, we must also answer the second and third, which deal with the short-run and the long-run consequences of violence, as well as with the level or intensity of violence.

In the second study reported in this paper, a positive linear relationship appeared between the frequency of occurrence of acts of instability and the frequency of occurrence of acts of government coercion. Also, the higher the level of intensity of government acts, the higher the level of intensity of political instability. In the third study, the same linear relationship was found between level of government coercion and the intensity of political instability stemming from ethnic/racial conflicts.

Table 19 Patterning of Predominant Behaviors of Government and Minority

Predominant Behavior of Government	Predominant Behavior of Minority				Total Countries
	Amicable Acts	Hostile Acts (Mild)	Hostile Acts (Moderate)	Hostile Acts (Severe)	
Hostile Acts (Severe)				Indonesia Lebanon Peru 3	3
Hostile Acts (Moderate)			Ceylon Egypt Philippines South Africa Yugoslavia 5	Belgium Cyprus Iran Iraq Morocco Syria 6	11
Hostile Acts (Mild)					
Amicable Acts		Canada Israel 2	Czechoslovakia India United Kingdom United States 4	Pakistan Tunisia 2	8
Total Countries		2	9	11	

The higher the intensity of government coercion, the more violent the minority group's actions. These relationships held only in the very short run, however; the level of government coercion was related to the level of political instability within the same one-month period. In the second study, when the time dimension was varied, empirical support emerged for the deterrent effect of force. It was found that high levels of coercive acts on the part of political regimes led to a low intensity of political instability one month later. The time dimension is crucial in these analyses; only with a time lag of one month did an inverse relationship appear between the acts of one party and the response of the other party.

The level of intensity with which force is applied is of considerable import. A curvilinear relationship was hypothesized between the level of intensity of government coercion and the intensity of political instability. This curvilinear relationship is, at least partially, predicted on the notion that low levels of force serve primarily as frustration, but have little deterrent power. High levels of force, on the other hand, suppress and deter responses of counterforce. Thus low levels of force should breed counterforce, while high levels of force will deter violence.

In the first study, the relationship between level of regime coerciveness and level of political instability was also explored. In this case, regime coerciveness was viewed as a dispositional property of government and was measured by means of structural variables, not coercive acts. Evidence was found for both linearity and nonlinearity in this relationship. The strength of both measures of association was significant, considering the universe of cross-national data. The finding of curvilinearity, however, was somewhat stronger and it was judged more persuasive. It is supported by other research findings. In the cross-national field, various researchers, using different cross-national data bases, different measurements, different definitions of variables, different segments of the cross-national universe, and different time periods, have all found empirical support for this proposition (Bwy 1968, Feierabend and Feierabend 1971, Gurr 1968, Walton 1965). This cumulative evidence gives some confidence to the finding of curvilinearity.

The fifth question concerns the consequences of inconsistency in the application of force. It was explored by relating the degree of fluctuation coerciveness of political regime to the level of political instability characterizing the nation. A positive linear relationship was hypothesized between fluctuation and instability. The first study explored this relationship, using the degree of change in structural characteristics of government over a 22-year period. Degree of change was related to the intensity of political instability during this time period. A strong linear relationship emerged between the two variables, as hypothesized. This finding is based on a large sample of nations and a considerable data base. Although the relationship has not been explored elsewhere in the cross-national literature, it appears to be of considerable import. Furthermore, inconsistency in regime coerciveness, in combination with the level of intensity of coerciveness, shows a very strong relationship to the level of political unrest. From a knowledge of these two aspects of political regime behavior, the level of political instability within a nation can be predicted considerably better than by chance. While prediction is never foolproof, errors may be minimized to the point that 58 percent of the variance in political instability within the sample of nations may be explained from a knowledge of the level of coerciveness of their political regimes and the consistency with which this force level is maintained.

The consequence of a legitimate versus an illegitimate use of force was raised in the fourth question. Unfortunately, the implications of legitimacy were not tested directly in these studies. Since legitimacy involves the perceptions of individuals, it is a difficult concept to measure with cross-national aggregate data. Some efforts to explore the impact of legitimacy on political unrest may be found in the cross-national literature (Bwy 1968, Gurr 1968), however, although these studies view legitimacy as an aspect of the political system rather than as a perceived attribute of violence. In this sense they do not come directly to grips with the fourth question. Yet their findings suggest support for our propositions. Both studies show that the higher the level of legitimacy of a political regime, the lower the level of political unrest within the society. This is an important question, since many of the propositions elaborated in the theoretical section of this paper are predicated on the distinction between legitimate and illegitimate uses of force. Proposition 1, for example, postulates counterviolence as resulting from the use of illegitimate force; Proposition 2 suggests quiescence as the response to legitimate force. To some extent the rationale for the inhibitory mechanism, as well as for the frustration mechanism of aggression, hinges on this distinction. Some indirect evidence may be found relating to legitimacy, however. It was argued in the theoretical section that the notion of legitimacy/illegitimacy is associated with the concept of an arbitrary and inconsistent use of force. Hence, we could claim that the strong empirical relationship discovered between inconsistency of political coercion and intensity of political instability bears on the notion of legitimacy. It is a plausible argument, but it provides only very

indirect and speculative evidence regarding the relationship between
legitimacy and force.

In summary of this presentation, it may be said that support has been
adduced for particular applications of the theoretical propositions. The
relationships uncovered in the data are interesting and suggest lines of
further research. For example, no other cross-national study has explored inconsistencies in coerciveness, although some parallel evidence
can be found in regional analyses (LeVine 1959). One question is
whether the relationship between inconsistency and violence holds for
other categories of political aggression, as well as for regime coerciveness and political instability. An even more immediate question would
probe the same relationship using coercive events rather than the dispositional aspects of coercion.

The question of the requisite time lag before the consequences of actions can be assessed still must be clarified. It has been given little attention in the literature. Tentatively, it appears that some time is
needed to make coercion "stick"; the immediate response to force is
counterforce. This is another avenue of further research: to explore
the consequences of actions at different points in time following the
event.

A final point is that this discussion presumes the presence of violence
in society in the first place, without explaining its antecedent causes.
An adequate discussion or theory of violence cannot avoid such questions, and we have explored them in previous research. For this essay,
however, we wished to focus on the consequences of violence and so
began with the assumption of a polarity between government and
people. Another omission is the lack of reference to the relative aggressive capabilities of incumbents and insurgents. Their game of power,
aggression, and violence must be considered in a more comprehensive
discussion of the violent consequences of violence. Nevertheless, we
have sought the consequences of violence within a limited set of possible outcomes and have found evidence of coherent patterns.

The patterning suggests that the consequence of a consistent use of
force by a regime is the maintenance of political stability. By implication, it seems plausible that this applies not only to coerciveness, but
to any use of force in the community, by insurgents as well as by incumbents. Furthermore, only minimal and maximal levels of force
have pacifying consequences. Medium levels must be judged as those
most likely to intensify, hence stimulate, violent reprisals. The evidence
stems from the coerciveness and level of political instability. Combining
these two answers, it appears that the strategy of either consistently low,

or consistently high, levels of the use of force is the safest in eliminating the likelihood of counterforce. Median levels, on the other hand, should be avoided; but if pursued, consistency must be the strategy. The surest way to provoke others is to treat them alternately with great force and with no force. Fluctuation between weakness and brutality is the deadliest of combinations. And this again applies not only to incumbents but also, at least by implication, to revolutionaries as well as to minority groups. Moreover, it seems that the immediate response to force is counterforce, and hence, in the short run, violence intensifies violence. In the long run, it does not, and the previous considerations regarding curvilinearity are more apt to be the long-run consequences.

ACKNOWLEDGMENTS

The generous support of the National Science Foundation is gratefully acknowledged. This support has made possible the collection of extensive cross-national data on political violence and political structures, as well as the analyses of the data.

REFERENCES

Bandura, Albert, and Richard H. Walters, *Social Learning and Personality Development,* New York: Holt, Rinehart & Winston, 1963.

Berkowitz, Leonard, *Aggression: A Social Psychological Analysis,* New York: McGraw-Hill, 1962.

Boulding, Kenneth E., *Conflict and Defense: A General Theory,* New York: Harper & Row, 1962.

Buss, Arnold, *The Psychology of Aggression,* New York: Wiley, 1962.

Bwy, Douglas, "Political Instability in Latin America: The Preliminary Test of a Causal Model," *Latin American Research Review, 3,* (Spring 1968), 17–66.

Davies, James C., "Toward a Theory of Revolution," *American Sociological Review, 27* (February 1962), 5–19.

Dollard, John *et al., Frustration and Aggression,* New Haven, Conn.: Yale University Press, 1939.

Feierabend, Ivo K., and Rosalind L. Feierabend, "The Relationship of Systemic Frustration, Political Coercion, and Political Instability: A Cross-National Analysis," in J. V. Gillespie and B. A. Nesvold, eds., *Macro-Quantitative Analysis,* Beverly Hills, Calif.: Sage Publications, 1971.

Feierabend, Ivo K., and Rosalind L. Feierabend, "Aggressive Behaviors Within Politics, 1948-1962: A Cross-National Study," *Journal of Conflict Resolution, 10* (September 1966), 249–271.

Feierabend, Ivo K., and Rosalind L. Feierabend, *Cross National Data Bank of Political Instability Events (Code Index),* San Diego, Calif.: Public Affairs Research Institute, 1965.

Feierabend, Ivo K., Betty A. Nesvold, and R. L. Feierabend, "Political Coerciveness and Turmoil: A Cross-National Inquiry," *Law and Society Review* (August 1970), 93–118.

Feierabend, Rosalind L., Ivo K. Feierabend, and B. A. Nesvold, "Intergroup Conflict: A Cross-National Analysis," paper presented at the Annual Meeting of the American Political Science Association, New York, 1969.

Gurr, Ted R., *Why Men Rebel,* Princeton, N.J.: Princeton University Press, 1970.

Gurr, Ted R., "A Causal Model of Civil Strife: A Comparative Analysis Using New Indices," *American Political Science Review, 62* (December 1968), 1104–1124.

Leites, Nathan, and Charles Wolf, Jr., *Rebellion and Authority,* Chicago: Markham, 1970.

LeVine, Robert A., "Anti-European Violence in Africa: A Comparative Analysis," *Journal of Conflict Resolution, 3* (December 1959), 420–429.

Lorenz, Konrad, *On Aggression,* New York: Harcourt Brace Jovanovich, 1966.

Markus, Gregory B., and Betty A. Nesvold, "Governmental Coerciveness and Political Instability: An Exploratory Study of Cross-National Patterns," *Comparative Political Studies,* 1972.

McClelland, Charles, "The Beginning, Duration, and Abatement of International Crises: Comparison in Two Conflict Arenas," unpublished manuscript, University of Michigan, 1967.

Mullick, Rosemary, and Rosalind L. Feierabend, "Intergroup Conflict and Conciliation: A Cross-National Analysis," paper presented at the Annual Meeting of the American Psychological Association, Washington, D.C., 1971.

Nieburg, H. L., *Political Violence: The Behavioral Process,* New York: St. Martin, 1969.

Schelling, Thomas C., *The Strategy of Conflict,* Cambridge, Mass.: Harvard University Press, 1963.

Walton, Jennifer G., *Correlates of Coerciveness and Permissiveness of National Political Systems: A Cross-National Study,* Master's thesis, San Diego State College, 1965.

10

Political Violence and Political Change: A Conceptual Commentary

JAMES A. BILL
University of Texas, Austin

Discussions of political violence become increasingly fashionable with time. In a world in which acts of political violence are dramatically evident, scholars from a wide variety of disciplines struggle to understand and to explain this phenomenon. Among the issues that demand systematic and rigorous investigation is the relationship that links political violence and political change. What role does violence play in the modification or transformation of political systems? How does violence shape the kaleidoscopic pattern of power relations that link individuals, groups, and classes in society? What is the relationship between violence and such processes as revolution and modernization? Surely these are among the most significant kinds of questions that can be raised as mankind seeks to understand change in the last quarter of the twentieth century.

A CONCEPTUALIZATION OF CHANGE: MODIFICATION AND TRANSFORMATION

Contemporary social science literature is increasingly riddled with terms such as change, dynamism, reform, revolution, development, modernization, progress, and transition. Phrases such as "the politics of social change," "the developmental process," and "the revolution of modernization" have become catchy and confusing clichés. Few observers have stopped long enough to discuss and develop the basic distinctions and definitions of change.

Analyses of social and political change often contain an implicit reference to different types of change. This is seen, for example, in works where the process of reform is contrasted to the phenomenon of revolution. The general references to concepts such as alteration, revision, adaptation, integration, and incrementalism indicate change of a milder and less than fundamental nature. Systemic change, radical change, or revolutionary change tend to reflect a deeper and more profound experience. In the terminology of this paper, the dichotomy is one that divides *modification* or *modifying change* from *transformation* or *transforming change.*

Those students of social change who have ignored the above kinds of distinctions or who have failed to discuss them explicitly and rigorously have consistently invested their analyses with ambiguity and distortion. Does modernization involve a process of modification or transformation? If the answer to this question is uncertain, then the role of violence in promoting political change or modernization cannot be ascertained. Certainly, violence may be used either to modify or to transform ongoing systems of power relations.[1] The important empirical task of determining which of these results prevails is dependent upon a clear understanding of the distinctions and definitions involved.

Using James C. Davies' imaginative article as a foundation, it is possible to construct a systemic scheme of power relationships that will enable us to analyze the related issues of political violence and political change.[2] Most important, an adaptation of the Davies formulation will assist us to bring into focus the more intricate distinctions within the variable of change itself. The issue of political violence is intrinsically intertwined with the patterns through which the modifying and transforming dimensions of change are interrelated.

The Davies domination–submission (or dominance–subordination) nexus is presented as a universal relationship in which individuals or groups are naturally bound to other individuals or groups. One side of the relationship is superordinate and the other is subordinate in a relationship in which both sides benefit in quite different ways. In all such relationships, both the dominant and subordinate groups must satisfy continuously and dynamically a series of innate and instrumental needs.[3] Davies summarizes the pattern as follows: "My thesis is that the dominance–submission relationship comes into existence because it serves the needs of the subordinate group."[4]

Transformation has been defined by Manfred Halpern as "that kind of alteration of a system which results in the exclusion of some existing elements and linkages and the entrance of some new elements and linkages sufficient to be recognized, at a given level of abstraction, as a new system."[5] Transforming change is fundamental and qualitative in nature. It involves change at the very roots and is therefore truly radical change. Transformation is a process in which the ongoing superordinate–subordinate nexus is ruptured and a fundamentally new relationship develops in its place.

Modification involves all processes of change that alter the superordinate–subordinate pattern without transforming it. Modifying change occurs when (1) the ongoing relationship is revised and reformed but is not torn, (2) the relationship is torn but another pattern is not constructed in its place, and (3) the basic relation is ruptured and then reknit, but in precisely the same pattern that existed prior to the break. In the processes of modification the basic linkages remain intact although there may often be a dramatic presence of sporadic reform and surface revision. Modifying change is a process of making adjustments. It does not concern or confront the roots of ongoing relations and often develops during a period of crisis as a result of the conscious need by an agent to react.

The various maneuvers and fluctuations that mark the pattern of superordination–subordination all classify as modifying change until the basic relationship itself is torn and a fundamentally new one is constructed in its place. The key empirical task is to discover when the relationship breaks and then to analyze the newly formed pattern to ascertain its nature. The process of the continuing rupture of old patterns of superordination–subordination and the formation of new ones may be termed *modernization.*

The politics of transformation demand that the new superordinate force that takes position following the rupture of the old pattern uproot the relations that infuse the traditional environment of power. Lupsha and MacKinnon are discussing precisely this type of change when they write that "we may be witnessing a different kind of revolution—namely, one in which the basic definition of what a power relationship is, is under contention."[6] The following questions must be answered affirmatively if the transforming dimensions of change are in effect at the level of the national political system. Will the new elite bring the subordinate forces effectively and continually into the decision-making process? Will the least powerful be allowed and encouraged to control and direct their own fate? Will the elite permit subordinate groups to enjoy the freedom necessary for them to develop independence and creativity? Will this dominant force sponsor educational and social systems that are open-ended and future-oriented? In James Davies' terms, will the new elite permit and promote an environment in which the important spectrum of innate and instrumental needs of all individuals and groups can be met? According to Davies, the relation of domination–subordination becomes pathological when the satisfaction of these needs is thwarted. In our terms, transformation is the process through which all these needs are persistently and effectively satisfied.

The developmental literature reveals a one-sided emphasis upon modifying change. Various approaches and problem areas have been heavily weighted towards the Parmenidean conception of man and society. Stability, order, balance, equilibrium, and harmony have been both the fundamental reality and the fundamental goal for most developmental scholars. The popular and prevalent "systems" and "structural-functional" approaches to the study of politics have decidedly emphasized such variables as homeostasis, equilibrium, and maintenance. Although the group approach has considered conflict within its theoretical purview, the bias has always been towards a balancing and countervailing competition that has enabled systems to resist transformation. The main strains of political culture and socialization literature have stressed benevolence and cooperation that have in turn promoted system preservation. Even the elite approach has cultivated an attachment for the study of modification. By focusing analysis on the politics and policies of elite actors, this approach accounts well for the conscious development of moderate programs designed to preserve the ongoing sociopolitical system.

The preoccupation with and glorification of modification in American social science has resulted in a serious state of underdevelopment in the overall study of political change. Patterns of conflict, tension, competition, and violence have been considered as aberrations and abnormalities in the political process. These abnormalities are intellectually tolerated only when they contribute to system stability, system preservation, or system maintenance. Only recently has the sterility of this kind of exercise become evident to an increasing number of scholars. To define development and modernization in terms of order in the midst of a world of change and in terms of stability in the midst of a world of instability was first criticized and questioned by those who studied either non-Western societies or subcultures within Western societies. It was manifestly evident that malevolent orientations and conflictual activities were integral and dominant characteristics of sociopolitical relations in such settings. It was also noted in these contexts that conflict and even violence were often the catalysts of order and stability.

In the recent drive to understand the more radical features of change, a number of social scientists have returned to the study of conflict and violence as fundamental processes in social and political relations. Imbalance, inequality, and discontinuity are increasingly considered at least as important as symmetry, congruence, and continuity. This current trend can be seen in the proliferation of studies concentrating on class analysis in particular and dialectical analysis in general.[7] The contemporary drive to develop various dialectical approaches to the study of politics and society represents an attempt to explore and explain dimensions of change hitherto largely ignored.

In the remainder of this essay we will attempt to analyze the modifying dimensions of change in direct relation to the politics of transformation and the issue of violence. By outlining the various methods by which the superordinate force introduces modifying change, we hope to make it easier to distinguish empirically between modification and transformation. At the same time we will recognize the formidable obstacles that exist with regard to the introduction of change that is transforming in nature.

THE METHODOLOGY OF MODIFICATION

The techniques and tactics used to preserve the basic dominant–subordinate relation represent a highly developed field of political activity. The essence of this process involves the introduction of various manifestations of modifying change in order to avoid a basic rupture in the ongoing relation itself. The methodology of modification has been a finely honed tool in the political repertory of the dominant force in the Davies power nexus. This has been the case whether the relation has been one of landlord–peasant, minister–deputy minister, monarch–aristocrat, master–apprentice, patron–client, or ward boss–constitutent. At the national political level, it is best understood in terms of political elite formation and policy. The classic studies of Pareto, Mosca, and Michels are handbooks that discuss the methodology of modification as developed and implemented by the dominant political forces.

At the subordinate level, the less powerful individual or group will move to sever the linkage whenever the costs of the relation are considered to be too high. From the dominant position, it is necessary, therefore, to shape the relation (or the subordinate force's perception of that relation) in a way that will keep it palatable to the subordinate. This process is essential to help muffle, deflect, or mellow the subordinate's challenge to the relation itself. Central to the strategy is a recognized need to introduce in carefully rationed doses various modes of modifying change that will quench the thirst for transformation. These doses must be administered in the smallest possible effective quantities since it is well understood that they must necessarily increase through time. The politics of modification are always incremental in nature.

There are several ways in which processes of modification serve to preserve and maintain basic systemic relations. In slightly different terms, these are methods by which modifying change can stave off transformation. In the first technique, the elite introduces programs of argumentation that are *directly* designed to alter the perceptions and attitudes of the parties linked in the power relationship. The most common variety of this technique is the attempt by the dominant force to legitimize its position by convincing the subordinate force that the relation ought to remain as it is. In other words, the elite develops and refines an elaborate case justifying and rationalizing its position as elite.[8] These "political formulas" have traditionally ranged all the way from arguments positing genetic superiority and otherworldly contacts to calls for nationalistic dedication and patriotic duty. One relatively recent and most effective tactic of modification by legitimation is for elite members to pose in the role of revolutionaries. The contemporary era, for example, is one in which monarchs quote Lenin and conservative democratic elites sprinkle their speeches with references to the need for change, reform, and even revolution. The Lupsha-MacKinnon article in this collection discusses the intricacies of this general form of modifying change, with specific reference to violence. Their analysis concludes that elite groups have successfully reserved legitimacy for only those violent acts engaged in by the dominant forces themselves. "To the system, only violence that comes from the bottom of the hierarchy is really 'violence' and hence requires repression if control fails. Antiauthority violence is always illegal."[9]

There is another form of this attempt to alter attitudes, and this concerns the changes that occur in the perceptions of the dominant subject itself. In this case, the attitudes of the elite undergo revision with regard to the political patterns within which they operate. These changes take place as a result of both the subjective and objective programs that the elite has targeted towards the subordinate forces. A fine example of how this operates is provided in the Lipsky-Olson paper in this volume, which analyzes the riot commission experience. This study argues that the policy of forming commissions represents an elite response to systemic challenges. The response, however, is a "symbolic response" that does little more than help "take the heat off." The authors place the policy of commission formation directly within the category of modifying change when they write that "the ritual itself serves to divert attention from the problem to the play, with consequent reduction in interest in positive action."[10] Lipsky and Olson point out that riot commissions are certainly more reassuring to the elite than to the less-powerful and more-frustrated rioters. In this sense, the elite engages in a form of institutionalized self-deception with regard to the fundamental and explosive issue of continuity and change. This second form of modification of attitudes is considerably less effective from the point of view of those seeking to preserve ongoing relations. The elite deceives itself into believing that it has done far more than it actually has in the process of placating the discontented.

A less subtle form of modification and one that is perhaps the most dramatic as well as the most common is elite policy designed to change the objective situation in which the nonelite lives. This program, which is developed as a surrogate for fundamental social and political change, is often cloaked in the language of reform or revolution. Such programs follow upon the promises and reasoning that accompany the forms of attitudinal placation discussed above. They in fact occur usually as a reaction to the expectations that have been aroused by the first kind of modification. The emphasis in this second general form of modifying change is upon the economic and the material. In non-Western societies, elites build roads, dams, steel mills, airports, hotels, skyscrapers, and theaters. Hospitals and schools are also projects that elites sponsor and portray as revolutionary aids to the people. These kinds of projects do indeed touch favorably upon the lives of the less powerful in society. They do not, however, introduce fundamental change into the basic sociopolitical relations that prevail. No matter how dramatic material concessions may be, they more often than not serve to strengthen rather than weaken the domination–subordination nexus described by James Davies.[11] In American society, this process of modification from above is seen in the numerous programs that sporadically result in new parks, sidewalks, and street lights for minority groups. Even the national housing, education, and occupational policies have been relatively piecemeal and have existed at the level of surface scratching. The basic power and authority relations have yet to experience transformation.

There are a number of other systemic mechanisms that keep domination–subordination relations from snapping and breaking. Although the dominant force does not play an important conscious role in shaping these kinds of modifying influences, there is little doubt that such mechanisms, nonetheless, are crucial factors in preserving the fundamental power patterns. One consideration, for example, is the entangling introduction of new forces into the Davies dialectic. Confrontation between the superordinate and subordinate forces is not always direct and straightforward. There are usually numerous other individuals and groups who have significant impacts upon the basic relationship. Key examples of these kinds of third parties include middlemen, intermediaries, and political brokers. Such forces help preserve the basic power relation and keep the inherent tension from exploding into violence. In the first place, they act to buffer the competition by separating the contenders. Secondly, they serve to narrow the power gap by maintaining a sphere of influence to themselves. In so doing, the intermediate forces tend to increase the leverage of the subordinate while decreasing the leverage of the dominant force.[12] Finally, the injection of outside forces into the basic dialectical pattern brings new linkages into existence. This permits the subordinate in one relation to become the dominant force in another relation. The result is a web of power relations in which subordinate forces at certain levels are dominant forces at other levels. Viewed from a broader perspective, therefore, subordinate actors are less likely to disengage themselves from a system in which they survive in the role of both domination and subordination.

A second series of mechanisms that contribute to system modification and the preservation of ongoing sociopolitical patterns are the cultural traits that prevail in many societies and communities. The struggle for power is cushioned by a blanket of linguistic and cultural proprieties that prevent shattering confrontations and violence. Overt politeness and courtesy often serve to obscure, publicly, who is in fact dominant and who is subordinate. Omnipresent tension and grim competition are kept beneath the surface where they continuously smolder but are seldom allowed to erupt. The dialect is coated with cultural conventionalities that demand civility, courtesy, hospitality, and amiability even between the most fierce and steadfast of rivals.

A final methodology contributing to the persistence of particular superordinate–subordinate nexuses involves modification by mobility. In this kind of change, the subordinate force improves its power position in the overall system. By so doing, this individual or group gains a greater stake in the ongoing system and therefore tends to become more committed and less alienated. Perhaps the most often recognized and discussed phenomenon within this category is the process of cooptation. In this case, the elite selectively absorbs members of the non-elite thereby lessening the dissatisfaction and weakening the challenge from below. There are, however, various forms of mobility. One type occurs when the subordinate force increases his power *relative to* the power of the dominant force. The gap between the two poles in the relationship is narrowed in some degree. The basic pattern, however, remains essentially the same. In the second form of mobility, both the superordinate and the subordinate parties improve their positions in the system. Their particular relationship moves forward relative to the other forces in the system. Usually, this occurs when the dominant individual or group catapults ahead in the system and the subordinate force is carried along with the promotion.

The final and most dramatic form of mobility occurs when the two forces in the power nexus reverse positions. This involves a temporary tearing of the relationship, which is soon reestablished, although with different faces occupying the two positions. In this case, a temporarily ruptured pattern is reknit in the same way that it existed prior to the break. This is a process in which servants become masters and subordinates become chiefs. A fine example of this kind of mobility at the national political level is the palace *coup.* In the Third World, this process of political musical chairs is common. The arrangement of the chairs and the relations between the occupants of the chairs remain the same. Only the occupants themselves change places.

The above outline of some of the techniques and manifestations of modifying change goes far to explain the extraordinary plasticity and elasticity of many traditional systems. Partially due to the political shrewdness of those who dominate and partially due to the systemic mechanisms that have developed through time, the transformation of ongoing sociopolitical relations is always a painful and difficult process. In attempting to assess the depth of political change that is occurring in a given instance, therefore, it is necessary to examine more than the reform programs and the movement of personalities. The focal point of analysis must be trained upon the linkages that bind superordinate with subordinate in the political system.

THE ROLE OF VIOLENCE

In this essay we are not concerned with whether or not violence begets more violence, nor are we interested in discovering what the incidence of violence was in a particular society over a particular period of time. These kinds of questions have been admirably addressed in a number of other essays in this volume. The question that we raise in rudimentary fashion concerns the relation between political violence and forms of political change. Does violence assist in the modification or transformation of the basic ways in which individuals and groups interact in society? Some preliminary observations follow.

Violence can emanate from above or from below; that is, it can be engaged in by either the dominant or the subordinate pole. From above it can take on the form of oppression and tyranny in freezing ongoing relations or it can even be used to increase the gap between the superordinate and subordinate forces. This use of violence is generally directed immediately against the less powerful groups in the system. In this form, the *threat* of violence is more common than its actual use. The dominant force undertakes an intensive campaign to build up its arsenal of tools of physical coercion with the hope of deterring any threat to its position of domination. Many times this kind of buildup is rationalized in terms of self-defense against some force exogenous to the basic power nexus. Moreover, the threat of, or indulgence in, violence by the dominant group against the subordinate group is often a substitute for modifying concessions of less disruptive nature.

Acts of violence by the dominant force in the dialectic can also be used as a fulcrum to assist in the modification of ongoing relations in order to protect the basic power pattern in the long run. In contrast to the first type of coercion, violence to this end is usually confined to the elite level. Here the more progressive and farsighted members of the group are in direct conflict with the more reactionary elements. When this disagreement breaks into violence, it is an intraclass phenomenon and the outcome of the struggle determines whether or not the superordinate force will pursue a policy of strict preservation or one of modification vis-à-vis the nonelite.

The final type of violence from above takes place to promote transformation. In order to carry out such a policy, it is essential that the power of the restraining forces be less than the power of the driving forces. This demands strong action by the superordinate actors against all groups that resist change. Such resistance is found at all levels of the sociopolitical structure. The use of violence to promote transforming change must be limited and moderate. If it is not, it rapidly undermines the very kind of change it is supposedly trying to support, since an elite that must rest its rule on violence soon is forced to the defensive position of protecting, buttressing, and reinforcing ongoing sociopolitical relations.

Violence can also erupt from below. This represents a rebellion against a "pathological" or oppressive dominant–subordinate relationship. A violent challenge to ongoing patterns may or may not lead to transformation. The revolt must first of all succeed. If it does not, it only acts as a catalyst in the formation of the kind of elite policy referred to above. A dominant actor that has just escaped a violent threat from below will continue to rely on the same tools that saved him, long after the confrontation point has passed. More often than not, a reactionary policy will even take precedence over a policy of straight preservation of the sociopolitical patterns. If the violence from below succeeds in destroying or supplanting the former dominant actor, there is still no guarantee that the new superordinate force will possess the will and capacity to introduce transforming change. As we mentioned before, it may result only in a game of revolving regimes or rotating rulers.

The politics of modifying change are deliberately designed to prevent and deter violence from occurring. Policies of piecemeal concession and selected cooptation have traditionally served as safety valves to siphon off the pressure that builds on discontent and dissatisfaction. The explosion of violence is one important indicator that policies of modification have ultimately failed. The actual mechanics of modification rely on violence only marginally. It is well recognized by elites that disruption of this kind is best reserved as a last resort. The well-documented essay by Ivo and Rosalind Feierabend concludes that there is strong evidence that violence does indeed beget more violence. Elites have generally been quite sensitive to this fact.

In the long run, however, modifying change leads inexorably to violent upheaval. An increasing number of studies indicate that political violence erupts out of situations in which the social, economic, and political positions of the subordinate forces had been improving for some time prior to the crisis point. In other words, violence explodes most often out of a sociopolitical atmosphere in which identifiable programs of modifying change have been under way. It is a fact of history that the reforming monarchs have been the last monarchs. In the contemporary United States, urban violence has tended to break out first in those cities and communities in which certain progressive programs had been initiated in order to modify the conditions of the ghetto dwellers. In essence, processes of modification are developed to buy time. There are few elites that do not have resources to do this for a limited period of time. There are no elites that can do this indefinitely. The price increases with time as the expectations of the subordinate groups heighten indefinitely and the intellectual and physical resources of the elite remain finite.

When the elite responds at the first crisis point by making one more adjustment, violence erupts.[13] Instead of a radical assault on the problem, the elite responds as it always had in the past. It is at this point that the failure to move from the level of modification to transformation carries disastrous results for the dominant force. The longer grievances are bottled up and dissatisfactions bought off, the more explosive is the mixture that ultimately bursts forth. Political violence that follows upon long periods of meticulous modification does not burn itself out as quickly, either. The difficulty in destroying the old power patterns is realized by all, and as a result those who destroy violently often become obsessed with chaos and disruption. In this kind of situation, it is most difficult indeed to move positively in the direction of constructing new social linkages and political relationships.

NOTES

1. Power relations herein refer to those relations in which one individual or group possess the ability to control the behavior of another individual or group. This definition of power is slightly broader than those provided by scholars who have chosen to reword Max Weber's original definition. As such, it most closely approximates the definitions used by Peter Blau, Herbert Simon, Kurt Mayer, and A. F. K. Organski. In all superordinate–subordinate relations, one side enjoys a power advantage over the other side.
2. See Chapter 3 of this volume.
3. The innate needs are the Maslowian physical, social-affectional, self-esteem, and self-actualization needs. The instrumental needs include the needs for understanding, security, and power.
4. See Chapter 3 of this volume. We would add that the relationship is also resisted when it no longer serves the needs of the dominant group.
5. Manfred Halpern, "The Revolution of Modernization," in Roy C. Macridis and Bernard E. Brown, eds., *Comparative Politics: Notes and Readings,* 3rd ed., Homewood, Ill.: Dorsey, 1968, p. 514.
6. See Chapter 1 of this volume.
7. See James A. Bill, "Class Analysis and the Challenge of Change," *Comparative Political Studies, 2* (October 1969), 389–400.
8. The great scholars of politics and society refer to this general policy by a number of different terms. It has been referred to as "political formula," "derivations," "general ethical principles," "ideology," and "political myth," by Mosca, Pareto, Michels, Mannheim, and Lasswell, respectively.
9. See Chapter 1 of this volume.
10. See Chapter 8 of this volume.
11. In the long run, however, the unintended consequences of this policy will lead to the destruction of the particular relationship. Modifications sharpen aspirations.
12. Recent studies of landlord–peasant relations in certain Third World societies document this point.
13. James C. Davies argues that revolutions are most likely to occur in a situation where there is a short period of sharp reversal following a prolonged period of socioeconomic modification. See his "Toward a Theory of Revolution," *American Sociological Review, 6* (February 1962), 5–19. Davies has recently written elsewhere, however, that "in addition to the J curve hypothesis there are alternative and additional explanations for the development of the revolutionary state of mind. It may be that gratifications do not suddenly fall but continue to rise, but not so rapidly as expectations rise, with the result that the gap between the two widens without a downturn in gratifications. There may be cases in which violence breaks out after a steady but too-slow rise in gratifications." See James Chowning Davies, ed., *When Men Revolt and Why,* New York: Free Press, 1971, p. 134.

PART FOUR

Conclusion

We come finally to the important normative question: How are we to decrease the increasing level of violence? Sheldon Levy's essay examines the present state of research on violence and proposes numerous ways to improve and expand our areas of concentration. Levy notes, however, that "these proposals, both long-term and short-term, are obviously preliminary suggestions. The specific forms in which conflict research becomes restructured may be substantially different from those that have been discussed. It is apparent, however, that acceleration in the accumulation of findings is both required and feasible. Because the substance of conflict research may bear so greatly on the human condition, the obligation to make efficient use of the available manpower and technical resources is of utmost importance."

Levy's proposals are necessary, but not sufficient, conditions to help us better understand the motivational and behavioral determinants of violence. If anything emerges from the essays collected in this book, it is the importance of the relationship between the rulers and the ruled, or, in Davies' terms, the dominant and the subordinate. Virtually all the papers in this volume concentrate in one form or another on the nature of this relationship. Some examine the responses of the superordinate, others examine those of the subordinate.

In the introduction to this volume we stated that it presents a variety of approaches to violence, which, collectively, represent a first step in the growing interdisciplinary study of violence. Here a group of scholars have attempted to confront forthrightly the nature and some of the issues that make up the violent politics of the human species. Not only must we continue such interdisciplinary communion, we must ultimately resolve to alter or change the nature of our own relationships with each other. If we refuse to so commit ourselves, those of us represented in this volume, as well as others in the academic community who are engaged in the study of that human behavior we call "violent," will not have to worry that our field of endeavor will fade away. In this spirit, there are few interests of the academic community that deserve obsolescence as much as ours.

11

Improving the State of
Research on Violence

SHELDON G. LEVY
Wayne State University

The major thesis of these comments is that research on human violence
has progressed slowly and that it is both necessary and possible for
more rapid achievements to be obtained. Optimism arises from both
the growing interest on the part of social scientists, as evidenced by the
contributions to this volume, and the rapid increases in relevant technology.

Two assumptions will be made about the philosophy of those who
work on problems of human conflict. The first is that there is generally
a commitment to a social ethic that seeks ways of obtaining justice and
well-being by means that will result in a reduction of the bodily harm
inflicted by one person upon another. The second is that there is a commitment to the scientific value that information should be accumulated,
that the knowledge at one time or from one person should be obtained
in a way that will allow it to be added to that obtained by a second
person-time unit.

This essay will, first, examine briefly the basis for the position that
conflict research has not progressed as far as one might expect. Then
examples of research will be cited to indicate some of the major difficulties that appear to exist within the scientific community of conflict
researchers. Finally, a strategy for more rapid accumulation of knowledge will be proposed.

This paper is a revision of one originally presented at the annual meeting of the
American Association for the Advancement of Science, Boston, December 30,
1969.

CONJECTURES ABOUT THE LACK OF
PROGRESS IN CONFLICT RESEARCH

Although the social sciences are far younger than are the physical sciences, this fact has assumed unjustified importance in explaining the lack of comparability in the states of knowledge. In the first place, a large proportion of all the human population that has ever lived has been alive during the past 75 years. Further, conceptual advances, such as statistical analyses, and technological advances, such as computer hardware, have been developed recently, and have therefore been equally available to all fields. Of course, there are advantages if investigators are spaced over time, since knowledge is accumulated more easily. The work of one can be made available to the next in fairly complete form. Contemporaneous investigators do not have similar opportunities, at least, not if traditional approaches to communication and interaction are followed. One purpose of this presentation will be to examine new relationships that might facilitate a more rapid accumulation of knowledge.

A major reason for the present situation is the lack of a common language in social sciences. The natural sciences have not only utilized mathematics to a far greater extent, but mathematical concepts have developed in conjunction with observations of physical systems. In contrast, social science has underutilized the available mathematical knowledge.

The use of mathematical language does not guarantee complete comparability, since elements in the mathematical model are undefined. Therefore, the same elements can be used to identify different aspects of the real world. However, there are characteristics of mathematical systems that do require great precision. These include the relationships among the elements, the logic that is accepted for deriving conclusions, and the implications of the postulated system, in combination with the accepted logic, for new relationships among the elements (deductions). Obviously, for comparability to exist among investigators, the real world operationalization of the elements must be specified. The acceptance of the logic in combination with specified operations for real-world elements and relations, which are in turn identified with the components of a mathematical system, leads to a universal language of research for which consensus exists about both the consistency of the conclusions within the system and the observations in the real world that are implied by the conclusions.

Another advantage that has been cited for the physical sciences is the closeness of physical concepts to intuitively understood or commonly observed attributes, such as length of weight. On the other hand, concepts such as force and acceleration seem no more intuitive than those of aggression and dominance. It would appear, therefore, that the major difference is in the degree to which ideas have been operationalized rather than in their innate quality.

It is possible that social science is more complex and that this has contributed to the lack of precision. Yet, the greater complexity of human behavior remains to be demonstrated. Organic chemistry—particularly, for example, the study of proteins or enzymes or genes—is extremely complex. In fact, there are probably several natural sciences in which the number of concepts that are related in an integrated theory are far greater than the number that have been used in any particular theory of social behavior. The greater complexity of human behavior may exist, but the point has not yet been reached in its study where this complexity accounts for the current level of knowledge.

A more reasonable explanation is that social science lacks a relevant set of concepts. This may have occurred because of the large number of unobservable and intervening concepts that have been used to account for behavior *in conjunction with* the source of the language for those ideas. The concept of emotions may be an appropriate one to illustrate the problem. A large number of emotions can be named—love, hate, desire, jealousy, fear, anger, calm, excitement, satisfaction, longing, loneliness, happiness, concern, pleasure, haughtiness, guilt, suspicion, hurt, for example. There are at least two possible explanations for why there are so many terms. One is that many of them may refer to the same concept. That is, if real-world operations were defined so that indices could be developed that would be taken as measure of the level of each emotional state, many of these operations might turn out to be identical. In addition, it is also reasonable to suppose that many of the concepts lie on essentially the same dimension; that is, the concepts themselves apply to different levels of an underlying emotional state. It would be as if the physical scientists, rather than labeling a dimension or attribute as speed, used, in a disjunctive fashion, concepts like slow, snailish, turtlish, unmotivated, crawllike, trudging, and, at the other end of the dimension, fast, speedy, lightninglike, quick, and so on, with other points between the end points of the dimension similarly labeled. The confusion that such a use of language would generate within a scientific enterprise is apparent.

It is difficult, however, to understand why social science may have stumbled in this way, compared with physical science. Perhaps the advantage accrued to the physical sciences once the decision was reached not to anthropomorphize. This decision forced the development of a language that was outside the everyday discourse of human interaction. As a result, a more limited number of concepts were developed. Social science, on the other hand, has utilized ordinary language and, consequently, has involved itself with an extremely large number of imprecise ideas. This language may itself have been one of the contributions to the lack of thinking in terms of dimensionality on the part of social scientists, as well as to the slowness with which the concepts have been operationalized. Since intuitive consensus (which is not necessarily precise, as the developments in the legal profession testify) had already been reached, the requirement to operationalize may not have appeared so important. This lack of operationalization may have further contributed to the use of multiple concepts that are basically identical and to the lack of dimensional thinking. In any event, the source of the language is proposed as another factor for limiting the state of social science research.

CURRENT RESEARCH DEFICIENCIES

This section will use actual research studies to examine some of the problems that exist in conflict research. Emphasis will be on empirical rather than interpretive or theoretical studies. The examples selected are from the best research available, since the purpose is not to demonstrate the defects of particular efforts but to indicate the necessity for a new framework to achieve a much-needed higher level of information.

Communication Problems

A prerequisite for data accumulation is adequate communication. Problems in communication can arise from several sources. Investigators may have difficulty in arriving at mutually agreeable definitions; they may view events from different perspectives; and their view may be affected by different filters that intervene between the real-world process and the presentation of results to other investigators.

The Problem of Definition

The problem of definition exists on at least two levels. One is the level of working relations in the real world. The other is the problem of definition among researchers. As to the severity of the problem in the real world, consider that, within the United Nations, countries do not seem to be able to agree that aggression should be defined, or, if it is defined, what the definition should be; or, if agreement is reached on the definition, what legal status the definition should have (*International Conciliation* 1969).

The problem among academic investigators of conflict is aptly discussed in the reviews by Fink (1968) and Converse (1968), which celebrated the first 12 years of the *Journal of Conflict Resolution.*

Several problems in communication result from the idiosyncratic way in which investigators approach their research. This egocentric approach results in an inability to communicate with others. The basis for the lack of communication may arise from the way in which the data universe is partitioned, from the contemporaneous perspective of the researcher, or from his cultural bias.

Partitioning the Data Universe. Perhaps the greatest problem that exists in the attempt to accumulate knowledge is the problem of the partitioning of the data universe. An example will best illustrate the difficulties.

Consider concepts such as the following: political leaders, opinion makers, elites, decision makers, opinion leaders, and, in order to avoid cultural bias, imperialists, warmongers, and capitalists. Each of these labels applies to a different collection of elements. In most cases, the elements overlap, but each definition also includes elements not contained in another. It must be clear that at least two problems exist in the studies that use definitions such as the above.

1. If the definitions are used imprecisely, an enormous number of different words could define exactly (or almost exactly) the same collection of elements.
2. Even if precise definitions are given, the selection of different and overlapping subsets of elements yields an almost infinite number of possible definitions.

Thus, consider a set of 1,000,000 elements. Further, suppose that words are used so that each one differs from all other words by at least 10,000 members. For example, "decision makers" refers to the first 100,000 elements in the collection. Then the next word, say "elites," would have to differ by at least 10,000 elements. These could be 90,000 through 100,000 of the first collection plus 10,000 additional elements, or could include all of the first 100,000 plus 10,000 additional elements. There are 100 units of 10,000 in 1,000,000. Consequently if each definition contained exactly 2 of these units there would be $\binom{100}{2}$ or $99 \times 50 = 4950$ different possible definitions. As a matter of fact, there are many more than this number of possibilities (over 1 billion). The main point is that even precise definitions do not necessarily limit the number of ways in which the data can be examined. Further, current research insufficiently examines the degree of overlap among even the precise definitions.

Of course, nothing above implies that creative examinations of the data should not be considered. In fact, these may be extremely valuable. But without a clear recognition of the problem involved, it is easy to expend resources wastefully in the name of creativity.

At a minimum it seems reasonable to ask that each definition specify the elements that make up a collection, either in terms of their attributes or in terms of the relationships that they have to each other and/or to other elements, human or otherwise. Further, this specification should be in terms of operational definitions so that someone else could, at least theoretically, replicate the study precisely.

Contemporaneity. Related to the problem of partitioning the data set is that of contemporaneity. Inadequate recognition of this problem results in new definitions being developed for each stage in human history. As a result, the past cannot be fully related to the present. Obviously, current intergroup conflict is a part of the available data. In fact, it may contain the most important topics of study, for at least two reasons. First, present events are closest to the future, which is the object of concern. Secondly, information is more complete about the contemporary scene because techniques of communication and collection have greatly improved and because the sophistication of scientific observation has been steadily increasing. Nevertheless, an infinite series of observations can be generated simply by studying contemporary events. It must be apparent that the study of present problems must occur within the context of a framework for the overall evaluation of historical trends in intergroup relations. Without such a concern, the analyses, though interesting and perhaps useful, will not allow the accumulation of sufficient knowledge for application to human events.

Cultural Bias. A third aspect of the problem is that of cultural perspective. The vast majority of research that is now in progress is being conducted by the United States or by English-speaking countries or by Western European countries, or is being funded by the United States. It is quite possible that if various points of view are not adequately represented, certain outcomes will be dictated or will be prevented from appearing, simply because of the vias in the definition of the research problem.

Consequently, the idiosyncratic approach, where idiosyncratic is used to denote an individualistic basis for partitioning the data or defining the set of attributes or relations, creates severe hindrances to the growth of a science. Thus other investigators may examine precisely the same data, but organize it in a different way so that the investigations are not readily comparable. The problem is more severe in the case of essays than in the case of quantitative studies because the former generally select a

greater number of concepts and have many unique or imprecisely understood definitions. Further, each new organization of data becomes a
part of the available pool of material. The idiosyncratic approach therefore suffers from the possibility of circularity, with each new investigator
using the material of those who preceded him and adding his version to
the available sources.

This is not to say that work is not quantitative, that is idiosyncratic,
cratic, that is contemporary, and that is from a particular cultural bias
may not be extremely insightful and valuable. The major point is that
there must be effort beyond this if the next 50 years are to yield applicable
results. (Some examples of insightful discussions that have one or more
of the attributes cited above may be readily given—for example, Deutsch
1962, Bernard, Oteenberg, and Redl 1965, Forster 1966, Hoffer 1966,
Clifford 1969, Gross 1970, Leiden 1969, and Spiegel 1969.)

Perspective of the Investigator. Finally, communication is affected by
the perspective of the investigator. Limited perspectives for the study
of any problem can arise from many sources, such as the information
selector (see Snider 1967 for a recent study of an editor responsible for
the selection of news stories), the physical means of communication
(see Shaw 1967 for a study indicating that the increased use of the
telegraph reduced the bias of newspaper stories about the presidential
campaigns in the 1880s), and the social situation or the discipline of
the investigator. This last problem is demonstrated in a number of different writings. Thus, Grier and Cobbs (1968) clearly indicate how
psychoanalytic interpretations are affected by knowledge of the social
history of blacks; Tilly (1969) indicates how history has been distorted
by perception of events from the top, so that records of conflict are
heavily weighted toward those affecting the upper strata of society;
Coser (1966) shows how the interpretation of the basis of revolutionary
activity is affected by the academic orientation of the observer; Berger
(1968) shows how the perceptions of the courts and of the justice that
the poor receive are influenced by a personal experience in the courts;
and Reiss (1968) shows how perceptions of the amount of police brutality, especially toward blacks, are influenced by the point of view of
the observer.

Even in the presumably controlled environment of the laboratory,
cues may be transmitted from the experimenter to the subject and consequently bias the results (see Duncan, Rosenberg, and Finkelstein
1969, and Evans and Rosenthal 1969, for brief research illustrations).

Obviously, perspective cannot be eliminated. But its role must be
more adequately recognized if rapid progress in conflict research is to
be attained.

Accumulation Problems

While communication is a necessary condition for data accumulation, it is not a sufficient one. Examination of current research indicates several additional problems that have restricted data accumulation. The problems that will be discussed include the need for precise definition of the data set, the importance of data for theory development, the need for continuity in research effort as well as the need for availability of data that have been collected, and the need to coordinate experimentation with real-world processes.

Coping with the Data Universe. In order for data to be useful, it must be specified precisely. Without such specification, the concept of data is itself ambiguous. For the most part, the components are commonly understood, although the brief discussion that follows will indicate that several requirements for data specification are frequently not met.

1. *The time frame.* All information is collected at a particular time and represents information that existed at a particular time. These attributes must be specified if additional research is not to be unnecessarily duplicative.

2. *The data source.* Each source—personal interview, participant observation, analysis of written documents, and so forth—must be specified.

3. *Filters.* A reporter who sees a riot is a filter. If he writes a news story that is not reproduced in its entirety, then at least one other human filter, the editor, has interceded. If a researcher then analyzes the published story, he becomes a third filter.

In addition to filters, there are physical transformations, such as writing, typesetting, printing, cardpunches, magnetic tape images, and analytic transformations, such as quantification, algebraic transformations, and the application of other mathematical procedures to the data.

The physical transformation is probably not of critical interest although it does restrict the nature of the information and may unconsciously affect the filtering process itself.

The initial human filters are important but infrequently studied. The researcher tries to be an objective filter by specifying completely both his observational procedures and the way in which he examines the data.

Even the specification of observational procedures has great difficulties, as anthropologists and public opinion surveyors have discovered.

The analytic procedures, however, are rather precise: correlation, analysis of variance, factor analysis, and so forth. While these procedures are well specified where appropriate, the evaluation of the same data from other analytic points of view is infrequent. Consequently, the restrictions that are imposed on the data by the analysis itself are not usually considered.

4. *The sample.* Every collection of data that is to be used to predict the future must be considered a sample of the possible observations. Further, in the strict sense, it cannot be considered a simple random sample of the universe of interest, because every element would be required to have an equal chance of being included. Obviously, future elements have no chance of entering the sample. Consequently, the assumption that there are a set of processes that are continuous through time is critical. (This continuity does not have to be equated with constancy but rather with orderliness.) In any event, the sample of elements studied must be clearly specified.

Although this may seem rather obvious, it is not. An easy illustration, and perhaps the most common, arises from interviewer surveys.

Generally it is assumed that the sample consists of the group of individuals that have been selected. But this is not so. An interview requires two people. Consequently, the interviewers are also a sample, but they are rarely seen as representative of a larger group. Nevertheless, if the results are to be "generalizable," the interviewers must be representative of others who might have conducted the interviews. Even if the interviewers are considered to be representative of others who could be similarly trained, the problem would not be solved, because the interviewer–interviewee situation is a social unit of two, not a group of two independent individuals. (As a matter of fact, interviewers are undoubtedly not representative of all who might be similarly trained. At most, some subset of interviewers may be representative of American, middle-aged, white females with at least a high school education.) The social situation of the interview, while recognized, has not been specified; that is, the relationships between the two elements have not been fully determined.

The above are merely examples of the considerations that are necessary before an adequate statement of the data that was collected can be given and, therefore, before a basis for the accumulation of knowledge can be obtained.

The above presupposes a particular orientation to the way in which a study is conducted. The proposal here is that the above requirements, as well as additional ones, must become the basis for the large-scale research effort that is needed.

The Need for Data. Empirical evidence frequently modifies long-held or commonly held theoretical beliefs. Without such evidence, theories may be perpetuated that are not useful for understanding conflict behavior. Two examples will readily demonstrate the influence of data on commonly held ideas.

Wolfgang (1966) has argued that "clearly, however, violence is deplored by all who have a stake in existing society. Hence, it should follow that the greater participation which members of society have in its maintenance, control, and direction, the less vulnerable that society will be to the emergence of collective violence designed to alter or overthrow it" (p. 5).

This statement is one with which most social scientists would be inclined to agree.

It is, therefore, surprising to read that, based on an actual study (Steiner 1969), such may not always be the case. One of the hypotheses obtained from the literature, with which the data in Steiner's study of Switzerland were consistent, was that *"democratic systems tend to regulate their political conflicts with relatively little violence . . .* if the political participation of the simple members of the system is relatively low" (p. 296). Further, the case of Switzerland indicated that relatively little violence occurred in the Swiss democratic system if the elites of the different subcultures interacted relatively often, out of public visibility and informally, and if political role-holders changed relatively seldom.

Admittedly, Switzerland may not be a nation from which generalizations can legitimately be made. Further, data based on participant observation may not be completely objective. And, finally, the issues that were studied may not have been particularly critical, either for Switzerland or for other nations (financial aid to cantonal universities, the founding of a new university, and a program for a federal election).

Another example will further illustrate this point. Wolfgang and Ferracuti (1967) have published an extensive review of the literature of criminology and have developed a theory called the subculture of violence. The United States is one of the cultures within which the subculture of violence is presumed to exist. Among the attributes of the subculture are a willingness to resort to violence in a wide variety of situations, the presence of a wider cultural norm of nonviolence, and the lack of feelings of guilt on the part of members of the subculture because they do not view the use of violence as illicit conduct.

However, Miller (1966) studied corner gangs in the middle and late 1950s. An extensive array of data was collected based on field-recorded behavior, field-recorded crimes, and court-recorded crimes. The major impact of the study as it relates to the thesis of the subculture of violence is that violence among city gangs is a stereotype that is largely contradicted by the evidence. For example, gang fights appeared to be mostly ritualistic and resulted infrequently in actual combat. Although gang members were not as reluctant to engage in individual as in collective fighting, most assaults involved no weapons of any kind, and the use of firearms was extremely rare. Further, there was little distinction between races in the rate of violence, and the violence rate decreased rapidly after the age of 18.

Another study, this one of blacks, by Pettigrew and Spier (1962), indicates that homicide rates are more likely to result from a homicidal culture as opposed to a subculture, especially when this is combined with high social change.

Of course, the above studies do not disconfirm the theoretical ideas that have been presented. The main purpose, however, is to illustrate the basic importance of readily available objective data in any strategy for the complete understanding of violence.

The Need for Continuity. Data collection in itself is not sufficient to insure the development of an integrated body of knowledge. There must also be continuity in research. Frequently, in conflict research, work of major significance has been performed but not adequately pursued by others. Although leaving additional research to others is a favorite concluding idea in reports of social scientists, there are instances where classical work has been published and then not extended. In fact, social science research is far more characterized by individual investigators who extend their own work through a series of steps than by groups of scholars interacting to advance a research idea. The picture is not completely one-sided, and both negative and positive examples will be given.

One of the classic works in quantitative historical analysis is *The Achieving Society* (McClelland 1961). Although many studies have been conducted on the achievement motive, the contribution of *The Achieving Society* is in the relationship that is examined between psychological concepts derived from experimental study and the economic activity of past societies. The creativity in the research comes not only from relating the experimental psychology to the historical activity of societies, but also from the inventive methods used to measure both the psychological and the economic variables. For example, Berlew, as reported by McClelland, obtained levels of need achievement from representative writing of ancient Greeks and measured economic activity by examining the area over which the remains of jars used for trading wine and oil were found. Equally creative was the measure of need achievement in pre-Incan Peru through the examination of ceramic designs and of the economic activity by measuring the volume of public buildings in each period.

The precise relation of the psychological achievement motive to the societal economic activity remains open to question (Brown 1965). McClelland feels that the evidence indicates achievement motivation precedes economic development; he has extended his work to the real world by trying to increase the achievement motive in entrepreneurs (Wallace 1969).

The important point for this discussion is not, however, the status of the theory of the achievement motive or even the additional experimentation that has continued using the achievement concept. Instead, the greatest lack of continuity derives from the failure by other investigators to extend the historical material and, even more importantly, from the lack of research that relates the achievement-economic characteristics of a society to its levels of conflict and modes of conflict resolution.

An even more current example is provided by the study of the Vietnam war by Milstein and Mitchell (1968). This study is comprehensive in scope as well as extensive in its quantitative analyses. Military, economic, public opinion, and communications variables were all examined. Among the variables measured were North Vietnamese and Vietcong military behavior, U.S. military effort, U.S. casualties, North Vietnamese and Vietcong attrition, South Vietnamese casualties, U.S. domestic support for the Johnson administration, Communist morale and support (based on the number of Vietcong and North Vietnamese defectors), confidence in the government of South Vietnam (as measured by "the black market dollar value of the piastre, hand-payment in Saigon," p. 169), international confidence in the government of South Vietnam, and the communications variables.

The analyses then involved correlational procedures including lagged correlations of up to 5 months and stepwise multiple regression. In addition, future data points were predicted from both real and previously predicted values.

One of the most valuable sets of results from the study consisted of tests of models of the war as determined from the communications data of policy makers. Some illustrations will indicate the value of the research effort:

We find no empirical evidence that the change in U.S. commitment predicts the change in Communist troop commitments (p. 176).

It appears that U.S. bombing of North Vietnam may physically decrease infiltration but escalation of the bombing is matched by North Vietnamese *escalation* of troop commitments (p. 176).

We find empirically that the more the U.S. bombs North Vietnam and escalates the bombing the *less* the North Vietnamese desire to negotiate (p. 178).

Further, it appeared that increased ARVN activity increased confidence in the South Vietnam government.

This sample of findings indicates the importance of the research. However, after the study was conducted, there were importance changes in the Vietnam war. A new administration came into power, and a policy of gradual withdrawal and Vietnamization was undertaken. But the lack of research continuity is evident in the failure of investigators to update the quantitative study of the Vietnam conflict.

A third example contains some, almost accidental, continuity, but again illustrates how often good ideas die. Shils and Janowitz (1954) made an important contribution to the study of army combat units in wartime. One of their conclusions was that the primary group was extremely important for maintaining cohesion in the Wehrmacht under battle conditions. Since World War II, there has been no cessation of international hostility. The United States itself has been involved in major wars in Korea and Vietnam. However, the Korean War brought an interest in brainwashing (see, for example, Kinkead 1958, and *The Journal of Social Issues* 1957), and Vietnam brought forth little analysis of combat units except for a study by Moskos (1969). It would seem that the area of investigation analyzed in detail by Shils and Janowitz is of great importance for trying to distinguish the reasons why nations decide upon war from those that lead men to fight them.

Before concluding this section, it is appropriate to note that some classic work on the study of intergroup violence does have heuristic value. Perhaps the most notable example is that of Richardson (1960a, 1960b). Undoubtedly, the deserved popularity of Richardson's work has been aided by Rapoport's (1957, 1960) clear exposition of its elements. In any event, the original studies have led to new analyses of the data (Horvath and Foster 1963) as well as elaborations of the basic model (Pruitt, 1969). In addition, the success of the approach has undoubtedly had a great impact on the subsequent quantitative study of international relations.

The Need for Data Availability. A significant contribution to continuity would be made if data collected by one investigator were available to others. The problem of data availability, as with all the problems being discussed, is not independent of the others. The major point is that even the best research that has been conducted could have been greatly extended had the data been publicly available. Thus, the problem of data availability is seen to be most closely related to the problem of research continuity.

Nothing in this discussion is meant to imply that researchers have deliberately withheld information. The point is that present methods of data publication are insufficient for the rapid and widespread investigation of problems.

In many studies, far more data are collected than will ever be used by the principle investigators. If these data could be utilized by others, the study of the problem under investigation could be rapidly extended.

The work of North, Brody, and their collaborators is an example. Although this material has been elaborated upon by those who have been closely connected with the research, other independent investigators apparently have not availed themselves of the data.

Another example would be the work of Singer and Small (1966a, 1966b). These investigators collected information on international alliances from 1815 to 1945 and related this information to the international conflict behavior of the nations. Even though they have published a complete list of the alliance information, they remain the only investigators who have used the data for research purposes.

Similarly, a series of investigators have done a great deal of work on the quantitative study of both internal violence and internation conflict, but, for the most part, their data remain independent collections. Thus Tilly (1969) has collected information on internal violence in France over the past 100 years, Levy (1969) has done the same for the United States over the past 150 years, Brown (1969) has studied vigilante movements in the United States, Gurr (1969) has made a comparative study of internal violence during the 1960s, Feierabend and his collaborators (1969) have done the same for the world between 1948 and 1965, Leiden has collected 1100 incidents of assassination attempts worldwide since 1917 and published the list in Kirkham, Levy, and Crotty (1970), and Rummel (1964, 1966) and Tanter (1966) have collected and analyzed information on both inter- and intranation violence. The above, of course, is only a partial list of the individuals who have collected data and published analyses.

The point, however, is that not only are investigators generally alone in the utilization of data they have collected, even when it is published, but data collections rarely are added to in a usable form by others. The Milstein and Mitchell (1968) example cited above is an important instance.

The data availability and research continuity problems are among the most important ones that must be considered in any strategy for the study of violence.

The Need for Relating Experimental Studies to the Real World. Experimental studies are extremely valuable. In addition to operationalizing variables, the experiment studies their relationships when other factors are controlled. But the control aspects of the experiment also create difficulties, since actual processes may result from the interaction of a large number of variables. In addition, the selection of the variables for manipulation in the experimental setting is based on intuitive understandings or upon agreement among a large number of investigators. There is a necessity to examine real-world events to determine whether the variables that have been selected are, in fact, the important ones.

Although the usefulness of experimental studies is evident, in many instances large numbers of studies have been performed in the laboratory using concepts that are extremely relevant to the problem of international conflict, but the studies (and the concepts) have not been adequately extended to the real world.

Exceptions to this deficiency are worth noting. The work by McClelland has already been discussed. Similarly, Osgood, Suci, and Tannenbaum's (1957) research on the semantic differential has led to a vast amount of activity, much of it relevant to the study of human conflict through the medium of quantitative content analysis.

More directly related to the study of conflict is the work of North, Brody, Holsti, Zaninovich, Choucri, and others on the perceptions of decision makers under stress. This series of studies has made major contributions to the study of conflict in several ways. First, the original research was initiated after an exhaustive examination of the experimental research in psychology on perceptions under stress. Then, a set of hypotheses were developed about how decision makers would react under stress. In order to test these hypotheses, documents produced by decision makers in World War I were analyzed using quantitative content analysis. Among the major findings was the confirmation of the hypothesis that if a nation perceives itself threatened by another, it will respond in a similarly threatening way.

Thus the arms conflict spiral prior to the outbreak of World War I that has been studied by Richardson (1960a) was confirmed by the escalation of hostile perceptions. Further, "input mobilization and perceptions of the other alliance as hostile are positively correlated ($r = 0.63, p < 0.01$). The correlation between one's expressions of hostility toward the other alliance and output mobilization also were positively correlated . . . ($r = 0.53, p < 0.01$)" (North, Brody, and Holsti 1964, pp. 12–13). Thus the study showed a relation between perceptions of hostility by key decision makers and the behavior of the nation as measured by the mobilization of troops.

The Cuban crisis afforded the researchers an opportunity to examine an international escalation that did not result in conflict and to compare it with the escalation to war that occurred in the two World War cases. (Holsti, Brody, and North 1965). Again, the documents generated by the decision makers (both U.S. and U.S.S.R.) were analyzed using a quantitative content analysis. The major discovery, and an extremely important one, was that whereas perceptions of Dual Alliance decision makers narrowed under stress in 1914, the U.S.S.R. and the United States reacted "appropriately" to each other in 1962. Examination of the case study material indicated several reasons for the approach that the United States took. First, decisions appeared to be based on a group decision-making process; secondly, President Kennedy kept his options open while at the same time trying to perceive what the Soviet reaction might be; and, thirdly, the lowest level of violence was decided upon, with threats used instead of violent actions. To what extent these changes were directly due to the awareness by decision makers of the capabilities of nuclear weapons is difficult to determine. No doubt it was substantial.

Other studies by this group of investigators have also been published. Thus, North and Choucri (1968) examined the tensions that preceded World War I by examining gross societal characteristics of European nations from 1870 through 1914. The basic hypothesis of the study was that "the defense allocations of states are responsive to distances between them on certain dimensions of national capability" (p. 130). Although the results are not definitive, the study is important because it represents an attempt to continue the study of the international system during a specific time period.

The specific use of quantitative content analysis was also utilized by Choucri (1969), who examined the attitudinal orientation of the non-aligned nations of India, Egypt, and Indonesia.

Finally, the study by Brody, Benham, and Milstein (1967) should be noted. First, a set of hypotheses about the international system was developed based on the existing literature. These primarily involved perceptions of threat on the part of decision makers and the relation of these perceptions to behavior. A simulated study was then performed using experimental subjects to test the hypotheses. This study illustrates the creative development of experimentation to test real-world variables that cannot readily be tested by examining the complex international system. Since the variables were primarily psychological in nature, the use of experimental subjects at early stages of the research is all the more appropriate.

The above examples contrast sharply with the usual procedure in social science, at least among psychologists. It is probably true that, within any particular subfield of psychology, the probability that a researcher will choose to investigate a problem is directly proportional to the ease with which the data can be obtained. Consequently, if the separate field of conflict studies is considered, it may be the case that, among psychologists, a greater number of people and a greater amount of time and resources are devoted to the study of experimental games than to all other conflict research combined. While this may be an exaggeration (it depends greatly on what is defined as conflict research) it is worth noting that the *Journal of Conflict Resolution,* an interdisciplinary journal, during the three-year period, 1969–1971, published as many research articles dealing with experimental games as with all other approaches combined. Further, in Volumes 7 through 16 (1967–1970) of the *Peace Research Society Papers,* also an interdisciplinary journal dealing with peace research, about 15–20 percent of the studies were devoted to game-theoretic material.

This is not to say that a great deal of interesting work has not been conducted (for example, Deutsch and Krauss 1962, and Morgan and Sawyer, 1969). But the innovative thinking in such studies as those by Schelling (1958), by Isard and Smith (1967), Isard (1968), and Howard (1968a, 1968b) have been too infrequent. Consequently, the real world has only occasionally been the source of experimental design, and the application of the implications of the experimental results to real problems has similarly been insufficient. Obviously, the experimental approach is an important one; therefore, the relation between it and real-world problems is potentially extremely valuable.

Use of Mathematical Models. Although operationalization of concepts and controlled observations are important aspects of the scientific endeavor, additional precision is obtained through the use of mathematical models. One example will be given for illustration. Naroll (1967) studied the cycles of world powers over a 5000-year period in order to try to determine when a world state might be expected. One of the bases for the research was Naroll's argument that the historical data for wars and boundaries should be accurate because it is difficult to keep this information secret.

The problem of boundaries between nations was independently examined by Dacey (1970). His examination was completely abstract and was based on the mathematical model of random walks. Both one-dimensional and two-dimensional cases were examined. It was possible for Dacey to show that, under certain conditions, boundary shifts would eventually lead to a single-nation world. This, then, was a mathematical examination of the problem that Naroll had studied empirically.

In both of the above cases, the concept of boundary was extremely important. It was, therefore, enlightening (to say the least) to learn from Nystuen (1967) about the line paradox. Basically, this paradox states that, as the unit of measurement gets smaller and smaller, the length of an empirical line (such as a boundary) gets larger and larger. Consequently, apparently because of different units of measurement, "to Yugoslavians their boundary with Greece is 262.1 kilometers long. To the Greeks the same boundary is 236.6 kilometers long" (p. 118). Nystuen describes how Perkal fortunately solved the paradox by using a concept he called an epsilon circle to define an epsilon length of a line.

Thus, the evaluation of the empirical work of Naroll has been refined in both conceptualization and rigor by the mathematical studies that have been cited.

Current Contributions

Several contributions to this volume are positive illustrations of the framework described above. For example, the Frolich and Oppenheimer paper illustrates quite clearly the power of even a limited mathematical model, particularly in generating precise deductions. Of course, many variables have not been included, and the real-world operations that define concepts such as costs, benefits, and taxes have not been specified. Nevertheless, the model allows one to examine the logical interrelationships and make predictions to actual events based on deductions within the abstract system. Further, as the authors indicate in their conclusion, the same abstract model might be applied to parking in New York or to riot behavior. The major point, therefore, within the framework of this paper, is not the limitations of the ideas, but the power available through their precise formulation.

The Berkowitz paper illustrates several positive approaches to the study of violence. First, the concept of aggression is operationalized through the experimental work. Second, many factors that might affect aggressive behavior have been carefully examined including justification for the aggression and identification with the aggressor. Third, the experimental study of aggression has a continuous history through the efforts of Berkowitz, his coworkers, and others in psychology. Finally, and perhaps most importantly, the consonance of experimental findings with real-world events and processes has been examined. It is this extension that will allow a determination of both the importance of the experimental variables and the extent to which the relationships observed in the laboratory are maintained in the more complex real world. The contribution of the research effort to the scientific understanding of conflict is obvious.

Finally, Tilly's research illustrates several facets of a more complete approach to the study of conflict. The historical perspective overcomes the problem of contemporaneity present in much work. Further, through examination of France rather than the United States, cultural bias is at least attenuated. Although the specifics are not defined in this particular paper, it is apparent that a well-specified sample has resulted in a data pool that other investigators may utilize and to which they may add. However, the major contribution arises from the collection of the data itself. As Tilly points out, traditional sociological analyses have claimed that urbanization was a causative factor leading to domestic violence. His study demonstrates, through the collection of actual data and correlational analyses, that the previous theoretical formulations are not supported. Further, this judgment is derived utilizing an operational definition of urbanization in terms of population in the cities, increases in urban population, and net migration into the department. The result of the investigation is an hypothesis that a critical factor associated with domestic violence is the integration of the individual into organizations. This hypothesis is consistent with the Theory of Reduced Alternatives (Levy 1970), which was developed from a national attitude study of adults in the United States. The theory proposes that the critical factor that leads to opposition to repressive governmental policies is the availability, through previous actions, of a wide range of behavioral responses. It seems quite possible that integration into organizations increases the range of behavioral alternatives.

This brief examination of three papers in the present volume reinforces the view that significant research on human conflict is being conducted. At the same time, these papers illustrate the fact that separate investigators participate in only a portion of the total strategy that is required for rapid advances in the field. The next section will consider a possible framework for conflict research.

A STRATEGY FOR THE STUDY OF VIOLENCE

If a research program is to be developed that will yield important results within a relatively short time, current procedures within the scientific community will need to be substantially altered. The present methods of information accumulation, as indicated in the review, are too inefficient to yield the required insights in the time that is available.

However, even with the development of different research procedures, no framework can guarantee success. Some of the reasons have been discussed, and they include the following possibilities:

1. The state of the universe may be under constant change by virtue of the availability of the new information. Since each reorientation of information is a change in state, it follows that the definition of the universe changes simply by virtue of the research that accumulates. If, for example, new relations, or relations among new groups of elements, develop as a result of the information, it may never be possible to study intergroup conflict adequately. Thus one major difference between the study of human behavior and the study of other aspects of the environment is that in the former case the information is processed by the elements under study and they may, as a result, be changed.

2. Related to the above, and a specific example of the problem, is the possibility that motives such as power, greed, and aggression so dominate human interactions that their satisfaction will simply become easier to express as more knowledge about them becomes available.

3. Both of the above points are relevant to the possibility that one society will so dominate the research that biased results will be inevitable.

It is apparent, therefore, that several assumptions must be made in order to proceed logically:

1. A reasonable probability exists that sufficient time and resources are available to yield effective results.
2. The accumulation of knowledge will not continuously alter basic modes of human interaction in unpredictable ways.
3. The public availability of knowledge will reduce the possibility of its misuse, compared with either the private accumulation of information or the total lack of such knowledge.
4. A sufficient number of points of view can be defined and studied to prevent the domination of one self-interested point of view in the accumulation of information.

The assumptions will be made and the discussion will proceed.

Components of the Framework

Fortunately, there are some ideals commonly held by members of the scientific community upon which a new approach can capitalize. These include the general agreement that research findings should be made publicly available as quickly as possible and the feeling that, while replication of results is desirable, two investigators should not merely duplicate each other's work. However, as discussed earlier, these ideals have not been most effectively achieved for several reasons, including the inadequate utilization of present technology and the lack of public availability of much of the data.

The major reason for proposing the framework is to develop a strategy that can have some favorable impact on the outcome. Ultimately, this means that decision makers in some way must be affected by the results. There is never, of course, any guarantee that those in power will use the results of the research to a desired end. One conceivable answer is to build into the research design itself questions that deal with influencing decision makers. This does not seem like a real solution since, in effect, it would make the researchers the decision makers and consequently merely set the problem back one step.

It seems reasonable, therefore, at least for the short term to set the goals somewhat more modestly. This can be accomplished by developing the state of knowledge to the point where accurate predictions about future events can be made.

Just as the research should use operational definitions, the evaluation also should be operational. Clearly, the best test of the increase in knowledge would be the extent to which conflict is reduced. Since this assumes that progressions in the state of knowledge become utilized by decision makers, this itself cannot initially be a basis for evaluation of research progress.

Instead, the proposal is that expert predictors be used to predict the occurrence and intensity of future conflict. Increased ability to predict would be taken as evidence of increased knowledge about events. Although it is possible to build predictability into the model that is used to conduct research, and this is the preferred approach, early stages of prediction will be based on so many studies that human judgment will be required to amalgamate and weight the various results.

Obviously, improvements in predictability will require as much precision about the basis for the predictions as will the research itself.

Ultimately, of course, a logical deductive field theory of conflict is required to remove the problem of human error in utilizing the current state of knowledge to make predictions. For this reason expert predictors are considered necessary on an interim basis.

The final problem is how a framework can be defined that capitalizes on the commonly held ideals and that will minimize biases, utilize technology, make data publicly available, and incorporate the application of the knowledge. Several requirements of such an effort seem apparent, such as:

1. The allocation of large amounts of resources.
2. The agreement on the part of a large number of researchers to work together at an interdisciplinary level of discourse.
3. The agreement of investigators to pool their data as it is collected.

4. International representation in the program at all levels of research and funding.

Assuming that such requirements were met, it is still necessary for there to be a system of coordination among investigators. The following ideas are an admittedly conjectural set that are offered to increase discussion concerning the best way to achieve the desired goals.

At least four divisions of labor are envisaged among the senior staff. One group would be the Formulators. These people would work with the second group, the Researchers, to operationalize concepts that are the basis of the research. The third group would be the Expert Predictors. The fourth group might be called the Field Theorists.

All data would be stored in a central facility. Researchers would use terminal facilities that connected with the central facility. All studies would be included in the central file. Among the aspects of a study that would be stored would be (1) the hypotheses that were the basis for the effort; (2) the complete description of the data that were collected, including the source and the sample; and (3) a description of the analytic techniques that were used, as well as the results. Since the data would be entered into the central file, they would become immediately available for use by other researchers. Because the hypotheses of the investigator responsible for the data collection would also be in the central file, secondary investigators would not duplicate research efforts.

Before an investigator actually began a study, either of original data collection or of secondary analyses, he would, through his terminal facility, obtain a record of the relevant hypotheses that had been tested, the data that had been collected, and the results. In other words, a quantitative procedure would be developed that would amount to an instant search of the literature. In addition, the Field Theorists could enter into the central data file judgments about the following:

1. Additional data that needed to be collected to test hypotheses that had already been conceived.
2. Research needed to test hypotheses that were deduced from logical models that had been developed by them or others.
3. "Critical experiment" research that is needed to choose between two or more logical models.

Thus the archiving system would not only be a storehouse of experiments, results, and data, but also a source of experimental questions and designs. Of course, other means of communication among Formulators, Researchers, Expert Predictors, and Field Theorists would also occur to aid in the design of the most important research. The above discussion has focused on those aspects that would be primarily contained in the central storage facility. This technique could also be used to allow more efficient communication among the various personnel.

Short-Term Efforts
The above strategy requires a major commitment of time, resources, and personnel. Consequently, the full effort is probably a goal toward which scholars of conflict might work. However, significant contributions toward that goal can be made now. For example, courses in conflict studies can be offered by individuals at various university centers. Such courses have several advantages. As more students enroll in such courses, demand for persons who can teach them increases, thus encouraging the development of graduate programs. In addition, courses induce the writing of textbooks, which can serve the function of integrating the field of study. Once faculty appointments in conflict studies become available, so does research time for the staff.

Focused conferences also can serve useful purposes. These conferences could be aimed toward several contributions. For example, researchers engaged in substantively similar fields could develop agreements in operational definitions. Or they could design a series of studies that were seen as contributing to the development of the field and that would yield data that would allow a choice to be made between conflicting theoretical views. Another goal of a conference would be to formalize theoretical ideas. These models would then yield deductions that would imply research investigations that would provide evidence of the appropriateness of the models.

Computer systems already exist among limited sets of institutions, and these should be used as completely as possible.

International cooperation and interaction might be provided by the publication of journals in more than one language, either through simultaneous translations in one edition or through the publication of several editions in different languages.

It should also be possible to encourage articles of broader coverage by having a process of sequential addition. Thus, when an author submitted an article, it would be passed on to another researcher, who might indicate other relevant data, or propose theoretical ideas that might explain the observations, or develop a logical model that would incorporate the findings. Several additional contributions to an original article might be allowed.

These proposals, both long-term and short-term, are obviously preliminary suggestions. The specific forms in which conflict research becomes restructured may be substantially different from those that have been discussed. It is apparent, however, that acceleration in the accumulation of findings is both required and feasible. Because the substance of conflict research may bear so greatly on the human condition, the obligation to make efficient use of the available manpower and technical resources is of utmost importance.

REFERENCES

Berger, C. J., "Law, Justice and the Poor," *Proceedings: The Academy of Political Science, 29,* No. 1 (1968), 52-59.

Bernard, V. W., P. Ottenberg, and F. Redl, "Dehumanization: A Composite Psychological Defense in Relation to Modern War," in M. Schwebel, ed., *Behavioral Science and Human Behavior,* Palo Alto, Calif.: Science and Behavior Books, 1965.

Brody, R. A., A. H. Benham, and J. S. Milstein, "Hostile International Communication, Arms Production, and Perception of Threat: A Simulation Study," *Peace Research Society (International) Papers, 7* (1967), 15-40.

Brown, R. M., "The American Vigilante Tradition," in H. D. Graham and T. R. Gurr, eds., *Violence in America,* New York: Praeger, 1969, pp. 154-226.

Brown, R., *Social Psychology,* New York: Free Press, 1965.

Choucri, N., "The Perceptual Base of Nonalignment," *Journal of Conflict Resolution, 13,* No. 1 (1969), 57-74.

Clifford, C. M., "A Vietnam Reappraisal," *Foreign Affairs, 47,* No. 4 (1969), 602-622.

Converse, E., "The War of All Against All: A Review of the Journal of Conflict Resolution, 1957-1968," *Journal of Conflict Resolution, 12,* No. 4 (1968), 471-532.

Coser, L., "Some Social Functions of Violence," *Annals of the American Academy of Political and Social Science, 364* (1966), 8-18.

Dacey, M. F., "A Probability Model for the Rise and Decline of States," *Peace Research Society (International) Papers, 14* (1970), 147-153.

Deutsch, M., "Psychological Alternatives to War," *Journal of Social Issues, 18,* No. 2 (1962), 97-119.

Deutsch, M. and R. M. Krauss, "Studies of Interpersonal Bargaining," *Journal of Conflict Resolution, 6,* No. 1 (1962), 52-76.

Duncan, S., Jr., M. Rosenberg, and J. Finkelstein, "Nonverbal Communication of Experimenter Bias," *Proceedings of the 77th Annual Convention of the American Psychological Association, 4* (1969), 369-70.

Evans, J., and R. Rosenthal, "Interpersonal Self-fulfilling Prophecies: Further Extrapolations from the Laboratory to the Classroom," *Proceedings of the 77th Annual Convention of the American Psychological Association, 4* (1969), 371-372.

Feierabend, I., R. Feierabend, and B. Nesvold, "Social Change and Political Violence: Cross-National Patterns," in Graham and Gurr, eds., *Violence in America,* pp. 632–687.

Fink, C., "Some Conceptual Difficulties in the Theory of Social Conflict," *Journal of Conflict Resolution, 12,* No. 4 (1968), 412–460.

Forester, A., "Violence on the Fanatical Left and Right," *Annals of the Academy of Political and Social Science, 364* (1966), 141–148.

Grier, W., and P. Cobbs, *Black Rage,* New York: Basic Books, 1968.

Gross, F., "Political Violence and Terror in 19th and 20th Century Russia and Eastern Europe," in J. Kirkham, S. Levy, and W. Crotty, eds., *Assassination and Political Violence,* New York: Praeger, 1970, 519–598.

Gurr, T., "Comparative Study of Civil Strife," in Graham and Gurr, eds., pp. 572–631.

Hoffer, E., *The True Believer,* New York: Harper & Row, 1966.

Holsti, O., R. Brody, and R. North, "Measuring Affect and Action in International Reaction Models, Empirical Materials from the 1962 Cuban Crisis," *Peace Research Society (International) Papers, 2* (1965), 1970–190.

Horvath, W., and C. Foster, "Stochastic Models of War Alliances," *Journal of Conflict Resolution, 7,* No. 2 (1963), 110–116.

Howard, N., "A Method for Metagame Analysis of Political Problems," *Peace Research Society (International) Papers, 9* (1968a) 47–67.

_____ , "Metagame Analysis of Cietnam Policy," *Peach Research Society (International) Papers, 10* (1968b), 126–142.

International Conciliation, Issues before the 24th General Assembly, Carnegie Endowment of International Peace. *574* (September 1969).

Isard, W., "The Veto-Incremax Procedure: Potential for Vietnam Conflict Resolution," *Peace Research Society (International) Papers, 10* (1968), 148–162.

Isard, W., and T. Smith, "On Social Decision Procedures for Conflict Situations," *Peace Research Society (International) Papers, 7* (1967), 1–30.

Journal of Social Issues, 13, No. 3 (1957). Entire issue on brainwashing.

Kinkead, E., *In Every War but One,* New York: Norton, 1958.

Kirkham, J., S. G. Levy, and W. Cortty, eds., *Assassination and Political Violence,* New York: Praeger, 1970.

Leiden, C., "Assassination in the Middle East," in Kirkham, Levy, and Crotty, eds., *Assassination and Political Violence,* pp. 689–699.

Levy, S. G., "A 150-year Study of Political Violence in the United States," in Graham and Gurr, eds., pp. 84–100.

_____ , "The Psychology of Political Activity," *Annals of the American Academy of Political and Social Science, 391* (1970), 83–96.

McClelland, D., *The Achieving Society,* New York: Van Nostrand, 1961.

Miller, W., "Violent Crimes in City Gangs," *Annals of the American Academy of Political and Social Science, 364* (1966), 96–112.

Milstein, J., and W. Mitchell, "Dynamics of the Vietnam Conflict: A Quantitative Analysis and Predictive Simulation," *Peace Research Society (International) Papers, 10* (1968), 1963–213.

Morgan, W., and J. Sawyer, "How Presumed Disadvantage Hurts Cooperation," *Proceedings of the 77th Annual Convention of the American Psychological Association, 4* (1969), 403–404.

Moskos, C., "Why Men Fight—American Combat Soldiers in Vietnam," *Trans Action, 7,* No. 1 (1969), 13–23.

Naroll, R., "Imperial Cycles and World Order," *Peace Research Society (International) Papers, 7* (1967), 83–101.

North, R., R. Brody, and O. Holsti, "Some Empirical Data on the Conflict Spiral," *Peace Research Society (International) Papers, 1* (1964), 1–14.

North, R., and N. Choucri, "Background Conditions to the Outbreak of the First World War," *Peace Research Society (International) Papers, 9* (1968), 125–137.

Nystuen, J., "Boundary Shapes and Boundary Problems," *Peace Research Society (International) Papers, 7* (1967), 197–128.

Osgood, C. E., G. J. Suci, and P. H. Tannenbaum, *The Measurement of Meaning,* Urbana, Ill.: University of Illinois Press, 1957.

Pettigrew, T. F., and R. B. Spier, "The Ecological Structure of Negro Homicide," *American Journal of Sociology, 67,* No. 6 (1962), 621–629.

Pruitt, D. G., "Stability and Sudden Change in Interpersonal and International Affairs," *Journal of Conflict Resolution, 13,* No. 1 (1969), 18–38.

Rapoport, A., "Lewis F. Richardson's Mathematical Theory of War," *Journal of Conflict Resolution, 1,* No. 3 (1957), 249–99.

_____ , *Fights, Games and Debates,* Ann Arbor: University of Michigan Press, 1960.

Reiss, A. J., "Police Brutality—Answers to Key Question," *Trans Action, 5,* No. 8 (1968), 10–19.

Richardson, L. F., *Arms and Insecurity,* Pittsburgh: Boxwood Press, 1960a.

_____ , *Statistics of Deadly Quarrels,* Pittsburgh: Boxwood Press, 1960b.

Rummel, R. J., "Testing Some Possible Predictors of Conflict Behavior Within and Between Nations," *Peace Research Society (International) Papers, 1* (1964), 79–111.

_____ , "Dimensions of Conflict Behavior Within Nations, 1946–59," *Journal of Conflict Resolution, 10,* No. 1 (1966), 65–73.

Schelling, T. C., "The Strategy of Conflict: Prospectus for a Reorientation of Game Theory," *Journal of Conflict Resolution, 2,* No. 3 (1958), 203–264.

Shaw, D. L., "News Bias and the Telegraph: A Study of Historical Change," *Journalism Quarterly, 44,* No. 1 (1967).

Shils, E. A., and M. Janowitz, "Cohesion and Disintegration in the Wehrmacht in World War II," in D. Katz, *et al.,* eds., *Public Opinion and Propaganda,* New York: Dryden, 1954, pp. 554–581.

Singer, J. D., and M. Small, "Formal Alliances, 1815–1939, A Quantitative Decription," *Journal of Peace Research, 1* (1966a), 1–32.

_____ , "National Alliance Commitments and War Involvement, 1815–1945," *Peace Research Society (International) Papers, 5* (1966b), 109–140.

Snider, P. B., "Mr. Gates Revisited: A 1966 Version of the 1949 Case Study," *Journalism Quarterly, 44,* No. 3 (1967), 419–427.

Spiegel, J. P., "Campus Conflict and Professorial Egos," *Trans Action, 6,* No. 11 (1969), 41–50.

Steiner, J., "Nonviolent Conflict Resolution in Democratic Systems: Switzerland," *Journal of Conflict Resolution, 13,* No. 3 (1969), 295–304.

Tanter, R., "Dimensions of Conflict Behavior Within and Between Nations, 1958–60," *Journal of Conflict Resolution, 10,* No. 1 (1966), 41–64.

Tilly, C., "Collective Violence in European Perspective," in Graham and Gurr, eds., pp. 4–45.

Wallace, S. R., "Review of *Motivating Economic Achievement* by David C. McClelland and David G. Winter," *Contemporary Psychology, 14,* No. 12 (1969), 635, 638, 640.

Wolfgang, M. E., "A Preface to Violence," *Annals of American Academy of Political and Social Science, 364* (1966), 1–7.

Wolfgang, M. E., and F. Ferracuti, *The Subculture of Violence,* London: Associated Book Publishers, 1967.

73 74 75 76   9 8 7 6 5 4 3 2 1